SOCIO-LEGAL FOUNDATIONS OF CIVIL-MILITARY RELATIONS

SOCIO-LEGAL
FOUNDATIONS OF
CIVIL-MILITARY RELATIONS

James B. Jacobs

Transaction Books
New Brunswick (U.S.A.) and Oxford (U.K.)

Library of Congress Catalog Number: 85-24657
ISBN: 0-88738-033-6 (cloth)
Printed in the United States of America

Library of Congress Cataloging in Publication Data

Jacobs, James B.
  Socio-legal foundations of civil-military relations.

  Bibliography: p.
  Includes index.
1. Civil-military relations—United States.
2. Civil supremacy over the military—United States.
3. Military law—United States.   I. Title.
KF7209.J33   1986   343.73'01   85-24657
ISBN 0-88738-033-6   347.3031

Contents

To
Morris Janowitz

Acknowledgments

Over the course of years many colleagues have read one or another of these essays, shared their thoughts and ideas, and offered their criticisms. I will always be grateful for this support and assistance. Lou Milford deserves special acknowledgment for his help with chapter 7. Above all, I am indebted to Morris Janowitz who stimulated, prodded, and nurtured me all along the way. My research assistant Jodi Saposnick, has helped immeasurably in the preparation of this manuscript. She too deserves my gratitude. I also want to thank the Filomen D'Agostino and Max E. Greenberg Research Fund of the New York University School of Law for a summer research grant and other support which enabled me to bring this project to completion.

Chapter 1, "Legal Change in the United States Armed Forces since World War II," is reprinted in different form from *Armed Forces and Society* vol. 4, no. 3 (May 1978): 391-421.

Chapter 2, "Aliens in the U.S. Armed Forces: A Historico-Legal Analysis," is revised from *Armed Forces and Society* vol. 7, no. 2 (winter 1981): 187-208.

Chapter 3, "The Role of Military Forces in Public Sector Labor Relations," is reprinted in revised form from an article by the same title published in *Industrial and Labor Relations Review* vol. 35, no. 2 (January 1982): 163-80.

Chapter 5, "Selective Service Without a Draft: The Dilemmas and Symbolic Politics of Draft Registration," is reprinted in slightly different form from *Armed Forces and Society* vol. 10, no. 3 (spring 1984) :361-79.

Introduction

It would be difficult to exaggerate the importance of the armed forces in United States society. Overshadowing all else is the military's awesome responsibility as caretaker of weapons of unimaginable destructive power. The military's annual budget stands at almost $300 billion, constituting over 30 percent of all federal expenditures, and 6.6 percent of the gross national product. More than a decade after the end of the Vietnam War, there remain approximately two million men and women in uniform in the four armed services, and the Defense Department employs just under one million civilians. Although a decreasing percentage of the population is participating in the armed forces, there are probably more than thirty million military veterans.

Despite the undeniable importance of the armed forces as a societal institution, they have not attracted the kind of scholarly attention that other perhaps less important fields have. Criminology, the subject with which I am best acquainted, has dozens of professional journals and thousands of specialist teachers. There are no figures like these related to the military. To be sure, there are a few flourishing subspecialities within military scholarship, including strategic studies and military history. The study of armed forces and society, however, thrives far less. There may be no more than a few dozen civilian scholars in the U.S. actively interested in this subject. There are only two journals of which I am aware. The Inter-University Seminar on Armed Forces and Society, which has done so much to promote scholarship and dialogue in this area has only 863 members, and its journal only 1607 subscriptions. In part, no doubt, low level attention reflects historic anti-military attitudes among American intellectuals. Even now, colleagues may feel something is wrong, or at least odd, about someone studying the military.

Until recently, the study of civil military relations usually meant the study of controlling the military. The issue was posed as one of civilian structures having to cope with an ever dangerous possibility of military takeover. On this subject there have been basically two competing positions. The implication of Morris Janowitz's work is that successful civil military relations requires professional soldiers who are knowledgeable and creatively involved in civilian governance. He argues that an isolated mili-

1

tary leadership cannot serve military or civilian goals effectively. Samuel Huntington seems to believe that the best way to prevent military leaders from encroaching upon civilian domains is to maintain a complete separation of military and civilian spheres. No doubt both men have captured an element of truth, especially as it emerges from U.S. experience. Neither Janowitz nor Huntington places much faith in the capacity of formal legal structures to prevent the military takeover or expansion of influence and power.

This book does not deal directly with civilian control over the military. This is hardly an indication that I undervalue the issue. To the contrary, I admit its centrality, even its primacy. But my goal has been to explore and map the role of the military in U.S. society. The more I have pondered this task, the more complex and expansive it becomes. One must come to grips with the fact that the military is the largest, strongest, and most pervasive institution in our society. It exerts its influence over individuals, groups and the nation as a collectivity. In dealing with such a subject, there is no hope of being comprehensive. There are many important and fascinating dimensions of civil military relations that are not dealt with in this book— for example, the military industrial complex, military spying on civilians at home and abroad, military influence on foreign policymaking. These and other topics must await future editions or perhaps future authors. For now I will be content if the essays presented in this volume extend the scope of civil military relations studies, raise some issues heretofore little considered, and stimulate greater interest in armed forces and society. I especially hope this volume will be of use to students, providing a framework for thinking about the pervasiveness of civil military relations and stimulating their curiosity to read further and think harder.

This is not a study in military law, but professional training necessarily shapes one's intellectual perspective. Therefore, there is a great deal of legal material presented in these essays. For the most part the statutes and cases that I draw upon are not analyzed for their doctrinal coherence, but are treated as data for describing the ties between the military and civilian sectors. Just as it would be wrong to treat military relations as nothing more than the sum total of relevant statutes and judicial opinions, it would be equally wrong to ignore or underemphasize the formal rules that set forth and regulate the interrelation of military and civilian institutions.

Chapter 1 focuses on the relationship between civilian legal norms and military organizations. This is the only essay in the volume that concentrates on civilian influences on military society rather than on military influences on civilian society. Since World War II, military criminal law has imported many, if not most, of the rights and protections afforded to criminal defendants in civilian courts. There has been a steady momentum toward greater and greater due process and toward a contractual model of military service. All this demonstrates that contemporary military institutions are deeply embedded in a national legal culture, despite ever present concerns about discipline and command control.

Chapter 2 turns to the relationship of citizenship and military service. Following the pioneering work of Morris Janowitz, it pursues the question: what impacts have U.S. military institutions had on the development of the political concept of "citizenship"? More specifically, a good deal of legal history is examined to determine the extent to which military service has been a special prerogative or obligation of citizens in the United States, and we speculate on whether military service could be explicitly used to assimilate new generations of immigrants.

Chapters 3 and 4 deal with two new but little noticed roles for the military in civilian society. Chapter 3 examines the military's, especially the National Guard's, role, as a replacement for striking public employees. Since the 1970 postal strike, such deployments have become increasingly common, despite a lack of either legal or policy analysis concerning the appropriateness of such activity. The issue that now arises is whether the National Guard's replacement function should be further legitimized and elaborated, or whether any further activity in this area would be counterproductive to effective civil military relations.

Chapter 4 deals with the fascinating entrance of the regular active duty armed forces into the battle against drug smuggling. In 1981 the old (1871) Posse Comitatus Act was amended to allow the Department of Defense to provide assistance to federal and state drug enforcement agencies that have become increasingly unable to cope with the air and sea capabilities of international drug smugglers. While military aid so far has been modest and extended with understandable hesitancy given the obvious pitfalls lurking in all drug enforcement efforts, it does mark a historic precedent and demonstrates a willingness to rethink the military's role in civilian society without the usual reflexive cries of military takeover.

Chapter 5 reviews the history of the Carter-Reagan draft registration program from its passage through the protests and up to the current enforcement dilemma. Ten years ago it may have looked like the nation's long stormy relationship with conscription had finally ended, but the new draft registration program raises many historic issues of equity, conscience, and state power over the individual. It also provides an opportunity for assessing the costs that would have to be borne in order to return to peacetime conscription.

Chapter 6 deals with the subject of National Service, a concept high on symbolism but low on administrative detail. I lay aside the philosophical debate between those who visualize national service as the ultimate expression of citizenship and those who define it as a form of totalitarianism. I inquire whether national service is administratively feasible. I do this by examining the most fleshed out national service proposals I know of, two programs offered as bills to Congress a few years ago and renewed periodically. I conclude that a large-scale mandatory National Service program is probably not feasible and that a so-called voluntary national service differs little from the situation we now have.

The final chapter reflects on the role of military veterans in U.S. society, with a particular focus on Vietnam veterans. Veterans constitute an important, albeit sometimes overlooked link between civilian society and military organization. The definition of veteran has expanded during the post–World War II period. The condition of Vietnam veterans continues to be assessed as the war recedes even further. Historical perspective shows that fears about maladjusted veterans committing crimes and undermining moral values have arisen in all our wars. Predictions about Vietnam veterans' problems have been proven exaggerated. Like veterans of America's other wars, the Vietnam and Vietnam-era veterans have mostly rejoined the societal mainstream, and like veterans of other wars have vigorously and persistently fought for more benefits. The key challenge for the foreseeable future is to formulate a veterans policy that makes sense for an all-volunteer force.

1

Legal Change within the U.S. Armed Forces since World War II

A review of the legal literature since World War II suggests at least three broad trends in military law. First, there is the extension of procedural and substantive rights to service personnel. Second, there is a shifting of emphasis from criminal to administrative law. Third, there is a reemphasis on the contractual nature of military service. This chapter briefly describes these trends before turning in section 2 to the forces initiating legal change and in section 3 to the possible consequences of legal change.

The Extension of Rights

The most salient post–World War II trend in military law is the extension of due process rights to those accused of crimes. More recently, attention has shifted to the administrative aspects of personnel management, where increasing emphasis has been given to due process and "administrative justice" in adverse personnel actions. In addition to procedural fairness, the armed forces have begun to import into personnel management equal protection norms as well as some concern for rights of expression and privacy.

The evolution of due process rights in the military began with the old Articles of War and Articles for the Government of the Navy, which were not codes of criminal law and procedure but systems of discipline and punishment (see Morgan 1952-53). Both codes reflected the contentions of military commanders, treatise writers, and courts that the goal of military law was not justice, but command control and combat readiness. As the eminent William Winthrop put it, "courts-martial are in fact simply *instrumentalities of the executive power*, provided by Congress for the President as Commander-in-Chief, to aid him in properly commanding the army and navy and enforcing discipline therein." (Winthrop 1896: 53-54)

The extensive use of courts-martial during World War II and the severity of the sentences led to public and congressional demands for reform. The first secretary of defense, James Forrestal, appointed a committee headed by Edmund Morgan of Harvard Law School to draft a new code. Secretary Forrestal instructed the committee that "the modernization of the existing system should be undertaken with a view to protecting the rights of those subject to the Code and increasing public confidence in military justice, without impairing the performance of military functions." Thus, an explicit objective of the Uniform Code of Military Justice (UCMJ) was to civilianize and liberalize the military's criminal law and procedure, as well as to extend certain rights of citizenship to service personnel.

The transition of military discipline and punishment to a more legal system of criminal justice was evidenced by the strong words of Article 37, which made it an offense for an officer convening a court-martial to attempt to influence the outcome. Many procedural and substantive rights were specifically guaranteed to general court-martial defendants. The accused had a right to qualified legal representation. Article 31 antedated *Miranda* by assuring the right to remain silent during all stages of interrogation. Pretrial investigations and pretrial hearings were mandated. Other Code provisions provided for a systematic review of court-martial convictions by the Judge Advocates General, Military Boards of Review, and in some cases by a three-judge Court of Military Appeals (CoMA) (see Willis 1972).

The creation of CoMA fulfilled the wishes of military law reformers since the 1920s, when General Samuel T. Ansell argued so vigorously for an independent civilian court with final authority over courts-martial (see Generous 1973; Willis 1972: 55-63). From the outset CoMA asserted its independence, identified itself with the federal appellate courts, and established its role as the "supreme court of the military." It did not hesitate to reverse court-martial convictions which did not conform to the letter and spirit of the UCMJ. The CoMA judges developed a doctrine of military due process which permitted the Court to scrutinize court-martial convictions for conformity with fundamental fairness. As early as 1953, in *United States v. Wappler*, CoMA struck down a Manual paragraph which authorized confinement on bread and water for more than three days plus a punitive discharge as being violative of the Code's proscription against cruel and unusual punishments. The voiding of Manual provisions continues to the present time (see *United States v. Ware* 1976). When the venerable Manual for Court-Martial (MCM) contradicted the UCMJ, the offending sections were either reinterpreted or struck down. Not only did the Court invalidate Manual provisions when it found them inconsistent with the UCMJ, it expanded its powers by judicial rulemaking as well (see *United States v. Donohew* 1969; *United States v. Rinehart*, 1957). More than any other institution, CoMA placed the military's system of social control under the rule of law (see *Military Law Review* 1984).

The Court also imported into the military most of the rights of criminal defendants which expanded so dramatically in the postwar period. Judge Ferguson, who joined the Court in 1956, agreed with Chief Judge Quinn, "that the protections in the Bill of Rights, except those which are expressly or by necessary implication inapplicable, are available to members of our armed forces" *United States v. Jacoby* (1960). Since the Jacoby case, most commentators have accepted the applicability of the Constitution to courts-martial. The Court's position on this crucial issue has varied with the makeup of the Court. Judge William Darden (1968-1974), for example, acknowledged an obligation to follow Supreme Court decisions on certain constitutional issues, while on others he based his decision solely on the UCMJ (see Willis 1972: 36-38).

Even those who believe that the Constitution applies directly to service personnel recognize an exception for "those [rights] which are expressly or by necessary implication inapplicable." The right to grand jury is expressly inapplicable (U.S. Const. Amend. V), as is the right of petit jury by historical implication. Beyond these two acknowledged exceptions, the meaning of the phrase is unclear, and it remains a point of debate and controversy (see Henderson 1957: 305-15).

Whatever the theory, the result of CoMA's activism is that almost all the procedural protections available to civilian defendants have been imported into military law.[1] From their prewar status as marginal citizens, service personnel have become fully vested with the rights of citizenship. Of crucial importance is the process of social learning to which the Court has committed the armed forces. For a quarter of a century CoMA has reiterated the value of respecting the rule of law and the rights of the individual in the disciplinary context. That message is by now an accepted fact of day-to-day life in the armed forces.

Momentum for protecting the rights of the accused has led to pressure to extend due process to Article 15 nonjudicial punishments, despite the fact that its stated purpose is to provide commanders a summary punishment with which to maintain unit discipline. The 1972 Task Force on the Administration of Military Justice in the Armed Forces (one-half of whose members were high level military officers) sharply criticized the Article 15 procedure for insufficient safeguards. In response, Secretary of Defense Melvin Laird issued a 1973 memorandum establishing increased protections (primarily a review procedure) for the "accused." Pressure for more due process continues, however. The Committee on Military Justice and Military Affairs of the Association of the Bar of the City of New York recently completed a Bill to Improve the Military Justice System. That bill proposes that the service member be given a right to consult with counsel prior to appearing at an Article 15 proceeding, to obtain one adjournment for further consultation, and to present witnesses and sworn statements in his own behalf.[2]

One consequence of elaborate due process procedures at general and special courts-martial has been increased reliance on the summary court-martial, a single-judge court authorized to impose maximum punishments of thirty days' hard labor under confinement or forty-five days' hard labor without confinement. However, the 1968 Military Justice Act provided that any serviceman facing summary court-martial could demand a special court-martial where full due process would be afforded; the serviceman would also be vulnerable to greater punishment. Several lower federal court decisions declared the absence of a right to assigned counsel at summary courts-martial unconstitutional (e.g., *Daigle v. Warner* 1973). In *U.S. v. Alderman* (1973), CoMA decided that assigned counsel must be available to a summary court-martial defendant when confinement is possible. The Supreme Court held to the contrary in 1976, in *Middendorf v. Henry*, emphasizing that the summary court-martial was more like an administrative proceeding than a criminal trial. Given that rationale, CoMA attempted to completely restructure the summary court-martial in *U.S. v. Booker* (1977) by holding that it cannot be used except to try minor military offenses unknown in civilian society. That holding was later vacated, however, and today *Booker* stands for the proposition that the accused must be advised of right to counsel in deciding to accept trial by summary court-martial, and must voluntarily and intelligently waive the statutory right of removal (see *U.S. v. Rivera* 1978; *U.S. v. Alsup* 1984).

The drive to extend due process to service personnel is also evident in the administrative context (see Heassing 1974). Department of Defense Regulation 1332.14, promulgated in 1965, assures a serviceman or servicewoman facing an administratively adjudged undesirable discharge the right to qualified free military counsel (or private retained counsel) before an impartial hearing board. It also permits women and minority personnel to request that one of the members of the hearing board be of their race or sex, thus extending equal protection norms beyond what is constitutionally required (or perhaps permissible) at civilian jury trials. The respondent at an administrative discharge hearing may challenge any voting member of the board for cause. He has the right to request the appearance of witnesses. At any time before the board convenes or during proceedings, he may submit any answer, deposition, sworn or unsworn statement, affidavit, certificate or stipulation. An individual cannot be administratively discharged for actions or omissions for which he had been acquitted (on the merits) at court-martial, nor "shall [a serviceperson] be subject to administrative discharge board action based upon conduct which has previously been the subject of administrative discharge board proceedings, where the evidence before the subsequent discharge board would be the same as the evidence before the previous board."

Where the convening authority approves an undesirable discharge for unsuitability or unfitness, the member has an absolute right of appeal to an Administrative Discharge Board. If a favorable decision is not obtained at this level, further appeal can be taken to the Board for Correction of Military and Naval Records, a civilian tribunal in Washington which functions as a kind of military administrative supreme court. The board has substantial power; it may correct retirement dates or a record of trial by court-martial, promote officers in the reserves, and change a discharge or dismissal adjudged by general court-martial or administrative discharge board.

Due process is only beginning to appear in revocations of security clearances, reductions in grades, bars to reenlistment and MOS reclassifications. Personnel in the grades of E5–E9 facing reductions in grade have a right to a hearing, free military counsel, witness, and cross examination. Still, the extension of due process to service personnel facing adverse administrative actions is by no means complete (see Ervin 1972). Critics continue to charge that authority is exercised too arbitrarily and that personnel have insufficient protections, given the career interests at stake. My point is not that the rights of the individual have been given their very fullest interpretation, but that expectations of fairness and due process have permeated the heretofore hierarchical, and perhaps even feudal, military organization.

Due process norms are also beginning to appear in nonadverse personnel decisions. Officer selection procedures are a good example (see Ford 1975). Although the regulations governing army promotions state that Selection Board action is final, they provide for convening a standby board "if a material error was present in the records of an officer when reviewed by a selection board" (AR 64-100 [1966]). The navy provides that

> adverse personnel matter shall not be placed in an officer's record without his knowledge. In all cases it shall be referred to the officer reported on for such official statements as he may choose to make in reply. If the officer reported on desires to make no statement, he shall so state officially in writing. The Chief of Navy Personnel is liberal in his interpretation as to what constitutes adverse matter. [U.S. Department of Navy, Bureau of Naval Personnel Manual Art. B-2201 para. 4(c).]

The extension of protections to service personnel in criminal and administrative contexts overshadows the importation of First Amendment freedoms (see Sherman 1971). Still some change is clearly evident. In *U.S. v. Daniels* (1970) and *U.S. v. Harvey* (1970), CoMA reversed the conviction of two Black marines who had been court-martialed for making antiwar statements to other soldiers. The Court applied the civilian "clear and present danger test" and stated:

> The right to believe in a particular faith or philosophy and the right to express one's opinions or to complain about real or imaginary wrongs are legitimate activities in the military community as much as they are in the civilian community. . . . If the statements and the intent of the accused, as established by the evidence, constitute no more than commentary as to the tenets of his faith or declarations of private opinion as to the social and political state of the United States, he is guilty of no crime.

The military itself responded to increased societal tolerance of antiwar protest in the late 1960s. A 1969 Army directive stated:

> It is important to remember that freedom of expression is a fundamental right secured by the Constitution. . . . Severe disciplinary action in response to a relatively insignificant manifestation of dissent can have a counterproductive effect on other members of the command, because the reaction appears out of proportion to the threat which the dissent represents. Thus, rather than serving as a deterrent, such disproportionate actions may stimulate further breaches of discipline. [Department of Army, Office of Adjutant General, May 2, 1969.]

Some liberalization has also occurred with respect to personal grooming standards and in the treatment of pregnant servicewomen (*Crawford v. Cushman* 1976).

Thus, there can be no question about the fact that military personnel today have far greater rights than their World War II counterparts. This is not to say that service personnel enjoy full rights of citizenship. They continue to have a special status in U.S. society, although that status is in flux. The rights of service personnel accused of serious offenses fairly closely parallel those of civilian defendants. Administrative protections for military personnel compare favorably with those of civil servants. In both criminal and administrative contexts the pressure for increased rights continues to be strong. In the four decades since World War II the military has become a society that exists under the rule of law.

The Shift from Criminal to Administrative Law

A second major trend in military law since World War II has been a shift of emphasis from criminal sanctions to administrative regulation. The numbers of personnel separated from the armed forces administratively increased. Types of administrative discharges proliferated. Article 15 nonjudicial punishment assumed increasing importance as a mechanism for social control.

New grounds have been established for discharging poorly performing servicemen and servicewomen from active duty. In July 1966 the army promulgated "a discharge for the good of the service" (AR 635-200 ch. 10). This procedure provided that personnel facing court-martial charges could request an administrative discharge, which, if agreed to, could not be classified as less favorable than "undesirable." In reality, almost all discharges issued under this procedure have been undesirable (see Hansen 1976). In 1967 the army processed 297 discharges for the good of the service; by 1972 the number had grown to 25,456. A decrease thereafter to 14,784 in 1975 may reflect a decline in troop strength plus a decline in AWOLs.

In the mid-1970s the army created two additional grounds for administrative discharges. Under the "expeditious discharge" a unit commander was given authority to separate personnel with poor attitudes, lack of motivation or inability to adjust (AR 635-200, para. 5-37; TRADOC Cir. 635.2). No discharge less favorable than "general" could be adjudged. The "trainee discharge" eliminates poor candidates for military service even sooner (AR 635-200, para. 5-39; TRADOC Sup 1 AR 634-200). A trainee who cannot adapt, meet enlistment standards or complete training can simply be processed out of the armed forces with an honorable discharge. According to figures provided by the Army Judge Advocate General (JAG) School, there were approximately 10,000 trainee discharges in the first six months of 1977 and 8,500 expeditious discharges during the same time period. Administrative discharges (no worse than undesirable) can also be imposed for unfitness, misconduct and unsuitability.

There was an average of 50,000 administratively adjudged less-than-honorable discharges between 1967-1972 (for a criticism of this see Starr 1973). The creation of the expeditious discharge increases that number substantially. The trainee discharge is also an important mechanism of social control, even though it does not carry a stigmatizing discharge. Table 1.1 indicates the increasing proportion of less-than-honorable discharges adjudged administratively rather than by court-martial since 1950 (*Harv. Civ. Rts. and Civ. Lib. Rev.* 1971).

This preference for administrative mechanisms of social control is fully consistent with the shift to pragmatic military leaders who rely less on coercion and more on positive incentives (Janowitz 1960). Faculty at the Army JAG School point out that at least two judge advocates general have put themselves on record as being in favor of removing JAG Corps resources from "the court-martial treadmill."[3] The attitude seems to be that

TABLE 1.1
Application of Less-Than-Honorable Discharges:
Percentage Issued through Administrative Procedures[a]

Fiscal Years	Army[b]	Navy	Marines	Air Force
1950-1954	64.49	40.16	42.62	c
1955-1959	78.88	59.66	45.23	74.76c
1960-1964	86.96	67.49	61.49	69.81
1965-1969	87.15	69.77	54.27	73.75
1970-1973	92.30	66.40	80.50	83.66
1981-1984	c	73.90	84.00	c

a   Undesirable Discharges as a percentage of total Undesirable, Bad-Conduct, and Dishonorable
    Discharges. The addition of General Discharges would show an even more dramatic shift away
    from court-martial procedures.
b   Years prior to 1961 do not include Army enlisted female discharges.
c   Data not available.

the army is best served by eliminating poorly performing soldiers as soon
as possible and with the least drain on administrative and legal resources.
Both judicial opinions and new professional training have withdrawn legitimacy from an authoritarian model of personnel management. Many civil
libertarians have charged that the widespread use of administrative discharges is a means of circumventing court-martial procedures (Starr 1973).
An official report of the Court of Military Appeals observed in 1960 that

> the unusual increase in the use of the administrative discharge since the Code
> became a fixture has led to the suspicion that the services were resorting to
> that means of circumventing the requirements of the code. The validity of
> that suspicion was confirmed by Major General Reginald C. Harmon, the
> Judge Advocate General of the Air Force, who declared that the tremendous
> increase in undesirable discharge by administrative proceedings was the re-
> sult of efforts of military commanders to avoid the requirements of the
> Uniform Code.

In 1962 the Senate Judiciary Committee's Subcommittee on Constitutional Rights held hearings on the subject of administrative discharges.
Subsequent bills to increase procedural protections in administrative discharge procedures failed to pass through Congress.

The shift to administrative processes is also indicated by increased emphasis upon Article 15 nonjudicial punishment. Article 15 provides a summary procedure for maintaining unit control. With the serviceman's
consent, a commander can impose a limited noncriminal punishment that
will not be recorded as a criminal conviction, but which nonetheless becomes part of an individual's record. A serviceman can refuse Article 15
punishment and elect trial by special court-martial, where he will be af-

forded the full panoply of procedural safeguards but where he faces harsher criminal penalties if convicted.

In the first decade after passage of the UCMJ, many military leaders felt that the maximum Article 15 punishments authorized under the Code were not severe enough and that control would suffer if the commander did not have the power to impose more potent summary punishments. From 1950 on there was constant pressure for a revision of Article 15. Punishments were increased (up to thirty days' custodial confinement) by executive order in 1963 and by the Military Justice Act of 1968. The 1964 report of the Judge Advocate General of the Army pointed out that, "although the number of general court-martial trials increased by 22 over Fiscal Year 1963, there was a decrease of 2,121 in the number of special court-martial trials from 32,316 last year to 16,926, or approximately 47 percent. *The decrease may be attributed primarily to the amended Article 15*" (emphasis added). With the increased judicialization of court-martial procedures brought about by the UCMJ, reliance on Article 15 for maintaining order and discipline is increasing. In 1964, for example, the air force adjudged 31,109 Article 15s and 7,551 courts-martial. Ten years later there were 37,556 Article 15s and 2,947 courts-martial; the ratio had changed from approximately 4:1 to approximately 12:1. During fiscal year 1983 the air force presided over 30,014 Article 15 and 1705 courts-martial; the ratio has risen to 17:1.

Military law reflects as well as contributes to a major change in the social organization of the armed forces since World War II. The shift toward less punitive mechanisms of social control indicates a new basis for personnel management and an emerging definition of the nature of military service that is less moralistic and less feudalistic than in earlier periods.

Redefining Military Service in More Contractual Terms

A reemphasis on the legal and contractual nature of military service is a third post-World War II trend in military law. It is evidenced by the Supreme Court's decisions narrowing military jurisdiction, CoMA opinions on the validity of enlistment contracts, the recent controversy over reenlistment bonuses, the decline of criminal sanctions and the creation of the all-volunteer force.

The authors of the UCMJ sought to create a criminal code which extended court-martial jurisdiction to its furthest historical limits. The Supreme Court whittled away this jurisdiction in a series of decisions between 1955-1969. In *Toth v. Quarles* (1955) the Court ruled that Congress lacked authority to bring a civilian back into the military to stand trial for a crime committed before he was discharged. *Reid v. Covert* (1956) and *Kinsella v.*

Singleton (1960) rejected the assertion of court-martial jurisdiction over civilian dependents of servicemen. *McElroy v. Guagliardo* (1959) held that overseas civilian employees of the armed forces could not be tried by court-martial. Ten years later *O'Callahan v. Parker* (1969) struck down court-martial jurisdiction over servicemen for offenses which are not "service connected." *O'Callahan* reemphasized the language of *Toth v. Quarles* that "free countries of the world have tried to restrict military tribunals to the narrowest jurisdiction deemed absolutely essential to maintaining discipline among troops in active service."

The *Toth-O'Callahan* line of cases in effect denied that a feudal relationship existed between the soldier and the military organization. *Toth* held that a citizen's relationship to the armed forces did not last a lifetime; military service was limited to the contractual enlistment period. *O'Callahan* rejected the claim that even a full time active-duty soldier was totally a creature of the military. It also rejected the claim that the relationship between the serviceman and the military transcends time and place. The case defines a serviceman as only segmentally related to the armed forces; off-duty and off-base the peacetime soldier is like any other citizen.

Since 1969, the Supreme Court and CoMA have backtracked somewhat from the *Toth-O'Callahan* view, emphasizing the military's need for its own specialized legal system. In *Relford v. U.S. Disciplinary Commandant* (1971), the Court interpreted the "service-connected" test more broadly than *O'Callahan* itself seemed to suggest. A serviceman who raped a civilian woman on a military base was held to be properly under court-martial jurisdiction. The Court was clearly not willing to remove civilian-type crimes from courts-martial (as is the case in West Germany), a position underscored in *Schlesinger v. Councilman* (1975). There, the Court stated that the issue of court-martial jurisdiction

> turns in major part on gauging the impact of an offense on military discipline and effectiveness, on determining whether the military interest in deterring the offense is distinct from and greater than that of civilian society, and on whether the distinct military interest can be vindicated adequately, in civilian courts.

CoMA subsequently decided that criminal offenses committed off-post may be service-connected because "they often have significant impact on the security and combat readiness of those within" (*U.S. v. Lockwood* 1983; see also *U.S. v. Trottier* 1980). In *Lockwood*, the crimes of forgery and larceny committed in a nearby town were considered service-related because the accused used a military identification card in perpetrating the offenses. In upholding court-martial jurisdiction, CoMA impliedly agreed with the Supreme Court that the military should be treated as a "specialized society" (*Parker v. Levy* 1974).

Recent developments in the law of military enlistments also lend force to the proposition that the relationship of the serviceman to the armed forces is becoming increasingly contractual (see Grayson 1976; cf. Schlucter 1977). The traditional understanding of the "enlistment contract" was stated by Winthrop:

> An enlistment contract is a transaction in which private right is subordinated to the public interest. In law, it is entered into with the understanding that it may be modified in any of its terms, or wholly rescinded, at the discretion of the State. But this discretion can be exercised only by the legislative body. [Winthrop 1920; 528-39]

Under this view, regulations placing restrictions or qualifications on enlistments were for the benefit of the military, not the serviceman. Enlistments which did not conform to regulations were voidable by the government but not by the enlistee. In a series of cases arising in the court-martial context, several federal courts and the Court of Military Appeals held that the military must follow its own regulations. Enlistment contracts in violation of statutes or regulations were held *void ab initio*. The courts were less willing to find a "constructive enlistment," despite actions by an enlistee consistent with a willingness to serve in the armed forces (e.g., *U.S. v. Brown* 1974; *U.S. v. Catlow* 1974; *U.S. v. Dumas* 1975). In *U.S. v. Russo* (1975), an enlistee was given the answers to the enlistment test by an aggressive recruiter who did not want him disqualified because of a visual handicap. Chief Judge Fletcher rejected the government's argument that the reading requirement for enlistment was solely for the benefit of the military. His opinion stated that "common law contract principles appropriately dictate that where recruiter misconduct amounts to a violation of the fraudulent enlistment statute, the resulting enlistment is void as contrary to public policy."

As a result of *Russo*, successful claims of fraudulent enlistment led to dismissal of the court-martial on jurisdictional grounds. In 1979, Congress countered this blow to court-martial procedure by enacting an amendment to the Uniform Code of Military Justice (Pub. L. No. 96-107, § 801; currently at 10 U.S.C. § 802). The amendment validates for the purposes of court-martial jurisdiction "the voluntary enlistment of any person who has the capacity to understand the significance of enlisting in the armed forces."

The contractual nature of military service has also emerged in suits brought by servicemen demanding satisfaction of an enlistment promise.

In *Bemis v. Whalen* (1972), the petitioner sought a discharge from the marine corps on grounds of false representations and breach of contract. Instead of being assigned to schooling in electronics, he was sent for training as a telephone/teletype technician. The federal district court held that there had been no "material breach of contract" since the military was ready to correct its mistake. A different result was reached in *Novak v. Rumsfeld* (1976), where a naval serviceman extended his enlistment by two years in order to attain eligibility for the Nuclear Field Training Program. The petitioner flunked out of the training course, but the navy refused to give him a discharge. The court found that there was a material breach of contract and ordered Novak released from military service.

The old definition of military service as a semi-serflike status in which the relationship between the soldier and state is only broadly defined, mostly in terms of the individual's obligations, is changing. It is becoming more equal and more contractual. Changes in governmental policy will no longer necessarily defeat an individual's expectancy interest and the deal he thought he had bargained for. The Supreme Court decision in *U.S. v. Larionoff* (1977) is an interesting example of this change. The case consolidated several disputes over variable reenlistment bonuses (VRB). The plaintiff had extended his enlistment in order to be eligible for an MOS covered by the VRB. Subsequently, the navy removed plaintiff's specialty from the list of "critical military skills," thereby denying him his VRB. Then in 1974 Congress repealed the VRB program altogether. Larionoff and other plaintiffs argued that despite departmental and congressional action, they were entitled to the bonuses which were in effect at the time they were induced to extend their enlistments. A closely split Supreme Court agreed. Justice Brennan held that Congress could not have intended to encourage reenlistments by offering bonuses which could subsequently be withdrawn. Although the opinion is based upon construction of federal statutes, it in effect recognizes the binding nature of government promises and upholds the serviceman's expectancy interest. Justice White's dissenting opinion recognized the larger significance of the case.

> As I see it, the legislation was not part of the re-enlistment agreement, which was executed in consideration of the re-enlistee's service. Those who executed re-enlistment agreements had no vested right in any particular level of pay, in any particular total package of pay, allowances or benefits.

The *Larionoff* case is consistent with the emphasis of the all-volunteer force on monetary and fringe benefits as incentives for military recruitment and service. Many supporters of an all-volunteer force equate military service with other types of workforce participation (Report of the

President's Commission on an All-Volunteer Force 1970). The legal redefinition of military service in more contractual terms thus contributes to and reflects the larger movement away from the mass mobilization army and toward a force in being.

Accounting for Legal Change

Military law consists of congressional statutes, the opinions of federal and military courts, and the plethora of directives, rules, regulations, and minutes issued by the Department of Defense and by various commands within each of the services. Changes in military law may emanate from any one or more of these sources. In addition, such background influences as public opinion, media, organized bar, and legal commentaries should not be overlooked in searching for an understanding of the processes of military legal change. Neither can the role of military lawyers and judges be ignored. The way in which the specialized military bar articulates with the larger legal environment may be one of the most crucial factors in the evolution of military legal norms.

The Role of the Federal Courts

After World War II the federal courts cautiously moved away from their "hands-off" approach to military disputes. The Supreme Court's 1953 decision in *Burns v. Wilson* permitted lower federal courts, which were so inclined, to more closely scrutinize court-martial proceedings. While the Supreme Court has somewhat expanded federal court review of court-martial convictions (see *Parisi v. Davidson* 1972), the decline in the hands-off doctrine has been modest rather than precipitous. In *Schlesinger v. Councilman* (1975), for example, the Court reemphasized the exhaustion requirement for military *habeas*. Review of court-martial convictions continues to be narrower than review of state criminal convictions (see *Harv. L. Rev.* 1970). The doctrine of nonreviewability of military administrative matters also underwent change (see *Harmon v. Brucker* 1958). Increased access to the federal courts combined with the upheavals of the Vietnam War to produce a massive increase in reported federal court decisions involving internal military disputes. However, with the war's end and the advent of the volunteer force the number of decisions plummeted.[4]

Throughout the late sixties and early seventies, there was judicial momentum toward opening up the federal courts to hear military cases, even if substantive relief was rarely granted. The Supreme Court decisions of this period seemed generally to be sensitive to the rights of service personnel; *O'Callahan* was explicitly hostile to the military establishment. Although many lower court opinions which held against the armed forces were reversed on appeal, some lower courts were seriously scrutinizing military practices. Thus, some observers and commentators anticipated the same full-scale judicial intervention in the armed forces that occurred in prisons, schools, mental hospitals and other state bureaucracies.

Despite these developments, however, direct judicial intervention in military management, except by the Court of Military Appeals, was limited. Military decision makers received greater deference from Article III federal judges than administrators of schools, mental hospitals, prisons, and other public bureaucracies. The Supreme Court intervened in military affairs only to narrow court-martial jurisdiction (as discussed above) and to rectify certain abuses in the administration of the draft law.

The high point of Supreme Court activism in matters of military personnel management involved the draft system. In *U.S. v. Seeger* (1965) and *U.S. v. Welsh* (1970) (see Greenawalt 1971: 31-68) the Supreme Court reversed criminal convictions of individuals who refused to be inducted into the armed forces after having been denied classifications as conscientious objectors. According to the plurality opinion in *Welsh*, section 6j of the Universal Military Service and Training Act had to be interpreted to include "all those whose conscience, spurred by deeply held moral, ethical, or religious beliefs, would give them no rest or peace if they allowed themselves to become part of an instrument of war." In other words, lack of affiliation with a pacifist church or belief in God or conventional religious training would not absolutely disqualify a draft registrant from conscientious objector classification. The decisions forced local draft boards to evaluate the "sincerity" and "strength" of a registrant's "opposition to all war." While purely political and sociological opposition to war would not qualify a registrant for CO status, the required opposition to war could stem from moral, ethical, and philosophical beliefs.

Shortly after *Welsh*, the Supreme Court indicated that limits to the carving up of the Draft Law had been reached. In *Gillette v. United States* (1971), petitioners argued that limiting conscientious objector status to opponents "of all wars" was unconstitutional because it unfairly discriminated against those opposed only to "unjust wars." Justice Marshall's majority opinion noted the Court's unwillingness to add to the burden already imposed upon the administration of the draft system.

Supreme Court pressure on the draft system also emanated from its decisions in *Ostereich v. Selective Service Board* (1968) and *Mulloy v. U.S.* (1970). In *Ostereich* the Court held that selective service classifications could be challenged in federal court prior to induction and in *Mulloy* the Court held that a local board must reopen its classification where a registrant makes a nonfrivolous claim concerning the existence of facts not previously considered by the board. Conscientious objection also surfaced within the armed forces and some lower federal courts did not shy away from reviewing discharge refusals (see Sherman 1969).

The court decisions may well have contributed to the dissolution of the draft system by undermining its legitimacy and by greatly complicating its administration. The *Seeger* and *Welsh* tests and the demands for increased procedural and substantive rationality may simply have been beyond the administrative competence of many local boards which were simply unaware of the Supreme Court decisions; others that were aware did not readily accept that views like Seeger's or Welsh's were "sincere" (see Rabin 1967: 657-71). The number of registrants classified as conscientious objectors (available for alternative service) sharply increased from 13 per 1000 in 1965 to 50 per 1000 in 1971 (Bureau of the Census 1976). Even so, in 1971 the New York Civil Liberties Union claimed a 50 percent success rate nationwide for those disputing CO classifications and a 90 percent success rate for cases tried by their attorneys (Civil Liberties in New York 1971).

The draft litigation and judicial disputes over in-service conscientious objectors are the exceptions which prove the rule. Recent Supreme Court opinions evince strong support for the current draft registration law (see *Rostker v. Goldberg* 1981; *Selective Service System v. Minnesota Public Interest Research Group* 1984; *U.S. v Wayte* 1985).

Even during the Vietnam War period the federal courts remained, for the most part, reluctant to review the complaints of unfair treatment brought by service personnel. Even when federal courts agreed to review such disputes, and even when they agreed in priniciple with an abstract assertion of a serviceman's claim, direct relief was rarely granted. Several of the most activist decisions were reversed on appeal. After the Vietnam War the federal courts, under the Supreme Court's leadership, have been withdrawing from even the limited intervention that occurred in the late 1960s and early 1970s. *Parker v. Levy* (1974) made it clear that judicial activism would not penetrate the armed forces. The decision, authored by Justice Rehnquist, reversed the lower court's holding that the General Articles (UCMJ Arts. 133, 134) were unconstitutionally vague and overbroad. Responsive to claims about the need to maintain institutional order and control, Justice Rehnquist stressed the importance of traditional military values, the distinctiveness of military society and its reliance on a unique body of military custom as well as positive law.

> This Court has long recognized that the military is, by necessity, a specialized society separate from civilian society. We have also recognized that the military has, again by necessity, developed laws and traditions of its own during its long history. The difference between the military and civilian commu-

nities results from the fact that "it is the primary business of armies and navies to be ready to fight wars should the occasion arise."

Rehnquist reached back to the nineteenth century to quote from *In re Grimley* (1890):

An army is not a deliberative body. It is the executive arm. Its law is that of obedience. No question can be left open as to the right to command in the officer, or the duty of obedience in the soldier.

He recalled an even older case, *Martin v. Mott* (1872), to find authority for the proposition that military law cannot be equated with a civilian criminal code:

Courts-martial, when duly organized, are bound to execute their duties, and regulate their modes of processing, in the absence of positive enactments. Upon any other principle, courts-martial would be left without any adequate means to exercise the authority confided to them, for there could scarcely be framed a positive code to provide for the infinite variety of incidents applicable to them.

If any doubt remained about the deference of the Supreme Court to military practices, it was dispelled by *Middendorf v. Henry* (1976), which rejected the argument that counsel at summary court-martial was constitutionally compelled. This holding actually retracted rights of service personnel, since the Court of Military Appeals had previously held assigned counsel to be required at such proceedings (*U.S. v. Alderman* 1973). (The air force and the army had moved on their own to assign counsel to summary court-martial defendants, and the navy and marine corps permitted retained counsel). Justice Rehnquist continued to develop his thesis that the military is "a society apart." There was no reference to social science scholarship documenting the substantial civilianization of the armed forces that had occurred since World War II. Instead Rehnquist quoted from precedents describing the military as it existed in the mid-nineteenth century.

In the same term, the Court handed down *Greer v. Spock* (1976). At issue was the constitutionality of the Fort Dix commander's refusal to permit presidential candidate Benjamin Spock to campaign on post. Only three years before, the Court had held that a base commander could not prohibit leafletting on a public access road crossing a military base (*Flower v. U.S.* 1972). It now took a very different view of the sanctity of the military enclave. Justice Stewart, who had dissented in both *Levy* and *Middendorf*, wrote the majority opinion (Justices Marshall and Brennan dissenting), reversing the Court of Appeal's injunction (*Spock v. David* 1972) in Spock's behalf. Stewart emphasized the need to insulate the military from civilian politics:

> One of the very purposes for which the Constitution was ordained and established was to "provide for the common defense," and this Court over the years has on countless occasions recognized the special constitutional function of the military in our national life, a function both explicit and indispensable. In short, it is "the primary business of armies and navies to fight wars should the occasion arise" (citing *Toth*). And it is consequently the business of a military installation like Fort Dix to train soldiers, not to provide a public forum.
>
> A necessary concommitant of the basic function of a military installation has been the "historically unquestioned power of its commanding officer summarily to exclude civilians from the area of his command." The notion that federal military reservations, like municipal streets and parks, have traditionally served as a place for free public assembly and communication of thoughts by private citizens is thus historically and constitutionally false." [*Middendorf v. Henry* 1976, quoting *Cafeteria Workers v. McElroy* 1961]

The decision again stressed the distinctiveness of military society, the sanctity of its enclaves and need for command discretion.[5]

The Court's view has not changed in the 1980s. In the draft registration case, *Rostker v. Goldberg* (1981), the court rejected the claim that the new draft registration program discriminated against men. Justice Rehnquist, writing for the majority, found that Congress acted well within its constitutional authority to raise and regulate armies and navies when it authorized the registration of men and not women. Rehnquist noted that, especially where Congress specifically considered the question of the law's constitutionality, "we [the Court] must be particularly careful not to substitute our judgment of what is desirable for that of Congress." Similarly in *Brown v. Glines* (1980), where the Court upheld regulations imposing a prior restraint on the right of military personnel to petition, Justice Powell stated that "the special character of the military requires civilian authorities to accord military commanders some flexibility in dealing with matters that affect internal discipline and morality."

The same reasoning inspired the Court's decision in *Chappell v. Wallace* (1983). There, navy enlisted men claimed they were discriminated against by their superior officers who allegedly failed to assign them desirable duties, threatened them, gave them low performance evaluations, and imposed penalties of unusual severity because of their minority race. The Court recognized the existence of two systems of justice—one for civilians and one for military personnel—and unanimously held that military personnel may not maintain a suit to recover damages from a superior officer for alleged constitutional violations.

The post–Vietnam period has been marked by strong judicial deference to those who command the all-volunteer armed forces. Perhaps the absence of a wartime situation and of a conscript force has lessened concern for administrative abuses. The contract military may simply be left to strike its own bargains, although within limits to be sure. While direct judicial intervention into the military has been limited, the indirect impact of court decisions may be significant. It is likely that commanders do not relish court litigation where they must defend procedures in a public forum, even when they ultimately win. Processes of social learning emanating from judicial opinions and the practicalities of litigation may influence the military to carry out its own legal reforms. Litigation over involuntary discharge of pregnant servicewomen is an excellent example. As the issue drew attention in the press and negative decisions by a few district courts (see *Crawford v. Cushman* 1976) the military's position changed. New regulations make substantial progress in accommodating pregnant personnel and keeping them in the armed forces. Thus, the impact of the federal courts may be indirect and diffuse. A comprehensive analysis of the relationship between military and civilian law would have to pay extensive attention to the diffusion of civilian legal norms into the armed forces.

Congress and Military Law Reform

Article 1 Section 8 gives to Congress the power to make rules governing the land and naval forces. Much of "military law" is congressional law. The most important statute is the Uniform Code of Military Justice which, in the wake of widespread public and congressional criticism of World War II disciplinary practices, brought about a major reform of military criminal law (see Generous 1973). The way the UCMJ was passed illustrates the pattern of legislative military law reform since World War II. Despite persistent criticism of military justice, reforms have come about on the military's own terms (see *Sherman* 1971: 25). This is not to say that military law reform would have occurred without pressure from the outside. A few congressmen have played important roles, but what results have been achieved have had at least the tacit approval of some segment of the military high command. The first major revision of the UCMJ, the Military Justice Act of 1968, for example, was passed after years of effort by Senator Sam Ervin, but the act did not include Ervin's most important reforms pertaining to administrative discharges. The military's clout in Congress remains strong and it continues to be extremely unlikely that military law reforms could be passed over the military's concerted opposition. Summarizing efforts at military law reform since World War II, William Generous concludes, "Again and again, it was demonstrated that nothing could be wrung from Congress unless all the services plus the Court of Military Appeals agreed on the point in question. And sometimes that was not enough" (Generous 1973).

Although congressional military law reform has been modest, changes have occurred. The Military Justice Act of 1968 did substantially strengthen the role of military lawyers and thereby contributed further to judicializing the court-martial system (see Sherman 1968-69: 45). The change of court-martial "law officer" to "military Judge" emphasized the transition to a system of military criminal justice. Similarly, transforming military "boards of review" to "courts of review" symbolized the movement towards civilianization. The act also provided for military judges at special courts-martial where bad-conduct discharges could be adjudged. At both a general court-martial and a bad-conduct special court-martial the accused was given the option of trial by a military judge alone.[6] In addition, the act assured the accused an absolute right to free, qualified, military defense counsel before general courts-martial and bad-conduct special courts and "in all other special courts-martial unless waived by the accused or when counsel is unavailable." The Act provides that defense counsel must be provided, except when such counsel "cannot be obtained on account of physical conditions or military exigencies," in which case the commander ordering the trial in the absence of a defense lawyer must make "a detailed written statement, to be appended to the record, stating why [lawyer defense counsel] could not be obtained" (Military Justice Act of 1968, §2[10] [B]). The role of the military lawyer has been greatly strengthened through CoMA decisions of the past several years (see Cooke 1977).

As opposition to the Vietnam War grew at home and within the ranks of the services themselves, several congressmen became more interested in "military justice." Senators Birch Bayh and Mark Hatfield introduced sweeping reform legislation into the 92nd Congress (see Sherman 1971). The Bayh-Bennet Bill would have abolished court-martial jurisdiction over all but typically military offenses and limited punishments to six months for violation of the General Articles. It would also have abolished Articles 88 and 89, which provide punishments for certain kinds of disloyal expressions ("contemptuous utterances against the President" and "disrespect" toward superior officers).

In addition to the Hatfield and Bayh-Bennet Bills, reform legislation was also introduced by Congressmen Charles Whalen, Jr., and Charles Price. Senator Ervin continued to reintroduce his legislation to protect the rights of service personnel facing administrative discharges (see Ervin 1972; Jones 1973). None of these bills won support from the military establishment; all languished within congressional committees.

Elements of the UCMJ were finally revised and streamlined in the Military Justice Act of 1983 (Pub. L. No. 98-209, 97 Stat. 1393; amending 10 U.S.C. §§ 801-940). The most important provisions of the Act allow the Supreme Court to review certain CoMA decisions. Either party in a case can seek review on a writ of certiorari and the high court has the discretion to accept or reject the case. Other changes in the appellate process include provisions permitting the government to appeal certain adverse rulings by the military judge and provisions allowing the accused to waive appellate review, except in capital cases. The Act also formalizes the procedure by which staff judge advocates make determinations concerning criminal charges. However, the base commander retains authority to decide whether a case should be referred to a general court-martial for trial. The base commander, as the "convening authority," is further authorized to review the sentence imposed after court-martial. His is not a formal appellate review, but rather a consideration of materials submitted by the accused rebutting the sentencing recommendation of the judge advocate. A final significant addition to the UCMJ is a prohibition against drug use and sale in which Congress expressly recognized "the substantial dangers to morale and readiness created by drug abuse." (see Cooke 1984)

The Manual for Courts-Martial was also updated recently. Among the revisions are a new type of pretrial restraint called a "condition on liberty" (ordering two soldiers to stay away from each other), the use of preventive detention in cases of "serious criminal misconduct," the giving of *Miranda*-type warnings as a prerequisite to confinement, and specific procedures for review of confinement. The 1984 Manual provides for broader discovery than federal criminal practice in order to eliminate gamesmanship from the pretrial process. One of the more controversial changes is a speedy trial standard which requires that the accused be brought to trial within 120 days no matter what the offense, level of court, or type of restraint. The specific rules governing summary courts-martial reiterate that there is no constitutional or statutory right to counsel for the accused, but they also state that if the accused has retained a civilian counsel, that attorney must be permitted to attend if it will not necessarily delay the proceedings. There are also major innovations in the Military Rules of Evidence reflecting the evolution of Fourth Amendment jurisprudence over the last dozen years. (see *Army Lawyer* 1984).

Other Sources of Legal Change

Admittedly, the analysis presented here is fragmentary; yet it suggests that legal change has not been imposed upon the military by outside actors.

The Court of Military Appeals is the only outside institution which has had a profound impact on military law. The federal courts certainly have not played the activist role in the military context that they have played elsewhere. Such interest groups as the American Legion, American Bar Association, the Bar Association of the City of New York (Committee on Military Justice and Military Affairs 1976), and the American Civil Liberties Union have persistently advocated military law reforms, but with minor successes. Congress, despite the passage of the UCMJ and the Military Justice Act of 1968, has not been a major initiator of military law reform.

This means that the evolution of military law lies largely, but not completely, in the hands of military leaders themselves. Therefore, students of military law must concentrate on the forces within the Department of Defense and the armed services that facilitate and inhibit the evolution of military law. Such analysis would do well to focus both on the nonlegal specialists among the high command and the legal specialists who constitute the JAG corps and military judges. That the military leadership is not monolithically opposed to the importation of civilian legal norms is indicated by the role of various generals and admirals in evaluating the military justice system from the time of the Code Committee to the present. The 1972 Task Force on Military Justice, which sharply criticized the military justice system in many areas, was composed of several generals and admirals (Report of the Task Force on the Administration of Military Justice 1977).

Much could be learned about the civilian Defense Department leadership and top officer corps by studying the internal dynamics of military law reform. We should like to know, for example, how the top officer corps is exposed to the larger society's legal culture and with what affect, and whether Janowitz's distinction between military leaders who are pragmatists and absolutists bears on the the rights of service personnel and the judicialization of military procedures. (Janowitz 1971).

The changing role and impact of military lawyers and judges has not, to my knowledge, received scholarly attention. Their social origins, education, and professional commitments might be of immense importance in explaining the day-to-day practice of military law. In order to understand the evolution of military law we need to understand the organizational development of the JAG corps. Did the creation of separate JAG corps bring about a more "professional," civilian-oriented military bar? Has the military lawyer contributed to a more legalized and litigious military? Did the noncareer lawyers who entered the armed services during the Vietnam period have a civilizing effect on policies of dissent, personal privacy and other such rights?

The service law schools, particularly the Army JAG School at Charlottesville, Virginia, seem to constitute important institutional links with the civilian bar and with civilian juridical institutions. The Army JAG School seems anxious to be recognized as a bona fide legal institution. Certainly, the school's law journal, the *Military Law Review*, closely resembles its civilian counterparts. Moreover, the bias in the *Military Law Review* articles favors greater civilianization. Whether dealing with federal court review of military criminal or administrative decisions or with constitutional rights or with due process, *Military Law Review* authors, many of them JAG School faculty, seem inevitably to advocate further civilianization.

The Implications of Legal Change for the All-Volunteer Force

Discipline and Command Control

The absence of empirical research makes it difficult to draw historical conclusions about the impact of legal change on military organization. Even if there were a corpus of such research, it would be difficult to attribute any particular transitions in military organization solely to legal change when other powerful forces have simultaneously affected the armed forces. The most important possible consequence of military legal change—a weakening of command control and combat effectiveness—is itself the subject of considerable debate. The extent of organizational breakdown in U.S. Vietnam forces is a matter of dispute (compare Moskos 1970, Hauser 1973, and Gabriel and Savage 1978). Even were it to be shown that there was a serious deterioration of discipline, it seems likely that the unpopularity of the Vietnam War, the politicization of minority youth, the antiestablishment orientation of youth culture and the one-year rotation system were all more important than the judicializing of military law.

Since the time of the UCMJ's passage, critics have persistently predicted that command control and combat effectiveness would be undermined by each new legal reform and CoMA decision. A 1952 poll of navy units found that

> Personal reactions in the fleet concerning the Uniform Code of Military Justice when it became effective one year ago were decidedly negative. In six months time the feeling abated to the extent that in the main the Code itself was considered sound and workable but that the Manual for Court-Martial needed drastic revision. The current opinion is that, generally, the concepts of the Manual are basically sound and workable. [Generous 1973:71]

The armed forces adapted to the UCMJ with relative ease despite the Korean conflict and the claims of popular military writers of the 1950s who spoke of "the dilution of military discipline resulting from the democratizing reforms of the Doolittle Board and the Uniform Code of Military Justice" (Moskos 1970).

The first in-service attack on the Code came in the 1960 Powell Commission Report to the Secretary of the Army (Committee on the Uniform Code of Military Justice 1960). The Report criticized liberal CoMA decisions for overlegalizing the court-martial system, thus making the Code cumbersome to administer and inadequate for maintaining proper discipline. Except for strengthening punishments available to commanders under Article 15, however, nothing came of the Report's recommendations for reversing a variety of liberal reforms in the military's criminal procedure.

Since the Powell Commission there has been no further organized in-service opposition to the military justice system, although sporadic criticisms continue. For example, at the Federal Bar Association's Annual Convention, San Juan, Puerto Rico, November 1977, the following speech is reported:

> Rear Admiral Penrose L. Albright of Arlington, Virginia, spoke on the problem of client determinism in the military justice system, and decried what he considered the "poor climate" presently existing in the military justice field. The state of discipline in the armed forces today, he said, is intolerable. A primary cause of this condition can be traced to the UCMJ and, more particularly to its development as an increasingly incomprehensible instrument for discipline by line military leadership. Before the enactment of the Code, the court-martial system was essentially a line-and-command function wherein the assistance of lawyers was helpful but not essential. But the Code has made military justice a specialization that exceeds the capability of the non-lawyer line officer. . . . [CoMA's] activity has produced an alienation and mistrust in the minds of the line leadership; they perceive the Code as unwieldy, unpredictable and unsympathetic to the needs of military discipline. Thus, the military has looked more and more to administrative measures to circumvent or avoid the military justice system; but such alternatives are not adequate substitutes for military justice.

How far norms of justice are now accepted as legitimate goals of military law is illustrated by a 1971 law review article authored by General William Westmoreland.

> The protection of individual rights is more than ever a central issue in our society today. An effective system of military justice, therefore, must provide of necessity practical checks and balances to assure protection of the rights of individuals. It must prevent abuses of punitive powers, and it should promote the confidence of military personnel and the general public in its overall fairness. It should set an example of efficient and enlightened disposition of

criminal charges within the framework of American legal principles. Military justice should be efficient, speedy and fair. [Westmoreland 1971:8]

Even though new reform proposals continue to be opposed, the military has made many legal changes on its own. Although prompted by executive order, the racial desegregation of the armed forces proceeded smoothly and expeditiously in the early 1950s. The 1969 Directive on Dissent was an important step in recognizing servicemen's First Amendment rights. The military is moving very rapidly to reevaluate the status of women in light of current equal protection norms. As was the case with racial integration, the military may in the near future reach further than many civilian institutions in extending equal rights to women. The press for further reform will, of course, continue. In the criminal procedure area, reformers seek to limit further the commander's court-martial role. There is demand for an independent defense corps within JAG. Additional protections at administrative discharge hearings and Article 15 proceedings and limitations on punishments for violating the General Articles are also being pushed.

The greatest unresolved tension is not in criminal or administrative procedures, but in the area of First Amendment rights (see *Brown v. Glines* 1980; *Secretary of the Navy v. Haff* 1980). As the peacetime all-volunteer force promotes itself as an alternative opportunity for skilled employment and educational advancement, there will be continued pressure to recognize the rights of service personnel as coextensive with those of civilian workers (see Marquette Law Review 1982: 684-88). Whether the military can absorb more dissent and more expressive individual conduct is uncertain. Too much dissent could conceivably undermine military authority and discipline, but suppression could cause alienation and loss of respect for commanders. As the Supreme Court noted in *Brown v. Glines* (1980) upholding the requirement of prior approval to circulate petitions, "Since a commander is charged with maintaining morale, discipline, and readiness, he must have authority over the distribution of materials that could affect adversely these essential attributes of an effective military force."

Civilian Workplace Model and Public Employee Unionism

We have been considering the contribution of several post–World War II trends to the redefinition of military service from status to contract. What consequences can be predicted for the volunteer force? First, the classification of discharges as honorable and dishonorable may wither away (Legislation to do so has been introduced in Congress). Approximately 97 percent of all discharges are classified as honorable, another example of the decline in the moral basis of military service. The adoption of many aspects of the civilian workplace model may lead inevitably to a more civilian-like system of hiring and firing. This shift may be especially attractive to military decision makers as the expansion of due process in the criminal and administrative contexts increases the time and expense of adjudging less-than-honorable discharges. Perhaps the military's need for the special sanction of a lifetime stigmatizing discharge to motivate personnel to perform on the job has diminished as salary and other benefits have improved. With a new generation of recruits choosing military service as an attractive work option, this special sanction may become more and more anomalous, as well as more expensive to administer.

A more legalistic military in which the relationship between the serviceman and the state is contractually defined may be ripe for some form of public employee unionism. Currently, there is substantial political opposition to the idea, but that opposition may weaken in the future, especially if bread-and-butter issues divide the rank and file from the Pentagon. What impact unionism might have on the all-volunteer force is beyond the scope of this paper (see Cartright and Thurmond 1977; McCollum and Robinson 1977; Ostan 1977), but collective bargaining is compatible with the move to the all-volunteer force and with the current emphasis upon the contractual nature of military service.

Notes

1. For decisions in recent years incorporating civilian due process norms into court-martial proceedings see *U.S. v. Douglas* (1976) striking down use of pretrial transcripts at trial; *U.S. v. Courtney,* (1976) striking down certain maximum sentences; *U.S. v. Ware* (1976) striking down convening authority's power to overrule trial judge; *U.S. v. Jordan* (1976) striking down evidentiary rules exempting certain foreign searches from the more exacting standards of search and seizure law; *Giles v. Secretary of the Army* (1980) striking down compulsory urine tests as compelled self-incrimination (see also Cooke 1977).
2. See, for example, Report to the United States Congress by the Controller General of the United States, *Military Jury System Needs Safeguards Found in Civilian Federal Courts,* 1977.
3. Personal conversations with Army JAG School faculty at Conference on Military Law, Charlottesville, Va. (June 1-3, 1977).
4. The number of reported federal court decisions on military issues (including the Court of Claims) for selected years from 1939-1981 are as follows.

Year	Number of reported decisions*
1939	222
1945	245
1950	194
1955	386
1960	372
1965	325
1968	1387

1969	1995
1970	1001
1972	1016
1975	282
1977	140
1979	122
1981	160

*Source: *West's Federal Digest.*

5. Three lower court decisions demonstrate a similar retrenchment of the lower federal courts in military matters. In *Carlson v. Schlesinger* (1975) servicemen in Vietnam sought invalidation of their commander's refusal to allow circulation of antiwar petitions and to expunge their arrest records. The D.C. Circuit Court of Appeals ruled against the servicemen noting that free speech is not an absolute and that in a battle zone it had to be balanced against military necessity. The court drew heavily on language from *Orloff v. Willoughby* (1953) and *Parker v. Levy* (1974): it was not the business of the courts to interfere in the management of the armed forces. In a subsequent case, *Culver v. Secretary of the Army* (1977) the D.C. court had the opportunity to limit *Carlson* to dissent on the battlefield. Faced with the question of whether the air force could court-martial two hundred servicemen for participating in an antiwar demonstration in London, the Court once again held that it was permissible to suppress expression of servicemen, because "it would be unseemly and possibly disruptive . . . for members of the military to engage in demonstration in the host country no matter what political interest was being pressed." In *Committee for G.I. Rights v. Callaway* (1975) the D.C. court again stressed the uniqueness of military life in upholding warrantless searches and intrusive controls over servicemen identified as drug abusers. "The fundamental necessity of obedience, and the consequent necessity for imposition of discipline, may render permissible within the military that which would be constitutionally impermissible outside of it." As in the case of the extention of counsel to summary court-martial, the Court of Military Appeals came to the opposite conclusion, striking down warrantless inspections used to uncover drug offenses (*U.S. v. Roberts* 1976).

6. Whereas in a federal civilian criminal trial the jury is selected from a broad base of eligible persons pursuant to a detailed federal statute designed to insure complete impartiality, the military "jury," or rather the members of the court-martial, are appointed by the convening authority. For a recent criticism of this court-martial feature and a recommendation to make court-martial panels more like juries, see Report to the Congress by the Controller General of the United States (1977).

2

Aliens in the U.S. Armed Forces: A Historico-Legal Analysis

with Leslie Anne Hayes

Growing interest in the relationship between military service and citizenship (Janowitz 1975:185; Feld 1975:191) stimulates the following question: to what extent has military service been the sole prerogative or obligation of citizens in the United States? While the answer might have some impact on current policy regarding the eligibility of noncitizens to serve in the All-Volunteer Force (AVF), the participation of aliens in the armed forces also throws light on the relationship between mass armies and a mass citizenry and on the relationship between war and nation building.

This chapter focuses on the way the distinction between citizens and aliens relates to military service, but one could also examine the relationship between the Civil War and the emergence of a concept of national citizenship (Kettner 1978) or on the relationship between lowering the draft age and passage of the Twenty-sixth Amendment.[1]

Our thesis is that with respect to military service, the United States has not made much of the distinction between citizens and aliens. In the early years of U.S. history, this partly reflected the weakness of the concept of national citizenship. It also reflected the need to recruit manpower during crises, a need that became even more acute during the Civil War and the twentieth century world wars. Aliens were not recruited as mercenaries, however. To the contrary, the country has consistently provided for the expeditious naturalization of alien military personnel, and under certain circumstances citizenship has been bluntly offered to aliens as a quid pro quo for a tour of honorable service in the U.S. armed forces. The idea that one who participates in national defense is entitled to become a citizen is deeply embedded in our traditions. Millions of immigrants have entered the societal mainstream, legally and socially, by serving in the armed forces.

The Eligibility of Aliens to Serve in the Armed Forces

From the birth of the Republic, service in the armed forces has been open to otherwise qualified noncitizens, at least during wartime or other periods when recruiting sufficient manpower was problematic. The role played by foreign troops in the American Revolution is well known; for example, Lafayette, Dekalb, Kosciusko, von Steuben, and their men fought with the Continental forces. It is true that after the Revolutionary War,[2] except during the War of 1812, the Army restricted enlistments to citizens, but this does not indicate a judgment that military service should be reserved as a special prerogative of citizens.

During this period the issue of a citizenship qualification for military service was academic since the standing army numbered no more than a few thousand (Weigley 1967:89-183). And since the concept of national citizenship did not emerge until the Civil War, an alien who wished to serve had only to become a citizen of a state, a rather simple matter. During the War of 1812 (Act of Dec. 24, 1811) and the Mexican War (Act of Jan. 12, 1847) when the nation needed military manpower, however, noncitizens were lawfully allowed to serve in the Army. From 1813 to 1864, the Navy did not permit the enlistment of foreign nationals from certain countries because of the sensitive impressment issue that assumed such importance in the events leading to the War of 1812. Congress reasoned, for example, that if no British seamen served on U.S. ships, the British could not "mistakenly" impress U.S. citizens into the British Navy (25 Annals of Congress 952-939 [1813]). But foreign nationals of countries which did not prohibit the employment of Americans on their ships were eligible to serve in the United States Navy (Act of March 3, 1913). In 1864, the citizenship requirement for seamen, but not for naval officers, was repealed (Act of June 28, 1864).

During the Civil War, aliens were eligible to enlist in the Union Army.[3] Not only were foreigners accepted, they were actively solicited. Aliens who were not subject to conscription could serve in regiments of their choice as substitutes for draftees (Murdock 1971:190). Federal, state, and local governments, as well as private organizations, offered bounties to encourage enlistment (Murdock 1967:20). In fact, newly arrived immigrants were often the victims of unscrupulous bounty-brokers (Lonn 1951:452-59).

European immigrants swamped United States consulates volunteering to serve in the Union Army in exchange for passage to the United States. The federal government did not officially recruit in Europe because of objections by European governments (Department of State 1864), but many state and local organizations did establish European recruiting operations since foreign recruits counted toward each state's draft quota.[4] Foreign officers were permitted to organize and lead their own regiments (Lonn 1951:92).

In 1894, in response to nativist protest against Eastern European immigration, Congress enacted a law to limit Army enlistments to citizens and aliens who declared on oath their intention to become citizens.

> In time of peace no person (except an Indian) who is not a citizen of the United States, or who had not made legal declaration of his intention to become a citizen of the United States, or who cannot speak, read and write the English Language, or who is over thirty years of age, shall be enlisted for the first enlistment in the Army. [Act of Aug. 1, 1894]

The House Committee on Military Affairs stated that "it is well known . . . that a very small proportion of foreigners are naturalized before entering the service or have taken steps to renounce their allegiance to foreign governments," and concluded, "there can be no good reason, in time of peace at least, why the Army should not be composed of persons whose allegiance is wholly and absolutely due to the United States government." (H.R. Rep. No. 339, 53d Cong 2d Sess. 2 [1894]). But even the 1894 Act did not pose a serious obstacle to an alien who wanted to serve in the military, since the declaration of intention was an easily executed formality.[5] The English fluency and literacy requirement, which was not repealed until 1920 (Act of June 14, 1920), might have been more of a de facto barrier to aliens and foreign-born citizens. Furthermore, the 1894 statute applied only in time of peace; even nondeclarant aliens were eligible to serve during wartime.

Still, the Adjutant General circulated a letter to recruiting officers on June 3, 1899, stating that "enlistments will be confined to persons who are citizens of the United States, or who have made a declaration of intention to become citizens thereof" (War Department Annual Report 1897-1898: 302), apparently blocking the participation of nondeclarant aliens in the Spanish American War.

During World War I, with manpower needs once again acute, all aliens except citizens of enemy nations were eligible to enlist (War Department Annual Report 1917:189-90). However, during the rapid demobilization following the war (Weigley 1967:358, 396), nondeclarant aliens were again subject to the 1894 prohibition against enlisting in peacetime. This restriction reflected the tide of antiimmigrant feeling sweeping the country during the so-called red scare. In 1921 Congress imposed the first immigration quotas in U.S. history (Act of May 19, 1921).

Up to World War II, military service was open to declarant aliens, but the distinction between declarants and nondeclarants disappeared during the war.[6] According to Army Regulations, aliens were classified in three groups: cobelligerent, neutral, and enemy. Aliens falling in the first two categories were "acceptable for induction, if otherwise qualified." Aliens who were nationals of countries with which the United States was at war were treated differently. Japanese aliens, except nationals of subject countries of the Japanese empire, were not accepted. Other enemy aliens could enlist, although they were subject to an investigation.

Immediately following World War II, when the key military manpower problem was demobilization, the Department of War issued a regulation providing that "First enlistments in the Regular Army are limited to citizens of the United States." (10 C.F.R. § 701.30 [1946 Suppl.]) However, by 1948, with the Cold War expanding (Weigley 1967:501), declarant aliens once more became eligible to serve (32 C.F.R. § 571.1 [1949]).

In 1961, Congress finally revised the 1894 statute. The new law reflected the fact that the declaration of intention requirement had been dropped from the Immigration and Naturalization Law.

> In time of peace, no person may be accepted for original enlistment in the Army (or Air Force) unless he is a citizen of the United States or has been lawfully admitted to the United States for permanent residence. [Act of Aug. 17, 1961]

Thus, all permanent residents, whether or not they intend to become citizens, are now eligible to enlist. In March 1979, for example, it was reported that 14,000 alien personnel were serving in the Army, and 12,800, 5,000 and 3,600 in the Navy, Air Force, and Marine Corps, respectively. Altogether, they constituted roughly 1.8 percent of the two million uniformed members of the armed forces.

Citizenship Qualifications for Officers

As we have already noted, during the American Revolution citizens of foreign countries served on the side of Continental forces in the very highest ranks. In 1808, Congress imposed the first restrictions against aliens serving as officers (Act of April 13, 1808).[7] During the Civil War, however, aliens could obtain commissions in regular and foreign language regiments of the Union Army (Lonn 1951:92). In 1892, one route to a commission, promotion from the enlisted ranks, was closed to aliens (Act of July 30, 1892). The National Defense Act of 1916 further restricted granting commissions to noncitizens. The Act limited the appointment of aliens to those who graduated from distinguished colleges and candidates from civilian life (National Defense Act of 1916).

Aliens were denied all opportunities of obtaining a commission in 1920 during the so-called red scare, when the Department of War made citizenship an absolute qualification for commissions in the regular Army (Army Regulations 605-5 [1920]). During World War II this requirement was relaxed (10 C.F.R. §73.121 [1943 Cum. Suppl.]), so that citizens of countries allied with the United States could be appointed as officers. After World War II, Congress passed the law which is still in effect: all persons appointed as officers in the regular Army and regular Air Force must be citizens of the United States (Officer Personnel Act of 1947). Some aliens, however, are eligible to serve as officers "in medical, dental, or allied specialist categories" under an exception created by the 1957 Selective Service Act. Alien doctors and dentists who serve as commissioned officers may take an oath of service and obedience rather than the usual oath of loyalty (Act of June 25, 1957).

The National Defense Act of 1961, which created the Officers' Reserve Corps, mandated that all reserve officers be citizens. But over the years Congress has loosened this requirement. The Armed Forces Reserve Act of 1952 permits the president to appoint as reserve officers declarant aliens and those aliens who had previously served in the armed forces. The present law, passed in 1963, allows aliens with permanent resident status to obtain commissions in the reserves (Act of Dec. 23, 1963). If activated, alien reserve officers may serve on active duty.

In sum, except during the first half of the nineteenth century, when the armed forces numbered fewer than 10,000, aliens with a declared intention of becoming citizens have been eligible to serve in the armed forces. During the Civil War practically any foreigner, otherwise qualified, was acceptable to the Union Army. Aside from barriers to aliens of enemy nations, enlistment opportunities during both world wars were available to aliens. After World War II those immigrants admitted to the United States for permanent residence became ineligible for military service whether or not they ultimately desired U.S. citizenship. The modern distinction is not between declarants and nondeclarants nor between citizens and aliens; the key distinction is now between aliens legally admitted to the United States for permanent residence and those aliens unable to obtain visas for permanent settlement. Immigration policies and procedures now place the only limits on eligibility to serve.

The nation has been flexible enough to utilize noncitizens as military personnel when manpower needs require it. Aside from the periods of hysteria about the overall negative effect of immigrants on U.S. society, concerns about loyalty have not convinced Congress or the Defense Department to impose restrictions on the recruitment of aliens. Only relations with foreign governments seem to have posed a persistent, if relatively unimportant, obstacle to enlisting foreign nationals.

Illegal or undocumented aliens, of course, are not eligible to serve in the armed forces as officers or enlisted personnel. In fact, knowing recruitment of an illegal alien can be punished by court-martial (10 U.S.C. § 884 [1976]). Yet, in spite of the law, illegal aliens have slipped into the All-Volunteer Force, and in some cases have been retained by the military even after their immigration status has been revealed.[8] According to Immigration and Naturalization Service (INS) operating instructions 242.1 (c), no action will be taken against a deportable alien serving in the armed forces until his discharge; thus, the armed forces have the option of retaining such a person. It seems highly unlikely that an illegal alien with an honorable discharge from the United States armed forces would actually be deported. An alien in this situation might be able to obtain an adjustment of status under the immigration law (8 U.S.C. §1255 [1976]), or by a private bill introduced in Congress by either a senator or representative.

Citizenship and Obligatory Military Service

On April 16, 1862, the Confederate States of America passed a first conscription act (Act of April 16, 1862). This, and later Confederate draft laws, authorized the conscription of all white male residents in the Confederacy of appropriate age who were not exempt by municipal or international law. The Confederate Congress never dealt explicitly with the draft liability of aliens, but several executive and judicial interpretations exempted aliens who could prove that they did not intend to establish permanent residence in the Confederacy (Lonn 1951:386). This exemption reflects the view that it would be unfair to impress visitors, foreign business men, and similar categories into a host nation's armed forces. In addition, of course, it would also expose the host nation's citizens to similar treatment when travelling abroad.

In the North, the Militia Act of July 17, 1862 gave the President authority to issue rules for calling up the state militia. Acting pursuant to authority delegated to him, Secretary of State Seward declared that any alien who had ever voted was subject to the draft, whether or not he had declared his intention to become a citizen.[9] In 1983, after considerable debate (*Congressional Globe*, 37th Cong.), Congress provided that all "persons of foreign birth who shall have declared on oath their intention to become citizens" were liable for conscription (Act of March 3, 1863). The following year's legislation broadened the category of aliens subject to the draft by including nondeclarants who had ever voted or held public office (Act of Feb. 24, 1864). The principle emerged that while not all inhabitants of a territory would be vulnerable to conscription, all those who passed some threshhold of minimum contact would be expected to serve if called. As Senator Trumbell, one of the authors of the 1864 act, put it, "one who voluntarily had taken part in the administration of government should be willing to perform military service." (*Congressional Globe*, 38th Cong., 1st Sess. 228 [1864])[10]

All aliens, declarants, and nondeclarants had to register with the Selective Service under the World War I draft law (Act of Aug. 31, 1918). Of 20,000,000 registrants, 3,877,000 were aliens: 2,607,000 were nondeclarants. The Selective Draft Act of 1917 allowed nondeclarants to claim an exemption from actually being drafted.[11] Despite this fact, as of September 12, 1918, according to the provost marshall general, 191,491 nondeclarants (in the 21- to 31-year-old age group) had waived their exemptions (Provost Marshall Gen. Rep. 1917:96). Assuming that the same proportions of citizens and aliens actually served, we estimate that approximately 9 percent of World War I military personnel were noncitizens.

The World War II draft provided that every male citizen and "every other male person residing in the United States" was liable for the draft (Act of Dec. 20, 1971); the distinction between declarants and nondeclarants was dropped. As in World War I, neutral aliens could apply for exemption, if willing to forego future citizenship. Aliens from enemy nations were only liable for the draft if the selective service system wanted to take them. The Selective Service regulations, which became effective on February 16, 1942, gave aliens residing in the United States until May 16, 1942, permission to leave the country if they wanted to escape liability for service (3 Dir. Sel. Serv. Rep. 233 [1943-44]). By early summer of 1945, 127,371 aliens had been drafted (4 Dir. Sel. Serv. Rep. 209 [1944-45]).

The 1948 draft law also established draft vulnerability for every prime age man residing in the United States. Any alien could claim an exemption if willing to sacrifice the possibility of future naturalization (Selective Service Act of 1948). In 1951 Congress imposed draft liability on all permanent residents and all other male aliens who had been in the country for more than a year, permitting only members of the latter category to claim an exemption (Universal Military Training and Service Act of 1951). The 1971 Selective Service Act (50 U.S.C. App. § 453-454 [1976]) imposed a registration requirement on aliens admitted as permanent residents, undocumented aliens,[12] and aliens who entered lawfully as nonimmigrants but who violated the conditions of their status. All males residing in the United States for one year or more were subject to being drafted (50 U.S.C. App. § 455 [1976]) except those lawfully admitted to the United States as nonimmigrants, a category which includes foreign ambassadors and diplomats, temporary visitors, students, foreign press, and other similar groups (8 U.S.C. § 1101(15) [1976]). Of course, under the current draft registration rules, aliens are required to register (Presidential Proclamation 4771, July 2, 1980).

To summarize, when the United States armed forces have needed to conscript personnel, the net has been cast wide enough to include aliens, even those with no intention of ever becoming United States citizens, and even those who entered or remained in the country in violation of immigration laws. Draft liability has not been a special obligation of "citizens," but an obligation of persons who have chosen to live within the territory and jurisdiction of the United States. Other than the perceived unfairness of drafting visitors, the main limitation of conscripting noncitizens arises from concern over foreign policy ramifications.[13]

Citizenship as a Reward for Military Service

Exchanging expedited naturalization or even citizenship itself for honorable military service is an offer that has recurrently been made to aliens throughout U.S. history. During the Revolutionary War, the Continental Congress offered land and citizenship (Franklin 1969:5) to enemy troops who would switch sides. After the war, the colonies rewarded those foreigners who fought with the Continental forces by making them citizens. The Marquis de Lafayette, for example, was made a citizen with all rights and privileges, by the assemblies of Maryland and Virginia. Maryland went so far as to extend citizenship to all male heirs of the Marquis forever (Maryland Laws vol. 2, ch. 12 [1784]).

During the Civil War, Congress provided that aliens who were honorably discharged from the Army could become citizens with or without a previous declaration of intention, with only a year's residency in the country, and with no proof of good moral character other than an honorable discharge (Act of July 17, 1862). The Confederacy also made special provision for the naturalization of alien soldiers (Act of Aug. 22, 1861). To induce aliens to volunteer for military service during World War I, Congress provided for the immediate naturalization of enlisted personnel without a prior declaration of intention or proof of residence (Act of May 9, 1918). No certificate of arrival[14] was required if the alien was actually serving in the armed forces. Thus the precedent for waiving lawful entry for wartime military personnel who wished to become citizens was established. Congress also showed special concern that aliens serving abroad have the opportunity to become citizens as soon as possible. The 1918 statute enabled alien servicemen while overseas to file petitions for naturalization, and to take the oath of allegiance. Because of administrative delays in processing applications in the federal courts, however, only 25,000 aliens were naturalized under these procedures (Hazard 1952:259-63). Altogether, during World War I, 123,335 alien soldiers achieved citizenship through military service (Bernard 1950:148).

The Nationality Act of 1940 eliminated both the five-year residence and declaration of intent requirements for those aliens who served honorably for three years. The Second War Powers Act of 1942 went further. It exempted wartime service personnel from practically all naturalization requirements; servicemen qualified after any lawful admission to the country, not necessarily for permanent residence. Later, even the requirement of lawful admission to the United States was waived for those military personnel who served outside the United States (Act of Dec. 22, 1944). More than 143,000 members of the United States armed forces—enlistees and draftees—were granted citizenship under these World War II provisions (Hazard 1952:279),[15] and 21,011 were naturalized abroad under a program similar to the one that operated during World War I (Ibid., 271).

The idea of exchanging citizenship for military service persisted after World War II. Various proposals for enlisting "displaced" Eastern European anticommunists stimulated a lively national debate. The Lodge (or Lodge-Philbin) Act, passed in 1950, originally provided for the enlistment overseas of 2,500 aliens from Eastern Europe.[16] The number of authorized enlistees was later increased to 12,500 (Act of June 19, 1951). The program, passed primarily for the benefit of the Army, permitted the recruitment of potential career military men with certain specialized scientific, technical, and professional skills. The Army particularly wanted persons familiar with foreign languages, customs, geography, and other local conditions (96 Cong. Rec. 9093-9108 [1950]). The quid pro quo was the opportunity to acquire citizenship. In support of the bill, the House Armed Services Committee reported:

> What the proposal now amounts to is an initial attempt—in a very limited degree—to secure badly needed, highly specialized career military men from a heretofore unused source. If the program is found to be extremely successful, it can be enlarged at a later date. As indicated, the enlistees would be aliens at the time of their admission in the Army, but the principal inducement for their enlistment would be the privilege of acquiring United States citizenship after demonstrating their fitness by honorable service in our armed forces. They are actually to be citizen candidates who, in return for the reward of the United States citizenship, will offer their own quid pro quo in the form of honest, faithful service in the Army of the United States. Unlike a foreign legion, which is merely a business transaction, this plan will be a matter of give and take from both a tangible and intangible point of view. On our side we give the advantage of a better life with the ultimate reward of citizenship. The citizen candidate, on his part, gives us rare human talents in highly specialized fields that will certainly be of substantial value to our country. The committee emphasizes that personnel enlisted under this program must have excellent qualifications for military service and possess special technical capabilities.

> The bill will afford our Government the opportunity of securing an appreciable number of badly needed, skilled military specialists and technicians who should make excellent American citizens after they have been carefully screened, selected, tried, and tested through service in our Armed Forces. [H.R. 2188, 81st Cong.]

Any alien who enlisted under this act, subsequently entered the United States or a possession under military orders, completed at least five years of honorable military service, and obtained an honorable discharge was deemed lawfully admitted to the United States for permanent residence for purposes of naturalization (Lodge Act of 1950). As of 1981, 1,029 persons had achieved citizenship under auspices of the Lodge Act (see Table 2.1). It appears from the brief congressional committee reports authorizing the program in 1955 and 1957, that the Army considered the program "highly successful," despite the fact that as of May 1957 only 1,302 aliens had been enlisted. The small number chosen from a much larger applicant pool was attributed to stringent security screening and high standards (H.R. 689, 85th Cong.).

Current naturalization provisions extend special benefits to aliens who serve honorably in the armed forces. An alien who performs three years of honorable peacetime service and is lawfully admitted to permanent residence is excused from ordinary residence requirements if he files a naturalization petition within six months after leaving the armed forces.[17] The applicant must comply with all other naturalization requirements, but the certification of honorable service is accepted as presumptive of good moral character and attachment and favorable disposition toward the United States (8 U.S.C. 1439 [1976]).

An alien who served in active duty during a specific wartime period—which traditionally extends long after the cessation of hostilities[18]—is entitled to more liberal naturalization benefits whenever he or she subsequently applies for naturalization (8 U.S.C. § 1770 [1976]).[19] Furthermore, an alien who served on active duty and was in United States territory at the time of enlistment or induction is exempt from the requirement of lawful admission to permanent residence.[20].

To conclude, the precedent for linking citizenship to military service is well established in American history. Since the Civil War, which marked the birth of the concept of national citizenship, military personnel have been afforded liberal and expedited naturalization opportunities. Other procedures have made it possible for individuals who failed to comply with the normal requirements of the immigration law to become citizens of the United States. Even "illegal aliens" who served in the wartime armed forces have been afforded the opportunity to become American citizens.

TABLE 2.1
Naturalization through Military Service, 1945-1975

Year	All Persons Naturalized Under all Provisions	Three Years Military Service	Active Duty in WWI & II, Korea, Vietnam	Lodge Act Enlisted
1945	231,402	25	22,695	
1946	150,062	39	15,213	
1947	93,904	83	16,462	
1948	70,150	98	1,070	
1949	66,594	450	2,006	
1950	66,346	343	1,724	
1951	54,716	300	675	
1952	88,6SS	194	1,391	
1953	92,051	192	1,383	
1954	117,831	61	13,684	
1955	209,526	36	11,922	
1956	145,885	75	7,129	
1957	138,043	229	616*	
1958	119,866	247	496	173
1959	103,931	730	399	179
1960	119,442	1,111	438	179
1961	132,450	1,175	492	52
1962	127,307	1,482	790	63
1963	124,178	1,640	820	100
1964	112,234	1,782	749	74
1965	104,299	1,696	1,365	24
1966	103,0S9	1,575	971	15
1967	104,092	1,648	1,040	3
1968	102,726	1,720	712	6
1969	98,709	875	4,578	5
1970	110,399	40	10,573	3
1971	108,407	14	9,479	56
1972	116,21S	22	8,446	5
1973	120,740	14	7,782	-
1974	131,655	13	6,832	3
1975	141,537	5	6,209	3
1976	142,504	5	5,623	3
1977	159,873	9	5,291	5
1978	173,535	10	5,111	5
1979	164,150	16	5,857	1
1980	157,938	11	4,584	0
1981	166,317	9	4,079	2

Source: Annual reports, Immigration and Naturalization Service (U.S. Dept. of Justice). As of late 1984, the 1982 Annual Report has not come out.
*Includes Lodge Act enlistees.

Military Institutions, Citizenship

In his essay, "Military Institutions and Citizenship in Western Societies," Morris Janowitz poses a challenging research agenda for students of the armed forces and society (see also Janowitz 1983). "The essential problematic issue is that of establishing the connection between military service in selected nation-states and the political concept of 'citizenship'" (Janowitz 1976). By "the political concept of 'citizenship'" Janowitz refers to the normative definition of the individual's relationship to a nation, and particularly to its governmental institutions. The emergence of nation building in Western societies was marked by the transformation of the individual's political status from *subject* to *citizen*. And, to follow Janowitz, universal conscription and military service must be seen as a form of citizen political participation that contributed to the shaping of democratic institutions. The term *citizen* serves to highlight and symbolize the dramatic transformation of the individual's relationship to the state that occurred with the breakdown of European feudalism and the rise of nationalistic democracies.

Citizen and citizenship are not only concepts having to do with the individual's participation in political culture, however, they are also legal "terms of art," which makes for some confusion. Constitutions and laws of state, in varying degrees of specificity, define who is to be included within the political community, and on what conditions. The legal term citizen is meaningful when contrasted with its opposites: *slave* and *alien*. In some societies, most particularly the Greek city-states and the Roman Republic, citizens constituted a minority of the total population and a caste with special privileges and obligations vis-a-vis the state. In the early Roman Republic, military citizenship was the special prerogative and obligation of citizens. By the late Roman Republic, military service became a vehicle for attaining citizenship (Goodfellow 1935). In democratic societies, where the vast majority of population participates equally (i.e., on the same basis) in political life, the legal term *citizen* sensitizes us to the existence of certain marginal and excluded groups.

In the United States, from a constitutional and legal point of view, whether an individual was a citizen was not particularly important, at least not until some of the highly discriminatory state legislation (against foreigners more than against aliens as such) of the early decades of the twentieth century. The preamble to the United States Constitution spoke of "We the people," not "We the citizens." The Bill of Rights protected "persons" not "citizens" against governmental abuse of power. The rights and obligations of persons residing in the United Stated did not depend upon their status as citizens or aliens. Aliens, who were not legally citizens, could in many states vote and hold office and were, of course, free to hold land and to engage in economic activity. Contrast the position of women, who although they were citizens, could neither vote nor engage in many occupations and commercial dealings. As the late constitutional scholar, Alexander Bickel, has pointed out, citizenship has not figured prominently in our constitutional history. He asserts that citizenship's main relevance "is international more than it is domestic, and domestic as a reflection of international. The citizen has a right as against the whole world to be here." (Bickel 1975:48).

The Civil War finally provided the United States with a definition of national citizenship. The Fourteenth Amendment, passed in 1868, stated that "all persons born or naturalized in the United States, and subject to the jurisdiction thereof, are citizens of the United States and of the State wherein they reside." To be sure, the main purpose of this statement was to normalize the status of those who had formerly been slaves. But the amendment could have laid the groundwork for a political caste system composed of citizens and aliens. Section I continues:

> No state shall make or enforce any law which shall abridge the privileges or immunities of citizens of the United States; nor shall any state deprive any person of life, liberty or property, without due process of law, nor deny to any person within its jurisdiction the equal protection of the laws.

A century of interpretation and elaboration of the Fourteenth Amendment decisively shows the nation's disinclination to establish castes of citizens and aliens. Had our constitutional history developed around the amendment's "privileges and immunities" clause, such a caste system might have materialized, with aliens occupying a completely different relationship to the government, like guest workers in some contemporary European states. Instead, the history of twentieth-century expansion of political, social, and economic rights has built upon the "due process" and "equal protection" clauses which protect the rights of *persons*. After upholding a variety of economic discriminations against aliens in the xenophobic early decades of the twentieth century, the Supreme Court reversed itself and in recent times has struck down most statutes distinguishing between citizens and aliens (Tribe 1978:1052-56).

Service in the armed forces was not defined as some special prerogative or obligation of a special class called "citizens," nor was it defined as a kind of punishment only fitting for a lower caste of "aliens." As we have shown, the opportunity and obligation of military service for the most part, has been open to and borne by citizens and aliens alike.

Of course, the military could not ignore issues of loyalty and matters of foreign policy. The nation has had to be somewhat sensitive to the foreign policy ramifications of drafting, and sometimes even enlisting, foreign personnel. Hence, enlisted or conscripted aliens were encouraged to become citizens, perhaps to reinforce solidarity and intensify commitment to military goals, certainly to remove any taint of divided loyalty. Gradually, the officer corps, although not the reserve officer corps, was reserved for citizens only. Perhaps this reflected heightened twentieth-century concern for treason, espionage, and subversion, or perhaps the citizenship qualification for appointment as an officer simply reflects an inchoate feeling that those who lead and govern should be fully and exclusively committed only to the nation which they serve.[21] To repeat Professor Bickel's observation, citizenship with respect to military service is significant in its international dimension.

In any case, the United States military has been a relatively "open" institution with respect to immigrants and has contributed to their assimilation into U.S. society. Even during xenophobic periods of U.S. history, the armed forces did not adopt the kind of discriminatory practices that were seen in other societal sectors. Conscription and universal eligibility for military service no doubt contributed to the formation and sustenance of democratic institutions.

Policy Implications for the All-Volunteer Force (AVF)

We hope to have shown that throughout most of U.S. history military service has not been the sole prerogative or obligation of citizens. Aliens have always been eligible to enlist in wartime and usually in peacetime. When the United States has had to conscript manpower during periods of military mobilization, the net has been cast wide enough to cover a high percentage of noncitizens who live within the boundaries of the United States. Approximately 35,000 aliens serve in the All-Volunteer Force (AVF). Obviously, the number of military volunteers is related to the number of aliens in the United States, a pool of approximately 4.5 million augmented by annual admissions of 500,000.[22] These total figures include persons of both sexes and all ages; thus, the pool of potential military recruits is much smaller.

United States immigration policy gives top priority to family reunification. In recent years, more than 70 percent of all immigration visas have been issued to relations of U.S. citizens and permanent aliens. A maximum of 10 percent of all immigration visas are allocated to those who have skills for which a need exists in the United States.[23] Willingness to serve in the armed forces does not currently qualify an applicant for priority status. We think it worth considering whether our immigration law should take into account this country's serious need for qualified military manpower. Some percentage of the immigration quota might be reserved for those willing to serve in the armed forces. In effect, such a policy would be tantamount to reviving the Lodge Act.

A second possibility for building upon the tradition of linking citizenship to military service is to permit undocumented aliens already living in the United States to become permanent resident aliens eligible for naturalization by serving a military tour of duty.[24] Compare this proposal to the Simpson-Mazzoli Bill which would grant amnesty and citizenship to those undocumented aliens who have been residing in the United States for a specified number of years.[25] Our proposal, while hardly a solution to the undocumented immigration problem, might present a politically acceptable, albeit limited, strategy for normalizing the status of a small number of undocumented aliens. Of course, a limited strategy may stimulate other programs linking the aspirations of undocumented aliens to national goals and priorities. Citizenship granted through military service may be more politically acceptable than a blanket amnesty.[26]

Notes

Leslie Ann Hayes, a graduate of Cornell University and Harvard Law School, conducted the research in chapter 2 while she was a student at Harvard Law School.
1. The Twenty-sixth Amendment to the U.S. Constitution states, "The Right of citizens of the United States, who are eighteen years of age or older, to vote shall not be denied or abridged by the United States or by any State on account of age."
2. In 1854, the Attorney General, (6 Op. Att. Gen. 474 [1854]), concluded that aliens had been barred from serving in the army only from 1802 (Act of March 16, 1802) until 1811 (Act of Dec. 24, 1811). However, in 1843, the Virginia Court of Appeals (1 Rob. [Va.] 615), stated in dicta that aliens were ineligible to join the Army, citing an 1815 statute that required the new peacetime Army to be "recruited in the same manner, and with the same limitations" as authorized in 1802 (Act of March 3, 1815). Whether or not aliens were ineligible to serve in 1843, as the Virginia court concluded, in 1847 Congress removed the earlier restriction (Act of Jan. 12, 1847). This statute authorized the enlistment of "men" rather than "citizens" during the Mexican War (see also Weigley, 1967:168).
3. According to Secretary of State Seward, "When [aliens] were found in the United States, exactly the same inducements to military service were open to them which by authority of law were offered at the same time to citizens of the United States." (Lonn 1951:406).
4. Some of these organizations lured immigrants with false promises of jobs or large bounties. Other recruiting efforts were more scrupulous, such as the one run by the City of Boston (Murdock 1971:317-21). Approximately 2.5 million men served in the Union Army between 1861 and 1865. Ella Lonn estimates that between one-fifth and one-fourth were immigrants. Of these 500,000 men, Germans comprised about 200,000 and Irish 150,000. Other groups included

Norwegians, Poles, Hungarians, and French. These are the total numbers of foreign born; it is not known how many of these soldiers were naturalized citizens (E. Lonn 1951:578-580). The Confederate Army also depended on the foreign born. Lonn estimates that "tens of thousands," perhaps 50,000 served in the Confederate forces. The number is considerably smaller than the number of foreign born in the Union ranks because only 13.5 percent of the foreign born population of the United States in 1860 lived in the Southern states.

5. A declaration of intention to become a U.S. citizen could be filed in any U.S. District Court or any state court of record at least three years prior to application for citizenship. It was also revocable at any time (Act of Jan. 29, 1795). In 1824, the waiting period between the the "first papers" and citizenship was reduced to two years (Act of May 26, 1824). An alien may still make a declaration of intention, but the requirement to do so was abolished by the Immigration and Nationality Act of 1952.

6. War Department regulations provided that "persons other than citizens of the United States will be enlisted or reenlisted only in accordance with general instructions or by special authority of the War Department" (7 Fed. Reg. 9223 (1942), codified in 10 C.F.R. § 71.2 [1943 cum. suppl.]). Army Regulations (615-500, section 2, 7e [Sept. 1, 1942]) set out the scheme for classifying and enlisting aliens.

7. Under this restriction, which applies only to eight new regiments, only citizens could be appointed officers (see Act of March 3, 1815, for application of this restriction after the War of 1812). Since 1813, citizenship has been a prerequisite for Naval Officers (Act of March 3, 1913).

8. The *New York Times* (April 24, 1978: 12) reports a Marine Corps investigation of the enlistment of 243 illegal aliens from Panama. Three recruiters were suspended from duty and placed under pretrial investigation. Apparently, the Panamanians used fraudulent birth certificates and high school diplomas. Of the 243 recruits, 137 had already completed their training. They were retained. After checking the performance and records of the recruits still in training, the Marines retained 54 and discharged 52; those discharged were turned over to the Immigration and Naturalization Service.

9. The governor of Wisconsin implemented this policy by announcing a presumption that anyone who had lived in the state for more than six years had voted. (Randall 1951:265).

10. Resistance to the draft was widespread and violent. The worst trouble occurred in areas with large immigrant populations, most notably in New York City where nearly one-half of the population was foreign born. The draft riot of July 1863 in New York was the bloodiest incident of civil disorder in U.S. history; roughly 500 people died during four days of rioting. Although the riot began as an attack on a drafting office, the rioters soon turned to burning, looting, and lynching (see A. Cook 1974).

11. The draft applied to "all aliens, not alien enemies, who have declared their intention [to become citizens]." Neutral aliens could escape the draft by withdrawing their declaration of intention, but could not thereafter become American citizens. (Act of July 9, 1918, ch. 143, tit. 12, §4, 40 stat. 845.) See generally Roh and Upham (1972).

12. That illegal aliens had a responsibility to register for the draft was the conclusion of Edith Lowenstein, editor of *Interpreter Releases*, (Lowenstein 1972: no. 39). David Carliner, an attorney specializing in immigration and nationality

matters, reached the same conclusion. "Aliens required to register included: . . . aliens who entered the United States illegally." (Carliner 1977:149).

13. Selective Service has traditionally taken account of United States treaty obligations. During World War II, under reciprocal agreements with cobelligerent countries, nondeclarant aliens could be exempted from service in the United States armed forces by serving in the forces of their own country. It has been estimated that only 10,000 aliens exercised this option during World War II (4 Dir. of Sel. Ser. Rep. 209 [1944-1945]). The 1955 Amendments to the Universal Military Training and Service Act provided that:

> any person who, subsequent to June 24, 1948, serves active duty for a period of not less than eighteen months in the armed forces of a nation with which the United States is associated in mutual defense activities . . . may be exempted from service . . . except that no such exemption shall be granted to any person who is a national of a country which does not grant reciprocal privileges to citizens of the United States.

Selective Service Regulations promulgated on September 2, 1972 provided a draft exemption for:

> any person who is a national of a country with which there is in effect a treaty or international agreement exempting nationals of that country from military service while they are in the United States (See 1611:2[c]).

14. Beginning in 1906, a certificate of arrival was generally required for naturalization. This certificate showed the date, place, and manner of the alien's entry (Act of June 29, 1906). With the Registry Act of 1929, an alien with no record of admission for permanent residence could get a record of registry (a substitute for the certificate of arrival) if he could show continuous residence in the United States since 1924. Under the current provision of the Immigration and Nationality Act of 1952, an application for petition for naturalization must contain an averment of lawful admission for permanent residence.

15. Of a grand total of 6,519,387 naturalizations under all statutes from 1907 to 1950 inclusive, 470,196 were by reason of service in the armed forces of the United States (Hazard 1952: 270).

16. Senator Lodge's second proposal (S. 238) was to raise a 250,000-man Volunteer Freedom Corps from the same population as the first group, but on a mass basis without careful screening. Members of the Freedom Corps would enlist and serve abroad for two years without being granted citizenship (S. 238, 82d Cong). Senator Johnson (of Colorado) introduced a bill (S. 609) calling for the enlistment of a 1,000,000-man freedom army made up of only Germans, Poles, and Czechs. After two years of honorable service the enlistees would be eligible for citizenship (S. 609, 82nd Cong). Neither bill was enacted.

17. More specifically, he may be naturalized without meeting the ordinary requirements: (1) five years residence in the United States and six months residence in a state, (2) residence within the jurisdiction of the naturalization court, or (3) 30-day delay period between petition and hearing, if he is still in the armed forces and if he and his witnesses appear before a naturalization examiner.

18. On September 18, 1978, President Carter signed Executive Order No. 12031, declaring the Vietnam War era over for the purposes of 8 U.S.C. §1440 (1976).

19. The benefits under this section originally enacted as of June 27, 1952, are: (1) naturalization regardless of age; (2) naturalization regardless of outstanding deportation orders; (3) the alien enemies provision does not apply; (4) the usual

period of five years' residence in a state is not required; (5) the petition may be filed in any naturalization court regardless of the person's residency; (6) the usual thirty-day delay period between petition and hearing does not apply.

20. An alien may be naturalized under this section "if (1) at the time of enlistment or induction such person shall have been in the United States, the Canal Zone, American Samoa, or Swains Islands, whether or not he had been lawfully admitted for permanent residence, or (2) at any time subsequent to enlistment or induction such person shall have been lawfully admitted to the United States for permanent residence."

21. But see *Sugarman v. Dougall* (1973) where the Supreme Court invalidated a statutory prohibition against employment of aliens in the state competitive civil service. The statute failed because, although the state has a legitimate interest in having loyal employees and in establishing its own form of government, the statute was "neither narrowly confined nor precise in its application."

22. The total immigration quota is set at 270,000 (8 U.S.C. §1151 [1980]). But this figure does not include special immigrants defined in § 1101 (a), immediate relatives of United States citizens, or political refugees. Altogether, 596,600 persons entered the United States as permanent residents in fiscal year 1981 (see Immigration and Naturalization Service 1977:25,33).

23. 8 U.S.C. §1153 establishes priorities for issuing immigration visas: 10 percent may be allocated to "members of the professions, or [those] who because of their exceptional ability in the sciences or the arts will substantially benefit the national economy, cultural interests, or welfare of the United States, and those services are sought by an employer in the United States;" an additional 10 percent may also be allocated "to qualified immigrants who are capable of performing specified skilled or unskilled labor, not of a temporary or seasonal nature, for which a shortage of employable and willing persons exists in the United States."

24. There is considerable debate about the number of illegal aliens in the United States. A decade ago the Immigration and Naturalization Service (1974: iii) estimated that there were between 6 million and 12 million undocumented aliens in the United States. More recent estimates have been scaled down, in the range of 3 to 6 million (see Schuck 1984: 42). Van Arsdol et al. calculated the net number of undocumented migrants coming into the United States from Mexico as between 82,000 and 232,000 per year with a preferred estimate at 115,700. They do not, however, estimate the total cumulative size of the population (Van Arsdol et al. 1979: 7; see also Select Commission on Immigration and Refuge Policy 1981).

25. Although the bill was passed by the Senate in May 1983, (S.529, 98th Cong.), and the House of Representative in June 1984 (H.R. 1510, 98th Cong.), public reaction to the jobs issue underlying legalization may thwart the bill's enactment.

26. It is important to bear in mind Morris Janowitz's observation that "From World War I onward citizen military service has been . . . a device by which excluded segments of society could achieve political legitimacy and rights" (Janowitz 1976:191).

Bibliography of Congressional Acts

Act of Jan. 29, 1795	ch. 20, 1 Stat. 414.
Act of March 16, 1802	ch. 9, § 11, 2 Stat. 132.
Act of April 13, 1808	ch. 43, § 9, 2 Stat. 481.
Act of Dec. 24, 1811	ch. 10, §2, 2 Stat. 669.
Act of March 3, 1815	ch. 79, § 7, 3 Stat. 224.
Act of May 26, 1824	ch. 186, § 4, 4 Stat. 69.
Act of Jan. 12, 1847	ch. 2, §2, 9 Stat. 117.
Act of Aug. 22, 1861	ch. 37, Prov. Cong., Confederate States of America, Stat. 189.
Act of April 16, 1862	ch. 31, lst Cong., lst Sess. Confederate States of America, Stat. 29.
Act of July 17, 1862	ch. 201, 12 Stat. 597.
Act of March 3, 1863	ch. 75, § 1, 12 Stat. 731.
Act of Feb. 24, 1864	ch. 13, 18, 13 Stat. 6.
Act of June 28, 1864	ch. 170, 13 Stat. 201.
Act of Aug. 1, 1874	ch. 179, § 2, 28 Stat. 215, current version at 10 U.S.C. §3253(c) (1976).
Act of July 30, 1892	ch. 328, § 1, 27 Stat. 336, current version at 10 U.S.C. §§ 3285, 8285 (1976).
Act of June 29, 1906	ch. 3592, § 4, 34 Stat. 497.
Act of March 3, 1913	ch. 42, §§ 1, 10, 2 Stat. 809.
National Defense Act of 1916	ch. 134, § 24, 39 Stat. 166, current version at 10 U.S.C §§ 3285, 8285 (1976).
Selective Draft Act of 1917	ch. 15, § 2, 40 Stat. 76.
Act of May 9, 1918	ch. 69, § 1, 40 Stat. 542, current version at 10. U.S.C. § 1440 (1976).
Act of August 31, 1918	40 Stat. 1918.
Act of June 14, 1920	ch. 286, 41 Stat. 1077.
Act of May 19, 1921	ch. 8, 42 Stat. 5, curent version at 8 U.S.C. §§ 1151- 1153 (1976).
Registry Act of 1929	ch. 539, § 1, 45 Stat. 1094.
Nationality Act of 1940	ch. 876, §323, 54 Stat. 1137, current version at 8 U.S.C. § 1439 (1976).
Second War Powers Act of 1942	ch. 199, § 1001, 56 Stat. 176, current version at 8 U.S.C. § 1440 (1976).
Act of Dec. 22, 1944	ch. 662, 58 Stat. 886, current version at 10 U.S.C. § 1440 (1976).
Officer Personnel Act of 1947	ch. 512, § 506(b), 61 Stat. 795, current version at 10 U.S.C. §§ 3285, 8285 (1976).
Selective Service Act of 1948	ch. 625, § 4(a), 62 Stat. 604, current version at 50 U.S.C. App. §§ 453-454 (1976).
Lodge Act of 1950	ch. 443, 64 Stat. 316.
Universal Military Training and Service Act of 1951	ch. 144, § 1(d), 65 Stat. 75, current version at 50 U.S.C. App. §§ 453-454 (1976).
Act of June 19, 1951	ch. 144, § 21, 65 Stat. 75.

Immigration and
Nationality Act of 1952

ch. 414, § 334 (f) and ch. 447,
§ 334 (b), 66 Stat. 163, codified at 8 U.S.C. § 1445 (1976).

Act of June 27, 1952

ch. 477, tit. III, ch. 2, § 329, 66 Stat. 250.

Armed Forces Reserve
Act of 1952

ch. 608, § 217, 66 Stat. 481,
current version at 10 U.S.C. § 591 (1976).

1955 Amendments to the
Universal Military Training and
Service Act

ch. 250, 69 Stat. 223.

Act of June 25, 1957

Pub. L. No. 85-62, § 4, 71 Stat 206, codified at 50 U.S.C App. § 455 (1976).

National Defense Act of 1961

ch. 134, § 37, 39 Stat. 166, 1961 current version at 10 U.S.C. § 591 (1976).

Act of Aug. 17, 1961

Pub. L. No. 87-143, 75 Stat. 364, codified at 10 U.S.C. §§ 3253, 8253 (1976).

Act of Dec. 23, 1963

Pub. L. No. 88-236, 77 Stat. 474, codified at 10 U.S.C. § 591 (1976).

Act of Dec. 20, 1971

ch. 602, § 2, 55 Stat. 844.

3

The Role of Military Forces in Public Sector Labor Relations

The intervention of military forces in labor-management disputes is highly controversial in a democracy committed to solving labor-management disputes through collective bargaining mechanisms and to keeping the military out of domestic politics. It is therefore quite remarkable that the repeated use in recent years of National Guard forces and, in two cases, of federal troops to replace striking public employees has attracted so little attention. There does not appear to be a single scholarly article on the subject in either the labor relations or civil-military relations literatures, despite a substantial number of such deployments since the 1970 postal strike.

History of Military Forces' Replacement Role

Despite the controversy it often provoked, military intervention in labor conflicts was common from 1875 to 1925 (Dulles 1966). Military forces, usually state militia, were frequently called upon during that period to preserve law and order in violent strike situations. In the great railroad strike of 1877, for example, 45,000 militiamen were called up in eleven states, more than 100 strikers were killed and several hundred were wounded. In fact, between 1877 and 1892, at least 30 percent of the militia's active duty assignments involved strikes (Riker 1957:55). And in a particularly notorious case, President Grover Cleveland sent federal troops to "preserve order" in Pullman, Illinois in 1894, despite the protests of Governor John P. Altgeld, who argued against the use of troops.

The role of the military, particularly the National Guard, as an industrial police force persisted into the twentieth century, but strike duty subsided by the late 1920s and all but disappeared after World War II. In recent years the National Guard has been called upon for such duty only in unusually violent situations, such as the 1974 truckers' strike, during which troops were called up in Pennsylvania, Ohio, Minnesota, Tennessee, Kentucky, Iowa, West Virginia, Illinois, Maryland, Indiana, and Alabama.

A less common form of military involvement in labor conflict throughout most of our history is the deployment of military personnel as replacements for striking employees. Blackman's history of presidential seizures traces the first such intervention to June 1863 when, in response to a strike by longshoremen, the government used federal troops and civilians to load and unload vessels at New York piers (Blackman 1967:294-98). During a 1917-18 loggers' strike that interrupted the supply of sprucewood for army aircraft, federal soldiers were assigned to logging camps where, under contract with private firms, they constructed and operated a logging railroad and a large sawmill. Twice in 1919, troops loaded, unloaded, and moved military cargo ships and troop ships. In 1941, the Navy Department recruited civilians to replace machinists whose wildcat strike disrupted work at ship repair yards in San Francisco. In August 1944, a few hundred sailors and soldiers cleaned out debris from government vessels in Bethlehem Steel Corporation's struck ship repair yards in New Jersey and New York. On several occasions in the ensuing thirty years, military personnel or civilians employed by the military loaded and unloaded strike-bound ships and assumed clerical functions related to the movement of military cargo. All these deployments appear to have been linked to military or national defense activities. In the New York harbor strikes, for example, the soldiers moved only military passengers and supplies, "leaving the private cargoes and passengers under the strike bans" (Blackman 1967:228).

Until 1970, troops had not been used to replace striking public employees, except for one instance—the 1919 Boston police strike, during which 4,500 members of the State Guard were called upon to maintain order in the face of looting and threatened mob violence. The Guard's capacity to carry out the police function effectively broke the strike. It is said that the Guard's success was responsible for catapulting Calvin Coolidge, then the Governor of Massachusetts, into the vice-presidency (Russell 1975).

For the most part, however, until the 1960's public employees were not unionized and did not strike. Those few public employee strikes that did occur apparently did not affect critical government functions, or at least not severely enough to provoke the call-up of military personnel as replacements. Perhaps important political and philosophical inhibitions prevented politicians from turning to the military to assure the continuation of struck public services.

From 1970 to the middle of 1983, however, military forces have been used as replacements for striking public employees on forty-nine occasions (see Table 3.1). The decline in call-ups since 1982 no doubt parallels the extraordinary decline in public sector work stoppages (see Table 3.2). The

TABLE 3.1
Military Call-Ups in Labor Disputes,
January 1970–August 1981

Dates	Place	Government Employees on Strike
1970: Mar 24-30	New York City	Postal Workers
1971: June 25	Nashua, New Hampshire	Firefighters
1973: Jan. 3	Milwaukee, Wisconsin	City Employees
1973: July 6-12	Puerto Rico	Firefighters
1973: Sept. 1-3	Texas	Traffic Safety
1973: Sept. 12-13	Texas	Prison Guards
1973: Nov. 5-10	Milwaukee, Wisconsin	Firefighters
1974: Mar. 12-13	Warm Springs, Montana	Mental Health
1974: Mar. 18-21	Galen-Boulder, Montana	Hospital Workers
1974: July 12-18	Lucasville, Ohio	Prison Guards
1974: July 16-17	Cranston, Rhode Island	Prison Guards
1974: July 18-19	Lima, Ohio	Mental Health
1974: Nov. 10-12	Cranston, Rhode Island	Mental Health
1974: Nov. 27	San Juan, Puerto Rico	Water Works Employees
1975: May 13	Lucasville, Ohio	Prison Guards
1975: Aug. 13-Sept. 8	Pine Bluff, Arkansas	Firefighters
1975: Oct. 3-9	Kansas City, Missouri	Firefighters
1976: Nov. 11-16	Warm Springs, Montana	Mental Health
1976: Nov. 12-19	Springfield, Illinois	Public Employees
1977: July 3-22	State, Wisconsin	Prison Guards
1977: Sept. 2-12	St. Croix, Virgin Islands	Prison Guards
1978: Mar. 12-13	Rhode Island	State Employees
1978: July 1	Memphis, Tennessee	Firefighters
1978: July 14	Louisville, Kentucky	Firefighters
1978: Aug. 17	Memphis, Tennessee	Police
1978: Sept. 6	Mach, New Hampshire	Firefighters
1978: Sept. 14	Wichita, Kansas	Firefighters
1978: Nov. 18-23	St. Bernard Parish, Louisiana	Firefighters
1978: Dec. 1-6	Huntsville, Alabama	Police & Firefighters
1979: Feb. 5-Mar. 14	Montana	State Employees
1979: Feb. 1-10, and Feb. 16-Mar. 6	New Orleans, Louisiana	Police
1979: Apr. 18-May 7	New York	State Employees
1979: June 27-29	Cape Girardeau, Missouri	Firefighters
1979: May 2-4	Birmingham, Alabama	Police & Firefighters
1979: Sept. 12-20	Cranston, Rhode Island	Mental Health
1979: Oct. 21-Nov. 16	Hawaii	State Employees
1978-80: Dec. 27-Jan. 3	Kansas City, Missouri	Firefighters
1980: Mar. 18-23	Kansas City, Missouri	Firefighters
1980: May 8-16	Nashville, Tennessee	Firefighters
1980: July 14-25	Mobile, Alabama	Firefighters
1980: Nov. 24-26	Marion, Indiana	Firefighters
1980: Dec. 6-7	Boston, Massachusetts	Commuter Transit

TABLE 3.1 (Continued)
Military Call-Ups in Labor Disputes,
January 1970–August 1981

Dates	Place	Government Employees on Strike
1981: Mar. 1-2	Milwaukee, Wisconsin	Firefighters
1981: Mar. 20-21	Milwaukee, Wisconsin	Firefighters
1981: June 23-25	Concord-Manchester, New Hampshire	State Employees
1981: July 10-14	Boston, other locations Massachusetts	Mental Health
1981: August	Nationwide	Air Traffic Controllers
1982: April 16-17	Boston, Massachusetts	Transit Workers
1983: May 15	Rhode Island	State Employees (standby duty only)

TABLE 3.2
Public Employee Work Stoppages: 1970-1983

Year	Number of public employee stoppages
1970	381
1971	298
1972	250
1973	317
1974	424
1975	235
1976	231
1977	298
1978	235
1979	187
1980	145
1981	96
1982	81
1983 (through June)	25

Source: U.S. Department of Labor, Monthly Labor Review.

precedent-setting action was the postal strike in March 1970 during which President Nixon sent 30,000 regular and reserve federal troops and National Guardsmen to replace striking postal employees in New York City. The strikers capitulated just two days after the troops assumed the task of sorting and delivering mail.

The postal workers' and air traffic controllers' strikes are the only recent occasions when federal troops have served as replacements for striking public employees. As Table 3.1 shows, however, National Guardsmen have been called upon at the state and local levels to work as firefighters, policemen, prison guards, and mental health attendants, among other jobs. While it may be premature to speak of a trend, it is worth noting (Table 3.3) that the number of National Guard interventions increased from 19 in the seven-year period 1970-76 to 30 in the seven-year period 1977-83. The largest deployment was in April 1979, when New York State Governor Hugh Carey activated over 12,000 Army and Air National Guardsmen to replace striking state prison guards (Zimmer and Jacobs 1981: 531-44).

TABLE 3.3
Yearly Summary of Recent National Guard Call-Ups
in Public Sector Labor Disputes

Year	Number
1970	1
1971	1
1972	0
1973	5
1974	7
1975	3
1976	2
1977	2
1978	8
1979	8
1980	5
1981	5
1982	1
1983	1

Legal Constraints

When can or should a governor (or a president in the case of striking federal employees) call up troops to replace striking public employees? What justifies the use of military forces? Must there be a serious threat to public health and safety? An imminent catastrophe? Or are we only dealing with an executive judgment call? To answer these questions requires, in part, an examination of federal and state constitutional and statutory law.

All but two instances of military personnel replacing public employees since 1970 involved state or local employees. Federal troops were used only in the 1970 postal workers' strike and, to a limited extent, in the 1981 air traffic controllers' strike.[1] This analysis begins, nevertheless, with the postal strike because President Nixon's use of military personnel set the precedent for subsequent gubernatorial actions. The fact that Nixon's action was not seen as significant by scholars at the time is partially explained by its having been overshadowed by the Vietnam War. In hindsight, however, the postal strike was crucial; since then, military deployments for public sector strikes have become unexceptional and are taken for granted. If one views the 1970 postal strike deployment as an extraordinary event in U.S. history, based as it was on questionable legal authority, the whole issue of using troops as replacements for striking workers becomes problematic.

The 1970 Postal Strike

On March 19, 1970, thousands of postal workers around the country walked off their jobs over a salary dispute. Work stoppages occurred nationwide—Philadelphia, San Francisco, Chicago, Denver, Pittsburgh, Cleveland—affecting about half of all mail service in the country. Hardest hit were banks, brokerage houses, insurance companies, publishers, public utilities, credit agencies, and government agencies. The strike was most severe in New York City, where mail service came to a virtual halt. Two federal judges issued injunctions ordering the president of Branch 36 of the National Letter Carriers Union to direct the carriers to go back to work. The union leader complied, but the rank-and-file did not. The Assistant U.S. Attorney pressing the government's case did not seek criminal punishment of the strikers, noting that "repressive measures will not get the mail delivered" (*New York Times*, March 20, 1970:40). The Government did, however, seek fines against the union and seven of its officers (*New York Times*, March 21, 1970:12).

After the injunction failed to bring the strikers back to work, President Nixon declared a national emergency and sent 2,500 regular military personnel, 15,300 Army, Navy and Marine reservists, and 12,000 New York State Army and Air National Guardsmen to New York City to sort and deliver the mail. The Declaration stated:

> As a result of [the postal employees'] unlawful work stoppage the performance of critical government and private functions . . . will impair the ability of this nation to carry out its obligations abroad, and will cripple or halt the official and commercial intercourse which is essential to the conduct of its domestic business. . . . Therefore, I, Richard Nixon, President of the United States of America, pursuant to the powers vested in me by the Constitution and the laws of the United States and more particularly. . . Section 673 of Title 10 of the Untied States Code, do hereby declare a state of national emergency, and direct the Secretary of Defense . . . to use such of the Armed Forces . . .[and] any or all of the . . . Army National Guard and of the Air National Guard [to maintain postal service and to execute the postal laws]. [Proc. 3972, 3 C.F.R. 473 (1970) (1966-1970 Compilation)]

Within two days the union capitulated and the strikers returned to work. The domestic use of troops to break the postal strike enjoyed widespread popular support, even in the liberal press (see *New York Times*, March 22, 1970:16; March 23, 1970:40). Perhaps this support explains why, in contrast to the massive legal literature on the legality of military actions in Southeast Asia (e.g. secret bombings and the invasion of Cambodia) not one article on the postal strike ever appeared in the law reviews.

Whatever caused this academic lacuna, presidential deployment of troops domestically raises profound questions about the proper role of the armed forces in a constitutional system and about the respective powers of the executive and legislative branches of government. The Constitution does not specifically provide for domestic deployment of troops, but to the extent that inferences can be drawn from the text, Congress not the president enjoys this power. Congress has the power to organize the militia and to provide for calling it forth to execute the laws (U.S. Const. art. I, § 8). Congressional control over the regular armed forces can be inferred from the powers to "raise and support armies and to maintain the navy," and to "make rules for the government and regulation of the land and naval forces."

When Congress uses its authority to regulate the use of the military, the president must conform his actions to the terms of such regulations (*Yale Law Journal* 1973:137-38). Legislative limitations on executive use of the military in domestic affairs go back to 1792, when Congress refused to grant the president the power to execute the laws with military force (Engdahl 1974:584). The Civil War and Reconstruction statutes that allowed domestic military deployments (10 U.S.C. §§ 331, 332, 333 [1976]), restrict executive use of the armed forces to specific types of emergency situations. In the Posse Comitatus Act of 1878 (18 U.S.C. §1385 [1976]), Congress specifically prohibited the use of the army to execute the laws, unless expressly provided for in the Constitution or in other legislation. The executive's power to deploy troops domestically, if any, must come either from congressional authorization or from the president's own constitutional powers as Commander-in-Chief (U.S. Const. art. II, § 2, cl. 1), as executor of the laws (Ibid., § 3) or arguably, from whatever inherent authority vests in the president as chief executive (Ibid., § 1).

Inherent powers

President Nixon never explicitly claimed reliance on inherent powers to justify deployment of troops in the postal strike; his emergency proclamation and executive order were vague and ambiguous. However, by declaring the postal strike a national emergency, President Nixon may have been setting up a plausible justification for calling out the troops to sort and deliver mail. There is no doubt that President Nixon had an expansive view of inherent powers, particularly war and military powers. In 1972, his adminstration's new regulations concerning the use of federal troops in civil disorders incorporated the view that the president has an inherent, constitutional right to use troops in a variety of vaguely defined domestic crises (32 C.F.R. § 215.4[c] [1] [i] & [ii] [1980]).

Constitutional scholars would no doubt accept the proposition that the president can use troops when the survival of the country is at stake. There is little doubt that the executive, acting on his own authority, can mobilize the armed forces to repel a sudden attack by a foreign enemy or to quell a domestic insurrection. This authority, based upon what has come to be referred to as *raison d'état*, is invariably raised only in hypothetical discussions about devastating threats to national security. It is hardly clear that such a theory could be comfortably applied to more mundane problems.

Does recognition of inherent presidential authority to prevent the nation's military defeat lead to the conclusion that troops can be called upon to deliver the mail during a postal strike? Disruptions of mail delivery cause inconvenience, even hardship, but other countries have weathered postal strikes without collapse. Canada survived a forty-two day postal strike in 1981; the Canadian government did not find it necessary to take legal action against the strikers, nor to rely on extraordinary measures to maintain mail delivery. Contrast this with the U.S. experience: when President Nixon issued the emergency proclamation, the strike had achieved only partial success in most cities. Postal officials had not yet had time to determine whether services could be maintained with supervisory personnel and other civilian replacements. Certain agencies, like Selective Service and Welfare, had postal strike contingency plans they did not even get the opportunity to test.

President Nixon did not elaborate on his conclusion that the postal strike had created a national emergency. However, in his television address to the nation he stated:

> The United States postal system is a vital element of our entire communications system. The poor depend heavily upon it for medical services and also for Government assistance. Veterans depend upon it for their compensation checks. The elderly depend upon it for their Social Security checks.
>
> The nation's business is dependent upon it as a way to stay in business so they can meet their payrolls. And our men in Vietnam depend on mail calls as their only link with their loved ones. [*New York Times*, March 24, 1970:16]

One wonders if there might have been alternatives for getting mail to each of these groups. Military personnel, veterans groups, and volunteers, for example, might have collected and delivered letters to and from those in Vietnam.[2]

It is possible to speculate that President Nixon's concerns went beyond the disruption of mail service. He spoke of the "survival of a government based upon law." (*New York Times*, March 24, 1970:16). His argument, in effect, was that the government's sovereignty itself was challenged by the postal workers' illegal strike.[3] Perhaps the president and his advisors saw the strike, or at least wanted to portray it, as a challenge to the national administration and to "law and order." They may have feared a diminution of governmental authority if the postal workers were able to force a settlement through an illegal strike. However, even if the postal strike enjoyed some initial success, the government could still have enforced criminal and civil penalties against the strikers, or fired them and hired replacements. It seems a gross distortion to have defined the strike, especially in its early stages, as a national calamity. Using the president's hazy, inherent authority to prevent national collapse to justify breaking the strike with military personnel was, at best, a drastic and unprecedented expansion of presidential powers. The very nature of constitutional government precludes the use of inherent executive power in all but the most compelling circumstances.

Commander-in-Chief

It could hardly be argued that President Nixon's use of federal troops in the 1970 postal workers' strike could be justified by the president's powers as Commander-in-Chief. The president's power as Commander-in-Chief is a war power and does not apply to internal affairs. As the Supreme Court noted in *Youngstown Sheet and Tube Co. v. Sawyer* (1952), "even though 'theater of war' be an expanding concept, we cannot, with faithfulness to our constitutional system, hold that the Commander in Chief of the Armed Forces has the ultimate power to take possession of private property in order to keep labor disputes from stopping production." The wide indulgence granted to the president when the nation is fighting a foreign enemy is not granted when the president acts domestically. When Congress authorizes domestic use of troops, the president assumes the role of Commander-in-Chief, but this power as "first general" cannot serve as a substitute for congressional action.

Executor of the Laws

In the postal strike deployments, President Nixon relied explicitly on presidential power to execute the laws; he seemed to be suggesting that since Congress provided for the establishment and operation of the postal system, military force could be used to ensure fulfillment of the postmaster's statutory obligations. Thus, his Executive Order began as follows:

Whereas certain employees of the Postal Service are engaged in an unlawful work stoppage which has prevented the delivery of the mails and the discharge of other postal functions in various parts of the United States; and

Whereas, the laws of the United States . . . require that the business of the Post Office Department, including the expeditious processing and delivery of the mail, be regularly carried on; and

Whereas the aforesaid unlawful work stoppage has prevented and is preventing the execution of the aforesaid laws relating to the Post Office Department; and

Whereas the breakdown of the postal service in the numerous areas affected by the said unlawful work stoppage is a matter of grave national concern; and

Whereas I am charged by the Constitution of the United States to take care that the laws be faithfully executed. [Executive Order 11519, 3 C.F.R. 909 (1966-1970 Compilation)]

If the president was suggesting that his authority to enforce the laws authorizes troop deployments to replace striking postal workers, his argument followed to its logical conclusion is that all federal employees could be replaced by military personnel if, in the judgment of the president, their statutory duties are not being satisfactorily discharged. The authority to execute the laws could be transformed into a charter for military rule.

Fortunately, the Constitution's "faithfully execute" clause does not provide the basis for military dictatorship. When executing the laws, the president may take only such actions as are not prohibited or preempted by Congress; he cannot violate the laws in order to execute them (Corwin 1978:191). The question therefore is whether use of troops in the postal strike was authorized or prohibited by Congress.

An answer to that question is suggested by the Supreme Court's decision in *Youngstown Sheet and Tube Co. v. Sawyer*. The Court held that the president had no constitutional authority to seize the nation's steel mills for the purpose of guaranteeing their operation during a strike; such authority had to come from Congress. Congress had impliedly prohibited such a seizure by defeating a proposed amendment to the Taft-Hartley Act that would have given just such power to the executive.

Justice Jackson's concurring opinion has achieved greatest prominence. Jackson argued that the president's power is at its maximum when he acts pursuant to an express or implied authorization of Congress. His power is in a "zone of twilight" when he acts in the absence of congressional authority and can rely only on his own independent powers. It is at its lowest ebb when he "takes measures incompatible with the express or implied will of Congress, for then he can rely only upon his own constitutional powers minus any constitutional powers of Congress over the matter." Clearly,

President Nixon was not operating in the first situation, since Congress had granted no power to use military forces to deliver the mail. At best, he was acting in the zone of twilight since it is arguable that Congress had given no indication of its position on this unprecedented use of federal troops. But the 1878 Posse Comitatus Act, outlawing the use of troops domestically, except in certain limited circumstances, places President Nixon's action most clearly in the third and weakest category of presidential powers.

The Posse Comitatus Act

In 1878, reacting to President Grant's frequent use of the regular military forces in labor disputes and other circumstances (20 Stat. 152 [1878]), Congress passed the Posse Comitatus Act. An excellent review of the history of the Posse Comitatus Act finds that its framers fully intended to limit the president's use of military forces in peacetime to those circumstances expressly provided for in the Constitution of the United States or in federal statutes (Seiner and Effron 1979:1-54). The context of the debate further underscores a common theme. Debate focused on opposition to use of the military in situations where the organized discipline and factors of a military force were not required, as for example in the collection of taxes, service of process, supervision of elections, and in response to labor strikes, when the task was within the existing or potential capability of state forces.

As amended in 1956 (70a Stat. 626) the Posse Comitatus Act provides:

> Whoever, except in cases and under circumstances expressly authorized by the Constitution or Act of Congress, willfully uses any part of the Army or the Air Force as a posse comitatus or otherwise to execute the laws shall be fined not more than $10,000 or imprisoned not more than two years, or both. [18 U.S.C. § 1385 (1976)]

"Posse Comitatus" literally means the power or force of the county, referring to the power of a sheriff to summon the entire population of a county above the age of fifteen for assistance.

The Act is the most significant legislative restriction on domestic use of troops. On its face, this law clearly prevents the president from assigning military personnel to strike replacement duty unless there is another law or Constitutional provision that expressly permits it.[4] It applies to active duty Army and Air Force Reserves and to the Army and Air National Guard when in federal service (Furman 1960:99). At the time of the postal strike, the Defense Department regarded the Act as an expression of policy applicable also to the Navy and Marine Corps (Meeks 1975:101). However, in 1972, the Nixon Administration broke with traditional policy by asserting that the Navy and Marine Corps were outside the ambit of the Act (*Yale Law Journal* 1973:130, 144).

An 1861 statute is most relevant to the use of troops in a domestic crisis. It provides, as one would expect, that troops may be deployed domestically in grave situations of insurrection and disruption of civil authority:

> Whenever the President considers that unlawful obstructions, combinations, assemblages, or rebellions against the authority of the United States, make it impracticable to enforce the laws of the United States...by the ordinary course of judicial proceedings, he may . . . use such of the armed forces as he considers necessary to enforce those laws or to suppress the rebellion. [10 U.S.C. § 332 (1976)]

History indicates that the lawmakers who passed this statute believed it permitted the use of federal troops only when civilian institutions were incapacitated in the course of a rebellion, insurrection, or riot (Engdahl 1974:581-617). Further, even had the statute been applicable, it would seem to authorize no more than firing or jailing strikers who disobeyed the court injunction, not establishing military operation of the postal system. When Arkansas state officials actively impeded the implementation of school desegregation in the 1950s, President Eisenhower relied on this statute (as well as on 10 U.S.C. § 333) to send the National Guard to Little Rock (Executive Order 10730, 3 C.F.R. §389 [1954-1958 Compilation]). The Guard's military presence was used only to prevent violence and to ensure that nothing obstructed the integration of the schools. The Guard did not assume the administrative, clerical, or educational duties of school officials.

Other statutes empower the president to deploy the armed forces when there is an "insurrection in any state against its government," (10 U.S.C. § 331 [1976]) and to suppress unlawful combinations or conspiracies that "obstruct the execution of federal law." (10 U.S.C. § 333 [1976]). Each of these statutes presupposes the inability or unwillingness of civilian institutions to perform their lawful functions.

President Nixon's executive order deploying federalized National Guardsmen to deliver mail did not cite any of these statutes. Instead, the President's executive order pointed to 10 U.S.C. § 3500, which authorizes the president to use Army National Guardsmen for domestic peacekeeping "whenever [he] is unable with the regular forces to execute the laws of the United States." The statute provides for the use of the National Guard as a last resort; presumably, the regular forces must first fail in their attempt to execute the laws. As in the case of the emergency proclamation, neither President Nixon in his executive order, nor Assistant Attorney General (now Supreme Court Justice) William Rehnquist in an internal memorandum on this subject, elaborated on the unprecedented decision to use Guardsmen as a replacement for strikers.[5]

Gubernatorial Authority

Most public sector strikes are against state and local governments. To determine when troops can be called up to play a replacement role at these levels, we must look to state constitutional and statutory law. State statutes, constitutions, or both, specify the conditions under which the National Guard may be activated. Each state constitution confers executive power upon the governor or names him the state's chief executive; designates him the commander-in-chief of the state's military forces; and charges him with the faithful execution of the laws. Thirty-six state constitutions specifically provide the governor with authority to call out the National Guard (National Association of Attorneys General [NAAG] 1973:10-20).

In every state but New York, this enabling power is governed by constitutional provisions strictly subordinating the military to civil authority (NAAG 1973: 10, 12). Moreover, under nineteen constitutions only the legislature can suspend the operation of civil law; these provisions are meant to avoid a situation where the governor might use a public emergency as an excuse for using the military irresponsibly. Half the states have civil defense statutes granting the executive wide discretion in emergencies (NAAG 1973: 13).

Only Tennessee's constitution places any legislative check on the governor's power to call out the militia. Notably, the legislature has circumvented that limitation by defining "militia" (Tenn. Code Ann. 7-106 [1970]) as excluding the National Guard. Some states limit the use of the Guard in emergencies by defining "emergency" narrowly enough to exclude labor strife (see Cal. Military & Veterans Code §1505 [West 1955]). Others establish a civil defense advisory council that may limit the governor's emergency powers (see N.C. Gen. Stat. 166-4 (1976); Vt. Stat. Ann. tit. 21 §4 [1958]). Although most states require a proclamation or executive order to activate these powers, few have any specific criteria for issuing a justificatory proclamation. A governor has even broader legal discretion than the president over whether, how, and when to call up the Guard (NAAG 1973:17-19).

Significantly, no state with a comprehensive public sector collective bargaining law provides for using Guardsmen as replacements. These laws are sufficiently flexible, however, to leave largely to the governor's discretion the decision whether or not to deploy the Guard in public sector strikes. While the courts, in theory, can review such deployments, in practice they are unlikely to second-guess the governor, given the strong tradition of judicial noninvolvement in executive military deployments (see *Luther v. Bordon*, 1845; *Gilligan v. Morgan* 1973).

A sampling of constitutional and statutory authority for gubernatorial deployment of the National Guard is presented in Table 3.4, which shows that several states permit the governor to use troops "to execute the laws of the state." Read broadly, this formulation could justify the use of troops in any illegal public employee strike. Since most states have laws prohibiting at least certain public employee strikes, the Governor could arguably deploy troops to enforce the law. Alternatively, it could be argued that troops are justified when necessary to maintain public services authorized by law. The latter justification would apply even to states in which public employee strikes are permissible, unless one interprets the acceptance of public sector strikes as an exception to the requirement that executive agencies maintain their operations.

In Montana, for example, prison guards are allowed to strike after they exhaust impasse procedures and give notice. In 1979, the guard union announced its intent to strike if wage demands were not met. State negotiators met with National Guard officers, devised a plan for sending troops to the prisons, and arranged to have Guard officers meet prison officials and tour their facilities. In effect, the Guardsmen were activated and prepositioned before the prison guards walked off the job. The justification was not maintenance of prison operations but rather anticipation of a likely emergency: when the strike occurred Governor Thomas Judge issued a "state of emergency" proclamation.

A number of states authorize the governor to call out the National Guard in case of "emergency." Since almost anything can be labeled an "emergency," a governor is free to deploy National Guardsmen in almost any strike by state and local employees. While every public sector strike creates severe problems for some governmental operations, sometimes adjustments can minimize service disruption and hardships for service beneficiaries; in other circumstances substantial disruptions are difficult, if not impossible, to avoid. So far there have been no reported judicial decisions concerning a governor's use of troops as replacements for striking public employees, perhaps because legal challenges would have little chance of success given historic judicial deference to executive authority in this area. In the federal courts, such suits would be unlikely to survive a motion to dismiss, since no federal statutory or constitutional rights are involved. A disgruntled Guardsman would have standing in state court to challenge an allegedly illegal call-up, but, as Table 3.4 shows, the constitutional and statutory authority for executive discretion to activate National Guard forces is broad enough to support any gubernatorial troop activation.

Nonlegal Constraints

We know very little about the decision making process leading to a call-up of the National Guard in strike and strike-threat situations. In the

TABLE 3.4
Gubernatorial Authority to Activate the National Guard in Selected States

State	Authority
Alaska	Alaska Constitution, Article III, §19. The governor is commander-in-chief of the armed forces of the State. He may call out these forces *to execute the laws*, suppress or prevent insurrection or lawless violence, or repel invasion.
Colorado	Colorado Constitution, Article IV, §5. The governor shall be commander-in-chief of the military forces of the state . . . He shall have the power to call out the militia *to execute the laws*, suppress insurrection or repel invasion.
	Colorado Rev. Stat. §28-3-104. The governor shall be the commander-in-chief of the armed forces . . . and may employ the same for the defense or relief of the state, the *enforcement of its laws*, and *the protection of life and property therein.*
Louisiana	Louisiana Constitution, Article 4, §5(J). The governor shall be commander-in-chief of the armed forces of the state . . . He may call out these forces *to preserve law and order*, to suppress insurrection, to repel invasion, or *in other times of emergency.*
	Louisiana Rev. Stat. Ann. Chapter 1, §7 (West). The governor may call into the active service of the state any part of the militia that is necessary in the event of insurrection, invasion, or riot, or imminent danger thereof, or in the event of public disaster from flood, fire, storm, or earthquake, or to assist civil authorities in guarding prisoners.
New Jersey	New Jersey Stat. §38A:2-4 (West). The governor may, in case of insurrection, invasion, tumult, *riot, breach of peace, natural disaster* or *imminent danger to public safety*, order to active duty all or any part of the militia.
New York	New York Military Law, Article I, §3. The governor of the state shall be the commander-in-chief of the militia of the state.
	New York Military Law, Article I, §6. (McKinney). The governor shall have power, in case of invasion, disaster, insurrection, *riot, breach of the peace or imminent danger thereof*; to order into active service . . . the organized militia.
Ohio	Ohio Constitution, Article 9, §4. The governor shall have power to call forth the militia, *to execute the laws of the state*, to suppress insurrection, to repel invasion, and to act in the event of a disaster within the state.
Rhode Island	Rhode Island Gen. Laws §30-2-6 (1968). In case of martial law, war, invasion, rebellion, insurrection, *riot, tumult, public calamity* or catastrophe, *or other emergency, or imminent danger thereof*, or *resistance to the laws of this state* or the United States the governor shall order into service all or any part of the militia.

absence of a literature based upon detailed case studies, it is useful to speculate on which factors may facilitate or constrain the use of military forces as replacements.

The Capacity to Serve: Practical Constraints

The National Guard is better suited to some replacement duties than others. Whether or not the Guard can play an effective replacement role depends upon the complexity of the operations to be performed and the consequences of faulty performance. We may hypothesize that where operations are very complex and consequences of faulty performance severe, there will be a greater reluctance to call upon the National Guard. The 1980 strike by New York City transit workers is an example. An informant who was close to the negotiations admits: "We never seriously considered using the Guard. The transit system was simply too complex; the potential for a cataclysmic accident was too great." It was also feared that angry workers might sabotage the system. Thus, although the decision to close down the transit system enormously inconvenienced New Yorkers and cost businesses millions of dollars, a call-up of the National Guard was not considered a viable option.

At the other end of the continuum lies a postal strike. Postal operations, especially mail delivery, require only low-level skills. National Guardsmen can be briefed and sent into action in a few hours. If their performance is poor, the mail may go undelivered, but there will be no loss of life, serious property damage, or catastrophe.

The job of prison guard lies somewhere in between. It carries major responsibilities, but requires little training (Jacobs and Retsky 1975:5-29). Most guards are trained "on the job" and much of their duty involves little more than watching prisoners. In a strike situation, the role can be simplified by confining prisoners to their cells around the clock. Under such a "lockdown," the danger of violence or escape is greatly reduced and the replacements' main task is to serve food in the cells.

The National Guard has been very successful at providing vital services and maintaining security during prison guard strikes. The Guard served without apparent incident, riots, killings, or escape during lengthy strikes in Wisconsin (1977), Montana (1979), and New York (1979) (see League of Women Voters 1978; Jacobs and Zimmer 1980; Zimmer and Jacobs 1981). In all three situations Guardsmen and prisoners enjoyed a honeymoon period. Some of the regular prison activities were resumed as the Guardsmen's confidence grew. Part of the Guardsmen's success in the New York prison strike may be attributable to their deployment in numbers far exceeding the regular complement of prison guards.

Institutions for the mentally ill and retarded and nursing homes are probably even easier than prisons for replacements to operate, since there is less need to worry about violence or escape. In addition, relatives of the patients and other volunteers may offer to assist military personnel.

Modern day firefighting, on the other hand, is a complex task involving the use of sophisticated equipment. Some fires, such as those in chemical plants or oil storage facilities, are extremely dangerous. Negligent performance by firefighters can result in the loss of life and property. Firefighting is thus not the easiest role for Guardsmen to fill; yet, as Table 3.1 shows, firefighters' strikes account for the greatest number of replacement call-ups. Government leaders no doubt believe that the risks in not providing any protection against fire outweigh those incurred by a National Guard call-up.

How have Guardsmen performed when called upon to replace striking firefighters? A review of newspaper reports reveal that troops, with the help of civilian supervisory personnel, have learned to use most civilian firefighting equipment and have performed adequately. In some instances, however, delayed reaction to alarms is reported to have "caused" major property damage.

In Great Britain, a nationwide firefighters' strike in 1977 led to the activation of 20,000 military replacements. They were outfitted with outdated firefighting equipment, apparently to soften the strikebreaking symbolism (seee Whelan, March 1979; December 1979: 222-34). Nevertheless, the military personnel performed adequately. According to Geoffrey Marshall:

> The strike ended on January 12, 1978, having lasted for three months. Subsequently published insurance figures have shown that the cost of fire damage to property was roughly twice that of the corresponding period in the previous twelve months. The evident unpopularity of the strike, together with the lack of sympathetic action by other unions or support by the Trades Union Congress, were factors that helped to bring about a settlement. But a major part was undoubtedly the size and effectiveness of the effort by which the strikers were replaced. [Marshall 1979:277]

Police strikes may pose a lesser challenge than firefighters' strikes. Some troops, especially military police, are already trained as police and can, without difficulty, carry out civilian police duties. Military police forces may deter more crime than civilian police, but they also present certain problems. Soldiers are trained to kill; they may have no experience in controlling individuals or groups with non-lethal force.

As studies of police have emphasized, police work often involves responding to simple requests for assistance and settling disputes (Wilson

1972). Many of these functions can be performed by untrained personnel or referred to other agencies, friends, or neighbors. Military personnel may not be able to respond as quickly to emergency calls as regular police, but most serious offenses occur before a call for assistance is made. Criminal investigations can usually be suspended during a short strike; and plainclothes investigators may well remain on the job in any event.

With the National Guard patrolling the streets, widespread looting and violence are unlikely to result from a police strike. The greatest concern is that the troops themselves will recklessly cause damage and possible loss of life. In several riots in the 1960s, National Guard units showed poor judgment in exercising force (National Advisory Commission on Civil Disorders 1968:497-506). Improved training and increased concern for general safety and peacekeeping would probably improve the Guard's performance during police strikes. By planning, training, practical exercises, education on abuse of force issues, and other measures taken since incidents in Detroit, Newark, and Kent State, the National Guard is said to have substantially improved its riot control tactics (NAAG 1973:81-84).

Political Impediments

Calling up troops to act as replacements obviously involves political risks; the potential for violent confrontations between strikers and Guardsmen, the possible opposition of uninvolved unions, and the spectre of sympathy strikes. Some politicians and most trade unionists, for example, sharply criticized the use of troops in the 1970 postal strike. Democratic political figures were virtually unanimous in condemning President Nixon's emergency actions. AFL-CIO president George Meany condemned it, but urged the employees to return to work. AFSCME president Jerry Wurf termed the use of troops a "shocking piece of strikebreaking." John DeLury, President of New York City's Uniformed Sanitation Men's Association, said "the use of troops in New York City is a step backward to the Stone Age of labor-management relationships with federal employees." (*New York Times* March 24, 1970:35)

For the most part, though, organized labor's response to troop activations has been surprisingly restrained. Several unions supported President Nixon, including the United Electrical, Radio and Mechanic Workers of America, the New York State chapter of the AFL-CIO, the Newspaper Guild, and the District Council 37 of the American Federation of State, County, and Municipal Employees (AFSCME) (*New York Times* March 24, 1970:35). The official position of AFSCME Nationwide, for example, supports legislation that "provides access to legislated interest arbitration for public safety employees as an alternative to the unlimited right to strike. "Where the public safety is not involved, AFSCME supports legislation allowing strikes but prefers "voluntary binding arbitration" as an alternative (AFSCME 1978).[6]

The leaders of public sector unions probably believe that opposition to the use of National Guardsmen to maintain essential services would be unpopular and might jeopardize the acceptability of public sector collective bargaining. AFSCME has acknowledged that public sector strikes are often counterproductive, adversely affecting the cause of public sector trade unionism and, in the case of public safety workers, negatively affecting the health and safety of a community. The public is not apt to tolerate both illegal strikes and a ban on the use of replacements. If troop deployment in public strikes were to become more prevalent, however, union opposition might intensify.

The Financial Costs

The financial cost of calling out the National Guard pales in comparison to strikers' demands for wage increases, although much depends upon the number of employees affected by the settlement and on the number of strikers. Deployment of the National Guard during the 1979 New York prison-guard strike, for example, cost about one million dollars per day, but state officials estimated that even a one percent permanent wage concession to state employees would have been more costly.

In making financial assessments, it is important to determine who will bear the costs of military deployments. In the case of state employee strikes, the money saved by not paying the strikers can be set off against the cost of the National Guard. In strikes by local employees, the city saves money by not having to pay the strikers and the state usually pays for the Guard. Thus, there might be an incentive for fiscally pressed cities with severe labor difficulties to request National Guard personnel. New York State has addressed this problem by requiring the county, city, or municipality that requests the Guard to pay half the costs of its mobilization and deployment (New York State Military Law § 212 [McKinney Supp. 1980]).

Resistance to Strike Duty

"The primary motive for the revival of the militia [in the 1870s]," according to William Riker, "was a felt need for an industrial police" (Riker 1957:55). This need gave the militia the ability to attract support from influential economic interests. But the industrial peacekeeping role was controversial and the unpopularity of strikebreaking among the working class created serious recruitment problems. It was crucial for the National

Guard's survival to deemphasize its strikebreaking role and find a different raison d'etre.

The problem was solved when the Guard became the bona fide reserve component for the United States armed forces in 1903 (32 Stat. 755, as amended, 35 Stat. 399 [1908]). This change was desirable for several reasons. First, the federal government assumed an ever increasing share of the cost of operations and payroll. Second, the National Guard gained prestige as a "real military force" with national defense responsibilities. Third, service was not suspect in any way; indeed it was popular and prestigious.

The 1903 Dick Act, which established the National Guard as the Army reserve, provided that training and equipment would be paid for in large measure by the federal government. The Guard was used in 1916 on the Mexican border and in 1917 in World War I. Guard forces also saw extensive service in World War II and in Korea. Under the "total force" policy developed by the Department of Defense in 1970-1972, reservists rather than draftees are currently the primary source of personnel for augmenting active forces in military emergencies (Coffey 1979:78). The National Guard is thus, by law, the nation's first line of military reserves (10 U.S.C. 263 [1976]). While the army reserve is oriented toward support and training, the National Guard's mechanized, armor, and infantry divisions are oriented toward combat involvement (Coffey 1979:97).

Service as a replacement force in public sector strikes is thus hardly relevant to the National Guard's mission or self-concept. One might ask, then, whether this is also true for emergency humanitarian deployments for floods, snow storms, and blizzards. Those traditional duties are distinguishable; they have a long history, and enjoy public support. They enhance the Guard's political strength and even its recruitment efforts.

Given the history of the National Guard, its leaders may well have doubts about serving in labor conflicts. For example, such duty takes time away from military training. More importantly, service as replacements in public sector strikes is inevitably controversial. The Guard may eventually have more clashes with strikers, as they did in New York's 1979 prison guard strike, and any such clashes may prod the ire of organized labor, as they did in the 1970 postal strike and the 1979 Montana prison guard strike. Guardsmen may be injured, as in the 1978 St. Bernard Parish (Louisiana) firefighters' strike. The presence of the Guard may trigger sympathy strikes, as was threatened when Mayor Lindsay proposed that the Guard be called out during the 1968 sanitation workers' strike in New York City (*New York Times* February 22, 1968:30). For all these reasons, it would not be surprising if the National Guard's leaders were reluctant to play a replacement role.

Policy Issues

Nearly all states that have extended collective bargaining to public employees have also denied public employees the right to strike. To enforce the ban, they provide for a variety of deterrent and punitive mechanisms. In New York State, for example, striking public employees incur a fine equal to the day's wages (in addition, of course, to losing a day's pay) for every day on strike (Peterson 1981:545-62). The union whose members are on strike faces the possible loss of checkoff privileges and, in addition, the employer is authorized to seek an injunction against the strikers and their union and to enforce the injunction through contempt proceedings (New York State Civil Service Law 210-211 [McKinney Supp. 1980]).

This analysis shows that the National Guard can also be deployed as a weapon for deterring and defeating illegal strikes. In a variety of contexts in which the Guard could play a replacement role effectively, it is already an implicit factor in contract negotiations. As bargaining by police, firemen, and correctional officers reaches an impasse, both sides begin to consider the role that could be played by the state's military forces. Indeed, state negotiators could alert and pre-position the National Guard to increase their bargaining leverage.[7]

If the military forces are already a part of public sector collective bargaining, the issue that must be faced is whether the role of the military should be made explicit and, if so, whether it should be enhanced or diminished.

Legitimizing and Enhancing the Military Role

Since public sector strikes are illegal, one might well ask why we should not recognize and encourage the deployment of military forces as effectively as possible in all illegal strike situations. Would it not make sense, for example, to train individual units to take over various agency operations? Why not have the National Guard account for the civilian skills of its personnel so that they can be deployed in public sector strikes as individuals rather than as units?

To legitimate and enhance the Guard's replacement role in the ways just suggested might strengthen the governor's hand in preventing strikes. Such a policy would not be without a price, however, for it might disrupt both the labor relations process and civil-military relations.

Most states do not permit public employees to strike, but neither do they choose to punish illegal strikers with the state's full police powers. While it would be a mistake to conclude that we have a de facto practice of tolerating public employee strikes, it would also be wrong to conclude that we unequivocally oppose them. In a country in which workers have the right to bargain freely over the terms and conditions of employment, there is considerable ambivalence about how to treat public employees who collectively withhold their labor.

To a degree, strikes in the public sector, like strikes in the private sector, are a test of strength. But in the public sector the state's strength has been augmented by a variety of legal enforcement mechanisms including injunctions and strike penalties. This gives the state an advantage, but one that is not necessarily decisive. To "unleash" the National Guard as a public sector strikebreaking force might prevent many strikes, at the cost of weakening collective bargaining. One has to ask if a strike threat, even a remote one, is necessary to make public sector collective bargaining effective. The potential for a strike may be necessary to keep the public employer bargaining in good faith. Otherwise, public sector bargaining, without interest arbitration, might be substantially undermined.

Another argument against enhancing the National Guard's replacement role is that it would increase conflict between labor and management. Unions would react bitterly to an explicit move to make the National Guard part of the state's negotiating team. Strikes might be more protracted and violent; to overcome the state, a union would have to take extreme action. To turn labor-management disputes in the public sector into battles would weaken the morale and commitment of public employees and destabilize the controlled conflict that may be necessary for public sector labor relations to work.

To enhance the National Guard's replacement role would also be too costly in terms of civil-military relations. Keeping the military at arm's length, out of entanglement with civilian affairs, has been a key feature of the American political system. Greater reliance on the military to help control workers may lead to weaker and weaker civilian governments. It is not healthy for a democracy to rely on the military to cure domestic ailments. The present need for the National Guard to moderate labor-management relations in the public sector underscores the need for more effective "institution building" in state and local government.

Diminishing or Eliminating the Military's Role

If one sees the use of military forces as replacements for striking public employees as at least a potentially serious problem in labor and civil-military relations, it is worth considering whether it would be advisable to diminish or even eliminate the military's role as a strike replacement force.

The Role of Replacements. This is not the appropriate place for a full-scale analysis of the role of replacements in the public sector collective bargaining framework. Briefly, though, private employers are free to continue operations in a struck plant by using replacements. There seems to be no reason that public employers should not have the same right. The question that arises is: what replacements are available to public employers?

In the past, supervisors, personnel from other agencies, trainees, individuals and units from other communities, and even volunteers have been used to keep government agencies operating. In addition, during most public sector strikes, some employees have continued to work. If one were firmly committed to using the National Guard sparingly, all other replacement and alternative services options would be utilized before resorting to the military trump card.

Even in the uniformed services—police, fire, prisons—it has not always been necessary to call on the National Guard. In the majority of strikes, public employers have either ceased operations or found ways to maintain services. Consider the following examples taken from Keith Ocheltree's *Six Strike Stories* (1969). In response to a 1967 strike by 217 social workers in Sacramento, California, the Board of Supervisors authorized new positions, thus permitting replacements to be hired; strikers who did not return to work were fired. In November 1968, 2,800 New York State mental hospital attendants went out on strike; the department continued essential operations by cancelling leaves, providing overtime for supervisors and nonstrikers, subcontracting for certain institutional services, and reducing the number of patients at the affected institutions. Seventy-five percent of the sanitation workers in Atlanta walked off the job in September 1968; with police protection, the remaining workers maintained essential services.

Even in police, fire, and prison strikes there appear to be alternatives to military forces (Gentel 1979). The police struck in Tucson in September 1975. Thirty-three patrolmen and fifty-nine supervisors, working on twelve-hour shifts, were able to maintain services. In October 1975, Oklahoma City experienced a police strike; 140 highway patrolmen and 434 nonstrikers carried on; and private security guards were hired to protect police headquarters. In February 1976, police and firefighters conducted a protracted strike in Los Cruces, New Mexico; nonstriking police officers went on twelve-hour shifts, sheriff and highway patrol departments were placed on alert, and trainees stepped in to assume firefighting responsibilities. Two weeks after the strike started, the city began firing the strikers and hiring replacements.

Even in the nation's largest cities, it has proved possible to weather strikes without National Guardsmen. Despite Mayor Lindsay's repeated requests for help during the 1968 sanitation workers' strike in New York City, Governor Rockefeller refused to activate troops. San Francisco's Mayor, Joseph Alioto, refused, despite intense pressure from the Board of Supervisors, to ask for National Guard assistance in an August 1975 police strike. In 1980, Mayor Jane Byrne of Chicago rode out a turbulent firefighters' strike by relying on supervisors and a variety of other personnel. Even in prison strikes it is not always necessary to turn to the National Guard. In 1973, Massachusetts correctional administrators operated the infamous Walpole, Massachusetts prison for seven weeks with the help of state police, front office personnel, guards from other prisons, and replacements hired off the streets.

It is clear that every strike by police, firefighters, prison guards, sanitation workers, or school teachers does not present an "emergency" requiring activation of the National Guard. The greater the commitment to solve civilian problems by civilian means, the greater will be the effort to rely on civilian replacements in public sector strikes or, better still, to avoid such strikes in the first place.

More Effective Legal Constraints. It would be possible to make constitutional and statutory changes to limit the kinds of strikes for which military forces can be activated. The law might provide, for example, that military forces could not be used as replacements except in strikes by members of the uniformed services, that is, police, firefighters, and prison guards. But this kind of formulation carries potential problems. It might legitimize and routinize strike call-ups in the uniformed services. It might deny governors the option of using troops when health and safety are severely threatened, as they are when staff strike against hospitals, nursing homes, and sanitation departments. Using the term "essential services" to delimit those activities for which the activation of troops would be permissible could raise similar problems. Some services are central to the state's governing role— for example, police, courts, and prisons—and their cessation could create a problem or crisis in governing. Other services the state has chosen to undertake—for example, hospitals, transportation, fire protection, sanitation, and welfare—and their cessation could cause severe inconvenience and hardship for users and beneficiaries.

To anticipate those strike situations in which the threat to life and property is sufficiently grave to require military forces as replacements, a standard such as "emergency" suggests itself. It is possible to refine the emergency trigger by adding requirements like "clear and present danger to life and property," but this leaves enormous discretion to the executive branch. If a governor were determined to use troops, he or she could find a "clear and present danger to life and property" in any public sector strike.

If enhanced legal constraints are necessary to prevent excessive reliance on military forces, rewriting the standard that governs the executive's authority to deploy troops will not be sufficient. A more stringent substantive standard will have to be complemented by stronger structures and procedures, most notably by relying on the popular American division-of-powers formula. The judiciary could be empowered to review the emergency situation via a procedure similar to that provided by the Taft-Hartley Act, which authorizes the president to seek an injunction against a strike that threatens national health or safety. Of course, judges are likely to show great deference to the chief executive in times of purported crisis: only twice have federal courts refused a presidential request for a Taft-Hartley injunction. Still, twice may be better than never, particularly if these precedents have given presidents pause in other cases. In addition, having to appear before a noninvolved decision maker would force an executive to articulate a justification for the use of troops. Any asserted justification would be available for scrutiny and criticism during and after the strike. A legislative veto is another possibility that could be explored.

Conclusion

The many problems associated with formalizing a policy for use of military forces as replacements make it worth considering whether the current nonpolicy should be preserved in the short run. Today's legal constraints on the use of military forces as replacements are weak, indeed almost nonexistent. Yet, certain practical and political constraints continue to present resistance to automatic activation of troops in public sector labor disputes. These constraints may dissipate over time if the tide of public opinion hardens against public employee strikes, and if government develops more confidence in the capacity of troops to serve effectively.

The temptation is to emphasize legal constraints. But the danger is that any formal standard will have the ironic effect of legitimating the use of military forces as replacements in a vaguely defined class of cases. Troops may then be used when the threat to life and property is minor or when other alternatives are available.

In the final analysis, the use of troops to back up civil institutions is a political problem. The best solution would be for wise leaders to make public sector collective bargaining work. But if civil institutions cannot govern themselves effectively, the attraction of a "military solution" may prove irresistible. There is a need to bring this subject into the open. Examination of the proper use of the military in labor conflicts will help constrain unreflective and excessive use of troops to solve civilian problems.

Notes

1. President Reagan's authority to use military air traffic controllers came from the Federal Aviation Act of 1958 (49 U.S.C. § 1343(i) [1976]), which provides for the

Federal Aviation Agency Administrator to "use . . . the available service, equipment, personnel, and facilities of other civilian or military agencies.

2. As for the criteria for declaring a national emergency, one recent commentator notes: "the test for when a national emergency exists is completely subjective—anything the President says is a national emergency is a national emergency" (see *Southern California Law Review* 1979:1458-1511). There were four declared national emergencies between March 1933 and September 14, 1978. In addition to the postal strike, President Nixon also declared a Balance of Payments Emergency in 1971. In 1976, Congress enacted the National Emergency Act (10 U.S.C. § 1601-1651 [1976]), establishing guidelines for both the declaration and termination of future emergencies. Only one national emergency has been declared since passage of the 1976 act. In 1979, President Carter declared a national emergency in order to freeze the assets of the Iranian government (Executive Order 12170, 3 C.F.R. 457 [1979 Compilation and Parts 100 and 101]).

3. 18 U.S.C. § 1918 (1976) makes it a crime for federal employees to strike.

4. Arguably, there was another federal law permitting President Reagan to use military personnel and equipment to maintain domestic air travel during the 1981 air traffic controller's strike.

5. In an unpublished internal White House memorandum to Assistant to the President, John Erlichman, Rehnquist stated:

> I have been unable to locate any square precedent for the use of 10 U.S.C. §3500 to authorize the Guard to actually perform a federal function, rather than simply guard or protect others who are performing that function, but the statutory language is broad enough so that a reasonable argument can be made in support of such use. [Rehnquist, March 22, 1970]

6. Similarly, the AFL-CIO's Public Employee Department resolved at its Fifth Biennial Convention in June 1981 that it:

> supports and will urge the Congress to provide federal legislation so that public safety employees of states and political subdivisions thereof, shall be subject to a national public safety employees collective bargaining law providing binding arbitration as an impasse procedure for settling labor disputes between employers and their employees . . . [and that it] . . . recognizes the inalienable right of public employees in other work sectors, other than the areas of public safety, to withhold his or her services in any collective bargaining legislation provided for those employees . . . [and that] for the purposes of this resolution, public safety officers shall be those uniformed employees in the fields of fire fighting, fire protection and law enforcement.

7. When another postal strike appeared likely in July 1981, Pentagon officials prepared to mobilize over 100,000 military personnel—regular forces, reservists, and National Guardsmen—to move 90 percent of the mail (*Chicago Tribune* July 21, 1981:16).

4

The Role of the Military in Civilian Drug Enforcement: Institution Building in Civil-Military Relations

Neither the military nor civilian society remains static; to the contrary, both sectors are transformed by technological, political, economic and other changes. Just as federalism, the relationship between the federal government and the states, has constantly adapted to new conditions over two centuries, civil-military accommodations have and must adapt to changing times, circumstances, and societal goals.

There is today a massive active armed forces, and a vast reserves and National Guard system. It is not surprising that the Department of Defense is regarded as a potential source of assistance by fiscally starved civilian sectors that are failing to meet their organizational goals.

One of the most overwhelmed civilian sectors is law enforcement, particularly those agencies charged with enforcing the drug laws. For years, smugglers of heroin, cocaine and marijuana have been running circles around the Drug Enforcement Administration, U.S. Customs Service, and Coast Guard, the agencies primarily responsible for preventing illicit drugs from entering the United States. It has been estimated that together these agencies stop only about 15 percent of the illicit drugs bound for the United States market (H.R.71, 97th Cong. 1982 [hereinafter Judiciary Committee Report]). The costs of the interdicted shipments are easily borne by the drug smugglers whose profits can reach truly dazzling heights.

The war on drugs is said to be a top priority of the Reagan Administration, yet budgetary deficits mean that civilian law enforcement agencies cannot expect much increase of resources. Consequently, it is not surprising that the Administration is interested in utilizing Defense Department assets in the effort to stop illegal drug smuggling. Carving out an appropriate military role is an exercise in "institution building," to use Morris Janowitz's phrase (1976).

Enlisting the military in the drug enforcement crusade raises the specter of military encroachment on a traditionally civilian function. Americans

77

have always resisted the idea of the military serving as a "super police force." Thus, even trivial military involvements in civilian criminal investigations have produced searching examinations of the military's proper role in our democratic system.

Much of this soul searching has been undertaken by lawyers, including advocates, judges, and members of the Justice Department. They have sought to understand and define our special brand of civil-military relations by interpreting the Posse Comitatus Act, an obscure criminal law passed during the Reconstruction Era (1878) in response to election abuses committed by civilian carpetbaggers with the aid of federal troops. The Act states that:

> Whoever, except in cases and under circumtances expressly authorized by the Constitution or Act of Congress, willfully uses any part of the Army or the Air Force as a posse comitatus or otherwise to execute the laws shall be fined not more than $10,000 or imprisoned not more than two years, or both. [18 U.S.C. § 1385 (1981)]

This single sentence has come to bear the lion's share of responsibility for defining American civil-military relations; this is all the more remarkable when one considers that no one has ever been prosecuted under the Act and that, until recently, the Act has been subject to little court interpretation. Nevertheless, issues involving domestic use of military forces have been debated in the context of this vague law.

When President Reagan's Attorney General's Task Force on Violent Crime recommended that the armed forces be deployed to assist in stopping drug smuggling, it was inevitable that there would be yet another reassessment of the Posse Comitatus Act. In this case, however, Congress sought to provide explicit approval for military involvement. A new law, passed in 1981, authorizes a larger, albeit still quite circumscribed role for the armed forces in the enforcement of the drug, immigration and customs laws.

The administration immediately sought to implement the new understanding through a coordinated federal effort to lessen the flow of drugs entering the United States through south Florida, by far the most important gateway for drug smuggling into the United States. AWACS and other sophisticated aircraft, helicopters and naval vessels were enlisted on the side of the drug enforcement agencies. While no revolutionary change in civil-military relations is at hand, the new law marks a new civil-military accommodation in the post-Vietnam War period. It remains to be seen whether the law merely authorizes what has been past practice or whether it points the way to greater military involvement in civilian law enforcement.

Background: From Riot Duty and Army Spying to Wounded Knee and Drug Enforcement

During the Vietnam War period, debate over the proper role of the armed forces in civilian law enforcement focused on the President's authority to utilize military units to quell race riots and to protect federal functions from the possible disruptions of antiwar demonstrators. Federal troops were called out four times in 1967-68 (Yarmolinsky 1971). These deployments were not controversial. The use of military troops in riot situations to preserve order and backup civilian police has a long history. For example, federal troops were used to quell riots stemming from labor strikes in the nineteenth century, and to replace striking public employees as early as 1919. Probably most citizens feel that when such emergency circumstances occur, "something must be done." It is generally accepted that National Guard units are the first line of defense, and if they are insufficient, that active duty forces reinforce them. While the particular civil disorder deployments in the 1960s were noncontroversial, the Nixon Administration asserted broad Presidential powers to deploy troops domestically, including authority to pre-position troops and to delegate deployment decisions to local commanders (see Engdahl 1974: 581-617). These regulations have not been put to a test. The Nixon Administration's decision to use active duty, reserve, and federalized National Guard troops during the 1970 postal strike, should have excited the concern of those interested in civil-military relations, but it hardly produced a raised eyebrow, perhaps because it was far overshadowed by the Vietnam War.

Another military foray into civilian law enforcement was revealed in congressional hearings on Army intelligence operations. The Army was charged with massive data collection on civilian antiwar activists and other "dissidents," including members of Congress (see, e.g., *Laird v. Tatum* 1972). Neither the President nor the Army defended these activities; instead, they denied or minimized them. Both military and civilian leaders agreed that the military should play no role in gathering domestic intelligence on Americans, except in espionage cases. This principle was embodied in comprehensive regulations issued by President Carter, later amended by President Reagan (E.O. 12,333, § 1.11, Fed. Reg. 59,941, 59,946 [1981]).

The military has played no dramatic civilian law enforcement or peacekeeping role in the post-Vietnam War period. The only operation of any kind occurred at Wounded Knee in 1973 when militant Native American groups seized a town, taking hostages in the process. Colonel Volney Warner, Chief of Staff to the 82nd Airborne Division, was dispatched to the scene to appraise the situation in case military troops were later needed.

Colonel Warner gave advice to the civilian law enforcement personnel; significantly, he counseled restraint and negotiation. The Army supplied logistical support, including armored personnel carriers, and a supply officer to keep an inventory. Military vehicles, maintained by the Nebraska National Guard, but crewed by Justice Department personnel, were used to seal off access routes into Wounded Knee. The Air National Guard provided reconnaissance. At no time did military officers take command of civilian law enforcement contingents, nor did military personnel engage in front line activities. Reports of the events suggest that active duty military officers paid scrupulous attention to the military's limited role.

The legality of the military's role was vigorously contested in four criminal cases involving persons who tried to break through the roadblock with weapons and other supplies.[1] Charged with interfering with a law enforcement officer in the lawful exercise of his duties, the defendants claimed that the military's involvement polluted the entire operation, making the law enforcement officer's actions unlawful. Two lower federal court judges agreed and dismissed the prosecutions. Two other federal judges sided with the government, finding a distinction in the Posse Comitatus Act between active and passive military involvement in enforcing civilian laws. The touchstone of the distinction is whether military troops coerce or regulate civilians; if they do, there is active involvement. While arrests and seizures are considered active involvement, sharing expertise, counsel, and equipment are not. Under this test, both courts approved the Army's role at Wounded Knee. Subsequently, lawyers in the Justice Department adopted this distinction, and it played a crucial role in the drafting of the 1981 law authorizing military assistance for civilian enforcement of drug, immigration and customs laws (H.R. 921, 97th Cong, 1982 [hereinafter Government Operations Committee Report]: 4-10; Judiciary Committee Report 1982: 6-12).

In the years since the Vietnam War, ingenious criminal defense lawyers have asserted a theory of absolute separation of civil and military authority to challenge drug prosecutions. They have attempted to suppress evidence against their clients by arguing the unconstitutionality of investigations, searches, seizures, and arrests in which military personnel have assisted civilian police. For the most part, courts have rejected these arguments, but on several occasions they have warned the military about overstepping its role. Generally courts define the scope of the Posse Comitatus Act narrowly to find that no violation occurred; this approach obviates the need for fashioning a remedy (*Am. Crim. L. Rev.* 1976; 703, 719-23).[2] Where violations have been found, courts have generally held the exclusionary rule inappropriate. (*Tex. Tech L. Rev.* 1982: 1467, 1483-84)

By 1980, no more than a dozen and probably as few as a half dozen federal judges had created a good deal of uncertainty about the extent to which the armed forces could cooperate with civilian law enforcement agencies by passing along intelligence information, carrying out joint investigations, lending equipment, and generally responding to requests for assistance. So scrupulous were military leaders in not violating the letter or spirit of the Posse Comitatus Act that, for example, if Customs or Drug Enforcement Administration officials wanted radar sightings from military planes, they had to have their own personnel on the planes monitoring the radar screens (97th Cong., 2nd Sess. 1982 [hereinafter Government Operations Committee Hearings]: 13). Many commanding officers had a policy against passing along information on drug smuggling obtained in routine military exercises.

The 1981 Law (P.L. 97-86 (Dec. 1, 1981); 95 Stat 1099)

The Department of Defense Authorization Act of 1982, Chapter 18 is entitled "Military Co-operation with Civilian Law Enforcement Officials (10 U.S.C. §§ 371-78 [1981]).

Section 371 permits the Secretary of Defense to provide federal, state, or local civilian law enforcement officials "with any information collected during the course of normal military operations that may be relevant to violations of any federal or state law." The provision seems eminently reasonable. The armed forces are particularly well situated to obtain information about suspicious aircraft and vessels which might be carrying contraband into the United States.

The law speaks of information collected during the course of "normal military operations"; the House Committee hearings make clear that the law's proponents desired military leaders to be alert for ways to assist in obtaining information on drug trafficking without compromising training and operational goals. For example, the Air Force was encouraged to consider routing Florida training flights over areas most likely to be used by smugglers, and providing smuggler profiles to aircraft crews (Goverment Operations Committee Report 1982: 12-13).

Section 372 permits the Secretary of Defense "to make available any equipment, base facility, or research facility . . . for law enforcement purposes." This had been somewhat controversial before the law's passage, as evidenced by the reversal of two Wounded Knee prosecutions. The consensus of those who testified at the congressional hearings was that lending equipment did not violate any of the values protected by the Posse Comitatus Act. Indeed, federal agencies, including the Armed Forces, already had authority under the Economy Act to lend equipment to other agencies (Government Operations Committee Report 1982:7). What the House Committee did emphasize, in response to concerns raised by Department of Defense, was that Congress did not intend the Department of Defense to become a routine supplier of equipment to fiscally starving law enforcement agencies (Judiciary Committee Report 1982: 9).

Section 373 permits the Secretary of Defense to assign military personnel to train law enforcement officials in the operation and maintenance of equipment made available under the previous section, and to provide expert advice about enforcement matters. The House Judiciary Committee on Crime noted that "Nothing in this section contemplates the creation of large scale or elaborate training programs. Neither does the authority to provide expert advice create a loophole to allow regular or direct involvement of military personnel in what are fundamentally civilian law enforcement operations." The Committee also stated that it would not be proper for the military to assume responsibility for training military-type police SWAT (Special Weapons and Tactics) units (Judiciary Committee report 1982:10).

Section 374 provides that the Secretary of Defense may assign personnel to operate and maintain equipment lent for the purposes of combatting violators of the drug, immigration and customs laws. This section probably goes furthest in authorizing a military role in civilian law enforcement— but it does not go very far. A subsection limits the role of military personnel to operating and maintaining equipment used for monitoring or communicating the movement of air and sea traffic, duties that are not likely to result in face-to-face contacts between military personnel and suspected civilian law violators. This provision would prevent military pilots from flying combat helicopters or driving ground vehicles on operations to interdict smugglers. The legislation explicitly states that in emergency situations outside the United States military personnel could play a larger role, if the Attorney General and Secretary of Defense jointly determine that an emergency exists, but they cannot be used to interdict aircraft or vessels within United States territory.

Section 375 explicitly prohibits military personnel from direct participation in "an interdiction of a vessel or aircraft, a search and seizure, arrest or other similar activity unless participation in such activity is otherwise authorized by law." The Senate bill originally had authorized these activities, but both the Justice Department and the Department of Defense (as well as civil liberties groups) opposed defining military authority so broadly (Government Operations Committee Report 1982: 9; Judiciary Committee Report 1982: 11, 16-19). In the end, something like the distinction between active and passive assistance, suggested by the federal courts in the

Wounded Knee cases, prevailed. Department of Defense regulations further circumscribe military involvement in enforcing civilian laws by prohibiting "use of military personnel for surveillance or pursuit of individuals, or as informants, undercover agents, investigators, or interrogators." At every point in the lawmaking process the military has sought to limit its potential involvement as much as possible without, however, appearing to rebuff the cries for assistance from congressmen highly concerned about the flow of narcotics into the United States.

Section 376 provides that the military should not provide assistance if it adversely affects military preparedness. Throughout the hearings, Department of Defense personnel expressed concern that nothing in the bill detract from the military's national defense responsibility. Congress responded to this concern (Government Operations Committee Report 1982: 12), by giving the military discretion to turn down requests if it so desires.

Section 377 is also an escape hatch for the Department of Defense. It provides that law enforcement agencies may be required to reimburse the Department of Defense for borrowed equipment and personnel. Needless to say, military equipment does not come cheaply. The meter on an AWACS aircraft, for example, runs at $7,000 per hour (Government Operations Committee Hearings 1982: 48). Hard-pressed law enforcement agencies hardly have this kind of loose change lying around. The Department of Defense claims that it requires reimbursement unless assistance is provided as an incidental aspect of an activity conducted for a military purpose. However, it will waive reimbursement when assistance to a civilian agency also provides the Department with training or operational benefits or when waiver will not have an adverse impact on military preparedness (DoD Directive 5525.5 [1982]). If the Defense Department sets stricter standards for waiver, it can, in effect, eliminate the majority of law enforcement requests for assistance.

Finally, Section 378 carefully states that the law is not meant to "limit the authority of the executive branch . . . beyond that provided by law prior to the enactment of this chapter." The Armed Forces thereby maintains maximum flexibility. The Department of Defense emphasizes that the Navy and Marines are not bound by the Posse Comitatus Act as they were not included in it originally, or in the amendments. On the other hand, Department of Defense regulations require these services to follow the principles adhered to by the Army and Air Force (Secretary of Navy instruction 5820.7 [1974]).[3] A DoD directive issued in response to the new law extends the Department's policy of cooperation to the Navy and Marines (DoD Directive 5525.5: 1 [1982]).

The new law is cautious. It only authorizes the military services to do what they have already been doing, albeit sporadically and on an ad hoc basis (Judiciary Committee Report 1982: 7). Except for section 375, which authorizes "the occasional use of military personnel to operate sophisticated equipment on loan to civilian drug law enforcement agencies for specific law enforcement operations," the Judiciary Committee viewed the new legislation as a clarification of military authority. Yet, the Act has at least symbolic significance. It authorizes a front line regular role for the military in a traditional civilian law enforcement area. This, in principle, is a departure from the kind of emergency role which has historically characterized military deployments in civilian law enforcement.

Implementation of the New Law

The Committee on Government Operations' Report, released October 1, 1982, observes that the president's South Florida Task Force, headed by Vice President Bush, immediately seized the initiative for implementing the new addendum to the Posse Comitatus law. In January, 1982, the vice president ordered immediate deployment to the Task Force of sophisticated downward-looking radar aircraft, the Navy EC-2 and the Air Force AWACS. These aircraft were flown by military personnel on missions specifically designed to detect drug smuggling. Cobra helicopters and a brand new Blackhawk helicopter were lent to Customs for a trial period; these were flown by civilian pilots trained by the military. The helicopters themselves were kept at military bases when not in use. The Air Force shared information obtained from the radar system embodied in its aerostadt balloon-borne radar. The Navy provided ships to assist with interdicting and towing vessels in the Caribbean's windward passage.

All in all, the Committee concluded that:

1. Despite some confusion the implementation of military assistance in the war on drugs has been quite successful.
2. There is a pronounced lack of effective liason between Department of Defense, the several services, and the civilian law enforcement community.
3. The civilian law enforcement community must accept responsibility for orderly implementation of the new law.
4. The Air Force has dragged its heels on the second balloon-borne radar system.
5. There has been a delay in implementing Department of Defense field directives.
6. U.S. Customs has not developed a national air interdiction strategy.

The Department of Defense issued a directive in March 1982, stating its policy to cooperate with civilian law enforcement officials to the maximum extent practicable (DoD Directive 5525.5: 1-2).

The Defense Department "letter" dated July 13, 1982, briefly reported the following acts of assistance to the South Florida Task Force:

> Navy has provided E-2C surveillance support in an attempt to halt the flow of contraband via small, low flying aircraft. They also provided to Coast Guard information on vessels of special interest obtained in the course of normal operations at sea, and have towed vessels seized by Coast Guard on the high seas back to port to enable limited Coast Guard assets to remain on station longer. Navy also provided high frequency radio equipment to the Drug Enforcement Administration in support of its operations.

> Army has made available three additional Cobra and two UH-lH helicopters to the enforcement agencies, together with the pilot training and mainte- nance support necessary for their proper utilization.

> Air Force continues to provide information obtained through the normal operations of North American Radar Air Defense (NORAD) network, has given Coast Guard access to our Skyhook radar facility in Cudjoe Key, Flor- ida, and is assisting the customs service with a test of Customs's own balloon- borne radar capability at Patrick Air Force Base. Air Force also conducted a test of the feasibility of certain reconnaissance assets providing information to DEA in the normal course of their military operations. The classified results of that test are now being analyzed.

In July 1983, Assistant Department of Defense Secretary Lawrence Korb reported to Congress that the Department of Defense desired to cooperate in the drug enforcement effort, and to find ways to use drug interdiction as a basis for realistic training missions for flight crews. The two most dramatic joint ventures described by Secretary Korb are the seizure of a "mother ship" ladened with marijuana, and a raid in the Bahamas which netted a sizable amount of drugs and currency.

Implications for Civil-Military Relations

Civil military relations require ongoing accommodations and adjust- ments between the armed forces and various civilian sectors. There can be no iron wall between the military and the rest of the society; in any case, such a wall would be counterproductive to a vigorous democracy. The accommodations which are worked out in light of new technological, eco- nomic, and political conditions must be consistent with historical values, but they must also be innovative. Cries of military usurpation should not be allowed to bury every suggestion for new military roles in the larger society.

Historically, the military role in enforcing civilian laws has been limited. Since World War II the military has been called upon to quell disorders and to assure that southern desegregation was carried out. The military has not functioned as a super police force, as may be the case in Italy, for example (see Pisano 1979).

Military assistance in defending the nation's borders from penetration by drug smugglers is not, in my view, "the first" step toward military domination of civilian society. To the contrary, it is entirely sensible and desirable that the military provide its unique assistance in support of this goal. One can hardly imagine a law enforcement effort more appropriate for military assistance. Drug smugglers are, in a real sense, challenging our national sovereignty and violating our borders. The drugs which they smuggle debilitate military as well as civilian society. The military possesses expertise and equipment useful in detecting and interdicting smugglers; this equipment is out of the price range of civilian agencies.

The distinction between an active and a passive military role in law enforcement discerned by two federal courts in the Wounded Knee operation makes sense. The paramount concern of the Posse Comitatus Act is military troops coercing civilians—ad hoc martial law. Sharing military advice, intelligence, and expertise, and lending expensive equipment to civilian law enforcement agencies violates no core principles of civil-military relations. It presents none of the symbolism that is so unsettling to the national psyche, military police coercing civilians with fixed bayonets.[4]

It could be argued that military equipment is too awesome for civilian law enforcement purposes and represents overkill and dangerous esclation of the internal arms race. While we need to be wary of police arming themselves with M-16s, it hardly seems like escalation for the DEA, Custom's Service and Coast Guard to be using advanced aircraft and radar systems to detect smugglers who use sophisticated equipment.[5]

If any dangers lurk in the emerging new accommodation between the military and the civilian law enforcement sector, they are ones that should worry the military. There will undoubtedly be an inexorable urge to ask for more and more military largess. It is one thing for Congress to counsel civilian law enforcement agencies to restrain themselves, it is another for an agency to exercise restraint when brother and sister agencies are augmenting their resources and budgets through acquisitions of military equipment. The military is an incredibly rich potential source of equipment and resources; telling civilian agencies to show restraint is like trying to control a 5-year-old in a candy store. Fiscal pressures might restrain civilian agencies. The Roundtable Discussion on the Use of the Military in the Control of Illegal Drugs, conducted by the National Governors' Association, the U.S. Department of Justice, and other criminal justice groups, found that the central issue in increasing the application of military assets to civilian law enforcement matters is the cost of such assistance (Round-table Report 1984: 4). However, labelling the drug problem a national defense issue, the Roundtable recommended federal reimbursement of state law enforcement authorites who avail themselves of military resources (Roundtable Report 1984: 5). Such a proposal would somewhat undermine the military's control of requests for assistance.

The military may find it disruptive to have to respond to requests for assistance from agencies all over the country. Is it the responsibility of the Department of Defense to decide which requests make most sense from the standpoint of overall drug enforcement? Must the Department of Defense develop a comprehensive blueprint for drug enforcement and strategies for best deploying military resources? This would absorb time, energy and resources and could complicate relations with various federal and state agencies. Inevitably some agencies will be disappointed. Defense Department judgments will be criticized. There will be appeals to higher-ups and interventions by Congressmen and Senators. The military will need to stem the tide of requests and demands, and dampen expectations that, with the cavalry's arrival, victory over drug smuggling is around the corner.

Furthermore, whatever success is achieved in south Florida will create pressure to expand military activities in behalf of the Drug Enforcement Administration, Coast Guard and U.S. Customs Service. Once they became convinced that south Florida has become too risky, smugglers will shift their air and sea routes. It makes no sense simply to displace smuggling from south Florida to other landing areas along the Gulf of Mexico. We can be sure that the drug smugglers are not simply going to give up because certain air and sea lanes have become more risky; the profits are too great and their motivations too strong. They will continue to test the air and sea defenses for points of vulnerability. Ultimately, it will be necessary to expand military assistance to the entire Gulf of Mexico, and beyond to the Atlantic and Pacific coastlines. In fact, during the summer of 1983 Vice President Bush, hailing the south Florida Task Force's success, announced the location of five new regional centers in New York City, New Orleans, Chicago, El Paso, and Long Beach (*Criminal Law Reporter* 1983: Vol. 33, p. 2291). When, as will happen inevitably, it becomes apparent that the war on drugs isn't being won, will the momentum to expand the war prove irresistible?

Political leaders and law enforcement personnel never envisioned the south Florida initiative as a short term mission that would end in the smugglers' unconditional surrender. Several of the witnesses who testified before the Congressional Committee stressed the importance of sending drug traffickers the message that the federal government and the Department of Defense are in the war against drugs until the end (Government Operations Committee Hearings 1982: 1-2, 18-19, 39-42). Military assistance in south Florida only makes sense if there is a permanent commitment. Yet, it is likely that the Department of Defense wants to avoid long term commitments, except for sharing information obtained incidentally on routine military missions.

Meanwhile, the limits of law enforcement are also becoming increasingly clear. What good is it to identify and track scores of vessels and planes meeting the drug smuggling profile, if there are insufficient personnel and resources to interdict these vessels and aircraft?[6] Indeed, interdictions alone cannot make for a successful antidrug effort; intelligence gathering on the most significant smuggling operations must be a top enforcement priority.

Once the initial commitment is made, how easy will it be for the military to withdraw? The new law is certainly flexible enough to provide a legal justification for lessening or terminating assistance, but it may prove difficult to disappoint popular expectations and influential politicians. For the military there is always the danger of being enveloped in drug enforcement politics, as well as the corruption that inevitably plagues narcotics enforcement. The Department of Defense has already come in for sharp criticism from citizens' groups and newspapers in south Florida because of a decision to remove one of the two EC-2 aircraft from full time use by the Task Force (Government Operations Committee Hearings 1982: 40).

The new law authorizes assistance in the enforcement of the immigration and customs laws as well as the drug laws. By some estimates, more than a million illegal aliens are entering the United States each year. The magnitude of this flow of human beings far outshadows the resources of the U.S. Immigration Service's meager border patrol. The imbalance between this agency's task and its resources is even greater than that between the drug enforcement agencies and their task (see also Morris and Mayio 1982). It takes little imagination to foresee that Congressmen and immigration officials will press for military surveillance, helicopters, jeeps, and other motor vehicles to assist in combatting this problem. No doubt there will be calls to deploy military personnel to patrol the Mexican border. The potential implications of such assistance, in terms of resources, personnel, and improper use of force are very sobering.

During a period of intense fiscal pressures on state and local governments, civilian political leaders will have no trouble thinking up new uses for military personnel and equipment. In 1980, New York State Republican gubernatorial candidate Lewis Lehrman suggested using reserve and National Guard forces to patrol New York City streets in order to prevent street crime. This proposal is the polar opposite of the kind of cooperative venture carefully prescribed by the new Posse Comitatus Act. No doubt, it is precisely this kind of proposal that is feared by those opposed to any breach in the wall between military and civilian law enforcement. It is well to recall, however, that Lehrman's proposal attracted very little support and much criticism (*New York Times*, August 4 1982: B3). A more moderate proposal for expanding the military's role in civilian law enforcement has been put forward by Representative Glenn English (D.-Okla.). He plans to introduce legislation that would expand the military's active role in the enforcement of marijuana cultivation laws. Troops would be used to cut and to cart away cannabis plants. This legislative effort, combined with the 1981 Act, suggests that there may be a trend toward further winnowing away Posse Comitatus restrictions (*Halbrook* 1983). It is possible to engage in creative institution building consistent with core values of our political tradition. Like any institution building, however, the developing military role in civilian law enforcement has the potential to create strains and produce unanticipated negative results. This is hardly cause for rejecting innovation; it is reason to proceed with caution.

The linkage of external and internal security is evident throughout world history. External security by no means assures continued prosperity or even the existence of a state, society or people. While abusive use of military forces in the domestic sphere can cause untold destruction to domestic values and political and social structure, judicious arrangements can nurture, support and bolster internal institutions and morale.

Notes

1. *United States v. Banks* (1974); *United States v. Jaramillo* (1974); *United States v. Red Feather* (1975); *United States v. Caspar* (1976).
2. For example, in *Hubert v. State* (1972), and *Hildebrand v. State* (1973), the courts found no violation of the Posse Comitatus Act when undercover military agents made a drug purchase that served as the basis for prosecuting civilian drug suppliers. Both courts pointed out that military authorities acted in concert with local police, and the *Hildebrand* court reasoned that because the purchase was made "outside the scope of their military jurisdiction . . . the agents assumed no greater authority than that of a private citizen."
3. The Government Operations Committee report points out that "the U.S. Court of Appeals for the Fourth Circuit in *United States v. Walden* (1984), relied upon a 1969 predecessor to the 1974 Instruction of the Secretary of the Navy to find the Navy bound by the restriction of the Posse Comitatus Act."
4. However, the case of *Jabara v. Webster* (1982) has added an unsettling twist to Fourth Amendment jurisprudence. Summaries of telephone calls legally intercepted by the National Security Agency (NSA) were turned over to the FBI, which was conducting an investigation of the caller. The caller's challenge to the FBI's receipt of the summaries as a warrantless search was dismissed on the ground that since NSA lawfully intercepted the messages, there was no search by

the FBI. The caller could not challenge the FBI's receipt of the messages because he could have no reasonable expectation of privacy with respect to information held by a government agency, the NSA. According to one commentator:

> *Jabara* implies that in the narcotics enforcement context any information obtained by an intelligence agency consistent with that agency's mandate may be turned over to domestic enforcement agencies. Thus, information which would be excluded from use in court if collected without a warrant by the DEA or FBI can now be used to prosecute individuals for narcotics offenses in U.S. courts if it is initially obtained by the NSA (*Journal of International Law and Politics* 1984: 398).

5. NASA satellites may also prove useful to law enforcement. A 1982 project conducted by the DEA, NASA and other federal and local agencies assessed the feasibility of using satellites to detect marijuana fields; decorrelation analysis of thermal infrared multispectral scanner data showed some promise [*Halbrook* (1983): v. 36].

6. On June 29, 1985, the U.S. House of Representaives overwhelmingly passsed another amendment to the Posse Comitatus Act. If it becomes law the new amendment would authorize the use of military forces in a drug enforcement operation, as long as the operation is under the control of federal law enforcement officials. The Secretary of Defense's vehement objections were waived aside by strong rhetoric likening the war on drugs to a war for national survival. (see Congressional Record H4989-5004, June 26, 1985).

5

Selective Service Without a Draft: The Dilemmas and Symbolic Politics Of Draft Registration

with Dennis McNamara

No issue has more significance for civil-military relations than the recruitment of military manpower. Who serves in the armed forces, for how long, and for what reasons are vital determinants of the military's role in the larger society and of the relationship between civilian and military sectors.

It is no exaggeration to state that for much of our history the military draft has been the most significant issue in civil-military relations to the vast majority of the population. This is true because a draft impinges on personal liberty and raises continuous complaints based upon real and perceived inequities (see *Society* 1981). Antidraft demonstrations and riots have been a feature of U.S. political life since the Civil War (see O'Sullivan and Meckler 1974). On the eve of World War II, President Roosevelt's conscription plan encountered enormous resistance in Congress (Cong. rec. 1940: 12160,12227). The Vietnam War triggered the most intense and sustained opposition in the United States history; there were thousands of demonstrations, many of them tinged with violence. During the Vietnam War era, 2,000 to 4,000 draft violators were prosecuted each year.

After intense national debate, the United States ended conscription in June, 1973; the president's authority to induct men into the armed forces was allowed to expire. Nearly two years later, the requirement that young men register with the Selective Service System upon reaching age 18 also expired. The president retained authority to reinstate registration only if he deemed it necessary; to begin inductions, however, would require congressional action. President Gerald Ford chose not to reactivate registration; in fact, he cut Selective Service's budget by $30 million and relegated the shrunken draft administration to standby status. At the time it seemed as though the country's long, stormy relationship with military conscription had finally ended.

Such a prophecy was soon proved wrong. Less than seven years later (July 2, 1980), following the Soviet invasion of Afghanistan and long debate, Congress provided the funds to implement draft registration for 18-year-old male citizens and permanent aliens. Despite the president's repeated assurances that he would not seek congressional authority to start inductions, protesters held antidraft marches, rallies, and teach-ins around the country. They also attacked draft registration in the courts, charging a plethora of constitutional violations, particularly sex discrimination.

Notwithstanding a few defeats in the lower courts, draft registration's legal foundation has remained intact. Yet, the success of the program is questionable. Perhaps as many as a million young men, for one reason or another, have failed to fulfill their obligation to register. A small number have been prosecuted, even jailed, but the number of nonregistrants continues to grow. The current administration must either initiate a much stepped up (and therefore expensive and divisive) prosecution policy or see registration deteriorate into a de facto voluntary program.

The current enforcement dilemma invites review of the entire registration program. Why was it passed? What purposes does it serve? What costs does it impose? What are its implications for civil-military relations in the 1980s?

The Politics of Draft Registration: Foreign Affairs, National Defense and Military Preparedness

Like all political events, the 1980 draft registration has multiple causes. No single variable accounts for reversal of the late 1970s' trend toward abandonment of Selective Service. However, three major sources of pressure to reestablish registration can be identified: (1) political and military leaders who felt registration necessary in case of a protracted, large-scale conventional war; (2) political and military leaders who believed the all-volunteer force to be a failure; and (3) political leaders who saw draft registration as an asset in the pursuit of U.S. foreign policy.

The Continued Attraction of Mass Mobilization

In the 1980 congressional debates, enhancement of the nation's preparedness for a military emergency was the most commonly voiced explanation for reviving draft registration (see e.g., Cong. Rec., H 2715), this despite the view of some civilian analysts that the realities of modern warfare (e.g., Coffey 1979:143) and the existence of military "forces-in-being" make mass mobilization irrelevant.[1]

As Morris Janowitz has explained (1975), Western military forces changed format after World War II in response to changes in the nature of warfare and international relations. In an age of nuclear weapons and highly mobile, conventional forces with enormous destructive potential, a nation could not wait six or more months after an international crisis for conscripts to be trained. A ready military force is needed to deter threats to national interests, and to defend those interests if deterrence fails. Janowitz spoke of the emergence of the "force-in-being."

The force-in-being differs from the mass mobilization force in that it does not rely on mobilization. The force-in-being is prepared to deter and fight wars at any time. While such a force must be credible it need not be as large as the mass forces that fought World War II.

During the debates, the potential contribution of draft registration to preparedness was not satisfactorily explained; registration came to symbolize "commitment." Had registration's advocates been forced to explain step-by-step how registration would enhance preparedness, their support might have weakened, or they might not have insisted on a registration program carrying adverse domestic, political overtones and straining civil-military relations. Their concerns about the nation's ability to mobilize sufficient manpower to deal with a protracted war might have been allayed by a standby registration plan that could be implemented in the event that Congress and the president agreed to start conscription. It is useful to recall that in both world wars registration did not begin until after Congress passed draft legislation. Although there had been extensive preplanning, for both wars millions of men were registered on a single day shortly after the draft legislation was signed (Selective Service System 1948).

The Selective Service stated in a January 26, 1980 report that premobilization face-to-face registration would save only 7 to 14 days and that a one-day postmobilization registration, utilizing state election procedures and machinery, would adequately meet defense needs. As an alternative, Selective Service proposed compilation of a standby list of eligible persons from Social Security and Internal Revenue Service records. In the event of a military emergency, persons on this list would immediately be sent draft notices, and a supplemental face-to-face registration would be immediately activated. Either of these alternatives would have produced less controversy than face-to-face registration (House Judiciary Committee 1980, No. 45).[2] But old institutions die slowly. The image of the World War II mass mobilization armed forces undoubtedly remains compelling for many political and military leaders.

Dissatisfaction with the All-Volunteer Force

The second source of pressure to reinstitute draft registration emanated from military and political leaders dissatisfied with the All-Volunteer Force

(AVF). Many had been skeptical from the outset. They were accustomed to conscription stimulating "volunteers" and making up shortfalls in force levels. The post-World War II peacetime draft made it possible to maintain a large force-in-being without having to pay personnel the market wage. This is what Milton Friedman and other market economists meant when they charged that the draft was a hidden tax on youth (*Report of the President's Commission on an All-Volunteer Force* 1973:25).

During the AVF's first few years it proved difficult to attract sufficient numbers of military recruits. Perhaps as a consequence force levels were continually reduced. The Army fell short of meeting its recruiting goals in 1973 during the transition from conscription to an all-volunteer force. From 1974-1978, even as force levels decreased, the military failed to meet its quotas by a few percentage points. In 1979, the active force strength of all the armed services was 30,000 below the congressionally authorized level. The situation improved markedly in 1982 because of the severe economic recession. But the sharp decrease in the number of young men turning 18 each year until the mid-1990s means that it will become increasingly more difficult to meet force levels (see Subcommittee on Manpower and Personnel of the Armed Services Committee of the United States Senate 1978 and 1979). It is likely that pressures to reduce force levels will continue. For example, during debate on the Defense Authorization Bill for fiscal year 1983, Senator John Tower (R-Tex.), Chairman of the Senate Armed Services Committee, stated that he would rather cut personnel than make major cuts in weapons procurement.

Recruitment shortfalls convinced many people that conscription should not have been terminated. As Senator Boren (D.-Okla.) put it during the 1980 congressional debates, "we have by our record demonstrated, at least in my mind, that we are not going to provide the funds . . . to meet the full cost of maintaining a military establishment short of some kind of required service." Other analysts were concerned with the quality of military personnel. They charged that the armed forces, particularly the army, was becoming a poor people's organization, and they cited high rates of attrition, absences without leave, drug abuse, and other problems. In addition, they criticized on fairness grounds the disproportionately high number of blacks in the armed forces (Janowitz 1975:432-49).

In July 1982, fifty-five prominent panelists, including retired Army General Andrew Goodpaster and former Secretary of Defense Robert S. McNamara, urged President Reagan and Congress to prepare to resume the draft in the near future. The panel, sponsored by the Atlantic Council, said the army needed more middle class white youths and fewer blacks, especially in combat arms, in order to achieve greater representation and to assure that casualities do not fall disproportionately on one group. At the time, the army's enlisted force was one-third black, while blacks constituted 13 percent of the overall population (see also *Society* 1981).

Many AVF critics favored reinstating conscription in order to improve the numbers and qualifications of recruits, but they were incapable of producing a congressional majority. Although registration cannot provide any remedies for the AVF, some of these critics, like Senator John Stennis (D.-Miss.), voted for registration in the hope that it would be a first step toward renewing the draft. Others opposed registration, fearing that the political effort necessary to pass registration would make it harder to reinstate conscription in the future.

Draft Registration as Foreign Policy

Undoubtedly, draft registration legislation would not have passed but for President Jimmy Carter's abrupt change of position following the Soviet Union's invasion of Afghanistan in December 1979. Carter reacted to the invasion by announcing a boycott of the 1980 Soviet Olympics, an embargo on grain and high technology equipment to the Soviets, and reinstitution of draft registration. Clearly, the first two measures were designed respectively to embarrass and penalize the Soviet Union, but it is not apparent how reviving draft registration could hurt the Soviets or further U.S. foreign policy objectives. As Representative Samuel Stratton (D.-NY) remarked in Congress, "The President has said that resuming registration is also an important symbolic act. What would it symbolize?"

It is difficult to understand what message the 1980 draft registration was supposed to convey to the Soviet Union. It surely did not convey the message that the United States was ready to improve the quality and increase the number of its military recruits, because registration cannot improve the AVF. The more plausible message was that the United States was ready to meet any extraordinary international crisis in the Persian Gulf or elsewhere with any means necessary. It is unlikely that the Soviet leadership was surprised to learn that the United States would be prepared to respond to an extraordinary international crisis by conscripting military recruits. Ironically, as events turned out, if the draft registration controversy conveyed any message to the Soviet Union, it may have been that the United States would experience serious domestic strife in returning to conscription.

President Reagan's Position

While campaigning in 1980 for the presidency, Ronald Reagan opposed a peacetime draft, and sharply criticized President Carter's draft registration program. The 1980 Republican platform called for registration's repeal. Reagan stressed throughout his campaign that the problems of the All-Volunteer Force could not be met by a return to the draft; instead he advocated improving military pay and benefits.

A year after moving into the oval office, however, he announced the President's Military Manpower Task Force's conclusion that registration could save "as much as six weeks in mobilizing emergency manpower" and his conviction that "the registration program should therefore be continued." Apparently, the president was thinking in terms of the old mass mobilization format. When the president was asked what it would take for him to reinstate conscription, he said, "I would have to hark back to the days preceding World War II and there for the first time we instituted a peacetime draft. But the rest of the world was at war; the whole world was going up in flames."

Draft, Registration and Domestic Politics

The draft has become more equitable over time as equal rights have become more important in our society. The Civil War draft, which permitted the wealthy to hire substitutes to fulfill their obligations, now seems outlandish and inconceivable. During the Vietnam War student deferments were a constant target of criticism and were eventually abolished. The lottery system, instituted in 1969, ended inequities based on the location of one's draft board. However, demands for increased fairness and equity are unceasing and probably could not be allayed.

Equity and Face-to-Face Registration

The Carter administration's decision to implement a preemergency face-to-face registration plan was determined more by equity norms of civilian society than by national defense requirements. Selective Service originally favored a postemergency one-day registration utilizing state electoral machinery. But the General Accounting Office criticized this plan on equity grounds—if some machinery broke down, some eligibles would not be registered, thereby creating inequities. As the GAO put it, "in addition to our specific concerns about implementing the emergency plan, an overriding issue centers around the concept of equity. Should any one of the planned procedures fail, serious legal questions could arise concerning fair and equitable treatment of those involved" (1979:3).

The Selective Service System's fallback position was a preemergency computer registration. Individual registrants would not be required to do anything. Selective Service would compile a list of eligibles utilizing Social Security and Internal Revenue Service records. As the draft registration debate proceeded, however, the Carter administration apparently became convinced that computer registration would be inequitable because it might fail to include from 15 to 40 percent of the draft-eligible population.[3] Selective Service's General Counsel Henry Williams advised (rather dubiously we believe) the Director that this type of registration could violate the Fourteenth Amendment's equal protection clause (House Judiciary Committee 1980, no. 45:175). The only fair system, in his view, was a face-to-face registration which would include the entire youth population. Apparently, he failed to anticipate that a significant number of young men would fail to fill out registration cards.

Domestic political concerns have dominated the registration controversy. Draft registration was meant to demonstrate U.S. opposition to Soviet aggression. Yet, the Carter administration believed that this symbolic move had to be reconciled with domestic politics. The decision to adopt a face-to-face registration program is strong evidence of the dominant role played by equity norms. The irony is that while face-to-face registration may be more equitable, it is also likely to provoke more protest.

Sex Discrimination and Rostker v. Goldberg

On January 23, 1980, for the first time in U.S. history a president asked for the authority to register women for a military draft, while at the same time asserting that women would not be eligible for combat positions. President Carter justified his position on the ground that women had established themselves as full working members of society, providing all types of skills in every profession. The president sought to defuse opposition by supporting the continued exclusion of females from combat positions. At the congressional hearings, the assistant secretary of defense explained that "the President's decision to ask for authority to register women is based on equity." Feminist groups spoke out strongly in favor of the president's proposal, seeing registration as a litmus test of equality for women (Hearings before the House Committee on the Budget's Task Force on Defense and International Affairs 1980).

Despite surprising public acceptance for the idea of registering women (about 50 percent in favor according to the 1980 Gallup Poll Index), there was little support in Congress. On February 27, 1980, the House Appropriations Independent Agencies Subcommittee blocked a proposal to fund the registration of women. On March 6, 1980, the House Armed Services Personnel Subcommittee voted 8 to 1 against registering women. When the full registration measure went before the House Appropriations Committee, an amendment by Representative Robert Duncan (D.-Oreg.) to add $8.5 million to register women was defeated by a voice vote. On April 17, the Senate Armed Services and Personnel Subcommittee disapproved the administration's proposal to register women. In mid-April, the full Senate

Armed Services Committee, pointing to moral values and administrative efficiency, recommended male only registration:

> Drafting women would place unprecedented strains on family life. . . . If such a draft occurred at a time of emergency, unpredictable reactions to the fact of female conscriptions would result. A decision which would result in a young mother being drafted and a young father remaining home with the family . . . cannot be taken lightly . . . nor its broader implications ignored.

The Committee also presented twelve specific findings as to why women should not be registered and drafted. These findings may have been included with an eye toward a court challenge (see Senate Committee on Armed Services 1980, No. 826: 154-60).[4] On April 29, the Senate Appropriations Independent Agencies Subcommittee voted against the registration of women. On May 6, the full Appropriations Committee added its disapproval. While several amendments to include women were offered in the Senate during the June 6-10 debate, they were all soundly defeated.

As soon as it became law, registration was attacked on the ground that it discriminated against men. On July 18, 1980, a three-judge panel in a Pennsylvania federal district court declared an all-male draft to be unconstitutional and enjoined Selective Service from proceeding with registration.

> Ordinarily, statutory classification based on gender are unconstitutional unless they are substantially related to an important government interest . . . the complete exclusion of women from the pool of registrants does not serve important governmental objectives and . . . unconstitutionally discriminates between males and females.

Supreme Court Justice William Brennan stayed the order, permitting the registration of males born in 1960 and 1961 to take place as scheduled.

Ultimately, in July 1981, the Supreme Court held, in *Rostker v. Goldberg* (1981), that a male-only draft did not violate the Constitution. Writing for the Court, Justice Rehnquist explained that since women were not eligible for combat duty, they were not "similarly situated" for the purpose of draft registration. Thus, there was no violation of the equal protection or due process clauses of the Constitution. Justice Rehnquist's opinion is notable for its insistence that on issues of military organization the Court will ordinarily defer to Congress's judgment. Dissents by Justice White and Marshall, each joined by Justice Brennan, emphasized that Congress had not concluded that all military posts must be filled by men. In their view, there was no justification for excluding women from the obligation to register. Nevertheless, the Court's decision put to rest the sex discrimination issue.

Time will reveal whether women themselves ultimately favor an equal obligation under Selective Service. Throughout U.S. history there has been a close relationship between service in the armed forces and the attainment of citizenship rights. Only recently, during the Vietnam War period, 18-year-olds won the right to vote, in large part because of their compelling slogan, "If we're old enough to fight, we're old enough to vote."

Draft Protest

Military conscription has triggered protest and conflict throughout U.S. history, most recently during the Vietnam War (see Useem 1973). In addition to opposing conscription per se, many activists use opposition to the draft to express dissatisfaction with the government, foreign policy, and the status quo. Likewise, many "super-patriots" use conscription as a litmus on loyalty to one's country and on commitment to national defense.

The reaction of traditional antiwar groups to face-to-face registration was swift and predictable. On January 26, 1980, the Central Committee for Conscientious Objectors announced the revival of its draft counselling network. Throughout February, protests occurred at many eastern universities including Cornell, Yale, Brown, Harvard, Williams, University of Pennsylvania and Princeton. Although more numerous in the east, anti-registration rallies also took place on west coast campuses, the largest at the University of California at Berkeley. There, a crowd of 2,500 listened to Daniel Ellsberg compare draft registration to mass suicide in Jonestown, Guyana, the similarity being "blind following." Although less prevalent in midwestern and southern campuses, notable rallies occurred at Michigan State, Houston and Northwestern (*New York Times* February 13, 1980:16). By mid-February, 1980, public opinion polls showed that on many campuses about half the students opposed registration. However, of the U.S. population as a whole, 83 percent favored registration. Opinion also supported reinstituting the draft; 59 percent were in favor and 36 percent opposed (Gallup Opinion Index 1980, no. 175:3-8).

While college campuses were the primary focus of protest, there were also street demonstrations. In early February, two thousand persons marched through mid-Manhattan. On March 23, 1980, the largest anti-draft protest since the Vietnam War took place in Washington, D.C. (*New York Times* March 23, 1980:24). A crowd of 30,000 marched from the White House to Capitol Hill and listened to veteran antiwar activists Rev. William Sloan Coffin, Jr., David Dellinger, and David Harris. Among the groups represented at the rally were the National Mobilization Against the

Draft, the Committee Against Registration and the Draft, the Central Committee for Conscientious Objectors, Students for a Libertarian Society, Americans for Democratic Action, Women's Strike for Peace, and the Communist Revolutionary Party.

No more large-scale protests took place after this Washington rally. From April-June 1980, while the registration bill moved through Congress, protests were small, isolated, and sporadic. A series of coordinated protests did occur in mid-June after Senate passage, but they drew small crowds and failed to produce broad-based support for draft resistance. A June 1980 Gallup poll reported that 80 percent of Americans favored registration of young men; 66 percent of the draft age population now favored registration. Nationally, 58 percent of all Americans and 37 percent of those of draft age favored returning to conscription.

In mid-June, antidraft groups announced a four-pronged strategy; protests at local post offices, a series of draft education programs at public places frequented by youth, nationwide distribution of antidraft tracts, and a series of press conferences featuring registration resisters (Terry 1980:4).

With this announcement, the F.B.I. entered the unfolding registration drama. The Bureau announced that it would investigate leaders in the antidraft program, for example for ties to the Communist Party. A spokesman for the Bureau noted that during the 1960s, nonstudents, some of whom were directly supported by foreign governments (Morehouse 1980:4), committed most acts of violent protest. For a time it seemed that the largely symbolic registration program might spark an equally large symbolic protest movement and the kind of confrontation that had so disrupted U.S. society during the Vietnam War era. But this did not occur. Protests remained small and peaceful.

The second round of mass registrations, for those born in 1962, took place during the week of January 4-11, 1981. Again, there were only mild protests, and no serious disruptions. Mass registration was replaced with staggered registration. Eligible young men have to register within 30 days of their 18th birthday. National attention would no longer be focused on a single registration week. The new registration system and President Reagan's silence on the future of the program may have combined to deflate protest activities during the remainder of 1981. The story in 1982 was the same except for a few isolated protests in response to the first indictments handed down on June 31, 1982, in San Diego. By 1983, the possibility of mass protest seemed remote, at least in the absence of large scale criminal prosecutions.

Compliance and Enforcement

All males born in 1960 and 1961 were required to register on July 22, 1980. Antiregistration forces predicted high levels of noncompliance.

However, in September, the Selective Service announced that ninety-three percent of the draft-eligible population had signed up. Registration opponents sharply disputed this figure. A General Accounting Office evaluation in December, 1980, put the compliance rate at 91 percent; nearly 350,000 young men had failed to register, a greater percentage than during the years of peak anti-Vietnam War protest.

In addition to estimating the level of compliance, GAO undertook to determine the accuracy of the records. Overall, it found no major problems. Most biographical data were correct. The total amount of error represented only 5 percent of the inventory. While this constituted a large absolute number, GAO concluded that Selective Service had corrected or was in the process of correcting, the errors.[5]

Compliance did not increase with the transition to the staggered process. In fact, an April, 1982, GAO report found that nearly one-third of draft-eligible youths had failed to sign up in the first nine months of 1981. Such massive avoidance of the law could hardly be ignored; failure to register is a federal criminal offense, punishable by five years in prison and/or a $10,000 fine (50 U.S.C. App. 462 12[a]).

By the time President Reagan assumed office, analysts estimated that there were approximately half a million nonregistrants. For the first year of the Reagan presidency, the issue of whether registration resisters should be prosecuted remained in limbo while the administration concentrated on whether to continue the program. There was no official statement on the subject for six months. In December, 1981, the Justice Department announced it would delay seeking criminal charges until the President decided the program's status. On January 7, 1982, President Reagan announced that his military Manpower Task Force had convinced him to continue registration on the grounds that it could save as much as six weeks in a mobilization. Three weeks later, Selective Service announced that 927,000 young men had failed to register, and that it was implementing a campaign to persuade them to comply with the law (*New York Times* February 28, 1982:1). Selective Service asked Congress for $400,000 to supplement the System's meager $150,000 public relations budget in order to implement a massive advertising campaign in newspapers, television and the radio. (The funds were never provided, and public relations had to rely on voluntary contributions).

On January 20, 1982, Director of Selective Service, Thomas K. Turnage, announced a grace period for nonregistrants. They could sign up without fear of prosecution until February 28th. In late February, Selective Service said that the grace period would be "informally extended a few days," and that the Justice Department would begin indicting youths in late April or early May. However, no indictments were returned in May. On June 23, 1982, the Justice Department announced that, in July 1982, approximately

160 young men who failed to register for the draft would face possible criminal prosecution. The first indictment was handed down in San Diego in late June. By September 1983, there were fifteen indictments; after that the administration seemed unsure about how to proceed (by January 1985, only seventeen nonregistrants had been indicted).

From the beginning, the Administration faced a sophisticated selective prosecution problem. To prosecute only those nonregistrants who are self-proclaimed antidraft activists raises constitutional problems and creates highly visible trials of publicity-seeking defendants, some of whom are anxious for the opportunity to promote their antidraft campaign in the judicial arena. On the other hand, to ignore the most vocal resisters might well undermine the credibility of the enforcement program, and ultimately, the registration requirement itself (see Jacobs and Travis 1985).

Most draft registration violators who have come to the government's attention have identified themselves through protest activities; a small number of others have been "turned in" by neighbors or others who disapprove of their unwillingness to shoulder this obligation of citizenship. Full scale enforcement, however, would require complicated and expensive investigation.

James W. Davis, a consultant to the National Advisory Commission on Selective Service in 1967, remarked that his work during the Vietnam War convinced him that "Selective Service had no satisfactory means of monitoring compliance." Davis further said that simply not registering and remaining anonymous was a good way to avoid both the draft and trouble with the law, but that if one registered and tried to evade induction, he would likely be identified (*New York Times* June 26, 1980:18). Selective Service claims that it could identify those who have not registered by using the Social Security System.[6] Perhaps so, but the Social Security System's computer system problems make such a plan dubious (*Wall Street Journal*, July 7, 1982). More important, even if hundreds of thousands of non-registrants could be located, there would be insufficient F.B.I. resources to interview and investigate, insufficient Justice Department resources to prosecute, and insufficient jail and prison space to incarcerate. As Curtis Tarr, a former Selective Service Director pointed out in the April 22, 1980 congressional hearings:

> I foresee the possibility of evasion by large numbers that would overwhelm the agencies for law enforcement and the judiciary. A law that cannot be enforced surely is worse than no law at all. The maximum step that should be taken by Congress would be to set new and reasonable penalities for non-compliance that might have some chance for application by the courts.

A federal district court in California dealt the administration's enforcement program a severe blow in November, 1982, when it dismissed an indictment against a nonregistrant on grounds of discriminatory selective prosecution. The court held that the nonregistrant, an antidraft activist, established a prima facie case of illegal selective prosecution by showing that, although the government had the ability to locate large numbers of nonregistrants, only vocal opponents of draft registration had been indicted, thereby chilling First Amendment rights (*U.S. v. Wayte* 1982). The Ninth Circuit Court of Appeals reversed, and the Supreme Court ultimately resolved the matter in *U.S. v. Wayte* (1985). Justice Powell began his opinion for the Court by stressing the government's broad discretion to decide whom to prosecute. While recognizing that prosecutorial discretion to prosecute is not unfettered, Justice Powell stated that "it is appropriate to judge selective prosecution claims according to ordinary equal protection standards." To succeed, a petitioner must demonstrate two things: that the prosecutorial policy had a discriminatory effect and that it was motivated by a discriminatory purpose. The Court held that Wayte and other registration resisters satisfied neither standard. Political dissenters were treated the same as anyone else. Anyone who turned himself in was targeted for prosecution. The government was not required to implement an active enforcement program, and even if it did, it could still target for prosecution everybody who turned himself in as a violator. "Those prosecuted in effect selected themselves for prosecution by refusing to register after being reported and warned by the Government."

Justice Powell had little difficulty dispensing with petitioner's first amendment claim. In evaluating a first amendment challenge to the exercise of prosecutorial discretion, he turned to a draft resistance case of a previous era. In *U.S. v. O'Brien* (1968) the Court had ruled that a draft resister could be punished for burning a Selective Service registration certificate on the steps of the South Boston Courthouse. The Court held that "when speech and nonspeech are combined in the same course of conduct, a sufficiently important governmental interest in regulating the nonspeech element can justify incidental limitations on First Amendment freedoms." The Court propounded a four-part test for determining when a government interest sufficiently justifies the regulation of expressive conduct.

> A government regulation is sufficiently justified if (1) it is within the constitutional power of the Government; it furthers an important or substantial governmental interest; the governmental interest is unrelated to the suppression of free expression; and if the incidental restriction on alleged First Amendment freedoms is no greater than is essential to the furtherance of that interest.

The Court quickly walked the registration program through the test. It readily found that a draft registration program is within the constitutional power of Congress, that the registration program furthers an important, indeed vital, national defense purpose. In the majority's view, the passive enforcement policy limits speech no more than necessary, and is a sensible program for enforcing the registration law particularly in the absence of a feasible active enforcement policy.

The Court's decision helped to clarify the status of the selective enforcement doctrine and the standard for evaluating First Amendment challenges to prosecutorial discretion, but it will have little practical impact on the registration enforcement dilemma. It is unlikely that the government will indefinitely rely on passive enforcement as the sole means for draft registration enforcement.

Not only does a nonregistrant face an almost negligible chance of being indicted, but, even if convicted, the likely punishment is not very severe. Despite the maximum statutory penalty of five years imprisonment and $10,000 fine, it remains to be seen whether such penalties will actually be carried out. Of the seven men convicted as of August 1984 only one has gone to jail (for 90 days), and one has been fined ($4000). We can only speculate on the political costs of large numbers of prison sentences for those who fail to cooperate with a symbolic program that is preparatory for a draft that may never materialize. If the administration moves forward with large numbers of prosecutions, increased criticism and protest are likely to follow.

Representative Les Aspin (D.-Wis) introduced a bill that suggested a way out for the administration; it makes the maximum penalty for failing to register a $200 fine. However, if conscription were reinstated, the penalty would revert to its present status. By providing for an administrative penalty, the strain on federal courts and prosecutorial resources would be reduced and potential protest might be diffused. However, a lesser penalty might result in widespread noncompliance, particularly among those who can readily afford to pay the fine. In any case, Aspin's proposal is unlikely to be enacted. The administration seems committed to increasing compliance by escalating the threatened consequences of not registering.

Widespread noncompliance with the registration program, coupled with practical, legal, and political difficulties of full-scale criminal law enforcement, produced a new enforcement strategy in late 1982. The Solomon Amendment, requires any person receiving federal educational aid to register with Selective Service (P.L. 97-252 [September 8, 1982]); if he does not register or refuses to provide proof, his educational assistance will be terminated.[7] Implementing regulations, issued by the Department of Education in February, 1983, placed responsibility for this regulatory system on the colleges and universities (48 Fed. Reg. 19, 3921-26 [January 27, 1982]).

Under the proposed regulations, a college student seeking federal financial aid must indicate on a Statement of Registration whether or not he has

complied with the Draft Registration law. If the applicant certifies that he/
she does not have to register, he/she must explain why; and the institution
may accept this explanation, unless it has information inconsistent with
the applicant's statement. If the applicant states that he has registered, he
must produce the Registration Acknowledgment Letter that Selective Service sends out after it has processed each registrant.

The Solomon Amendment provoked little controversy in Congress, although a number of Senators and Congressmen, conservatives and liberals,
expressed dismay at the mounting problems presented by the registration
program. Representatives Dellums and Goldwater condemned the bill as
"bandaids for a shoddy program." The issuance of the regulation predicta-
bly catapulted many universities into the registration controversy. Yale
announced that it would make up any loss of financial assistance occa-
sioned by refusal to register. New York University President and former
Congressman, John Brademas, spoke out against involving the universities
in the enforcement of the Selective Service laws. The American Council on
Education (ACE) submitted a strong statement in opposition to the proposed regulations. In addition to ideological distaste for being dragged into
the registration fracas as an ally to Selective Service, the colleges and universities object to the new administrative burdens. The ACE comment
states:

> The proposed regulations are flawed in several important respects. The pro-
> posed regulations are inconsistent with [the statute]. They would impose on
> colleges and universities administrative burdens exceeding those that Con-
> gress contemplated when it enacted the law. They would inaugurate an un-
> precedented and unsound administrative policy unduly entangling
> educational requirements. And a number of provisions would impose bur-
> dens on schools (and students) that seem wholly unnecessary to implement
> the objectives underlying [the statute]. [American Council on Education
> 1983]

On March 9, 1983, United States District Court in Minnesota, enjoined
implementation of the Solomon Amendment on the grounds that it was
highly probable that the Amendment would ultimately be held unconstitutional in violation of the Fifth Amendment and the Bill of Attainder clause
(*Doe v. Selective Service System* 1983). In effect, the court reasoned that the
Solomon Amendment is a law determining guilt and inflicting punishment
without judicial process. Further, it reasoned that this law forces nonregistrants to incriminate themselves.

The United States Supreme Court reversed, upholding the constitutionality of the Solomon Amendment (*Selective Service System v. Minnesota Public Interest Research Group* 1984). The Court stated that the law

is not a Bill of Attainder because those who failed to register "can become eligible for Title IV aid at any time simply by registering late and thus 'carry the keys to their prison in their own pockets.'" Conditioning receipt of aid on registration was found to serve the legitimate legislative purposes of improving compliance and furthering "a fair allocation of scarce federal resources by limiting Title IV aid to those who are willing to meet their responsibilities to the United States by registering with the Selective Service when required to do so." The Court also held that the Solomon Amendment does not force nonregistrants to incriminate themselves:

> A person who has not registered is clearly under no compulsion to seek financial aid; if he has not registered he is simply ineligible for aid. He has no reason to make any statement to anyone as to whether or not he has registered.

> If [nonregistrants] decide to register late, they could of course, obtain Title IV aid without providing any information to their school that would incriminate them, since the statement to the school by the applicant is simply that he is in compliance with the registration law; it does not require him to disclose whether he was a timely or late registrant.

Because of the storm of protest, the Department of Education announced in April 1983 that implementation of the Solomon Amendment would be delayed for two years.[8] But students are still required under DOE regulations to sign a form stating that they are registered with Selective Service or the basis for their exemption. Students who, although not required to register, were denied loans when they refused (on the basis of religious principle) to explain the basis for their exemption on the compliance form, attacked the regulations. The district court held that the regulations went beyond the power delegated to the Secretary of Education on the ground that a sanction Congress has targeted for a small group of law violators was being imposed on a much larger group of persons who had not broken any law and who had met the statutory requirements for aid. The Court of Appeals (1985) reversed, finding the challenged regulations reasonably related to the implementation of the Solomon Amendment.

Conclusion: Implications for Civil-Military Relations

Draft registration, even without conscription, constitutes a powerful link between the military and civilian society. The act of completing the registration form reinforces the notion of a citizen's obligation to serve in the nation's military forces and to participate in the common defense. Via registration, young men are forced to consider their relationship to their country as well as the rights and responsibilities associated with citizenship.

Imposing the obligation to register on men alone conveys the message that women will not play an equal role in national defense. Perhaps this defines citizenship differently for men and women. It perpetuates the stereotype of the male protector and the female dependent. Ultimately, it could be used to justify fewer citizenship rights for women.

Draft registration strains civil-military relations. Some young men feel it to be an unpleasant burden, more for what it signifies than for what it requires; others sincerely believe that any cooperation with the military is inconsistent with their religious values. Registration provides a highly visible target for antigovernment protest. The registration program could come to symbolize a melange of perceived governmental and societal injustices and inequities.

It is difficult to assess the significance of the reaction to the 1980 registration program. One could emphasize the demonstrations that did take place and the continuity with the tradition of antidraft protest, or the basic failure of a sustained antiregistration movement to develop on the scale seen during the Vietnam War period. In any case, the history of the 1980 draft registration demonstrates that a mere registration requirement does not impinge enough on young men's lives to motivate a mass protest movement. However, compliance problems, the protests that did occur, the mood on the campuses, and the attitudes reflected in public opinion polls, show that there remains widespread, if latent, opposition to military conscription and that efforts to renew the peacetime draft would trigger significant protest.

The registration program itself is in a precarious position. On the one hand, there may be symbolic costs, foreign and domestic, to its dismantling. On the other hand, the costs of enforcing compliance via prosecutions and restricting university loans will hardly be insubstantial. Registration, compared with actual conscription, offers few, if any, advantages for recruitment, military strategy or foreign policy. Perhaps it would be better for the United States either to bite the conscription bullet or adopt some computerized alternative to face-to-face registration, thereby defusing opposition and, more important, solving the compliance dilemma.

Notes

Dennis McNamara conducted the research in chapter 5 while an undergraduate student at Cornell University.

1. The weight of evidence suggests that even a full-scale war in Europe would last less than 60 days. European NATO forces have adopted this "short war" scenario

as a key assumption in strategies for defending Central Europe. The United States however, continues to assume a war in Europe could last many months and has committed a large proportion of its NATO resources to the "long war scenario" (Coffey 1979: 143).

2. Selective Service estimated that as many as 40 percent of the potential draftees would not be correctly identified, mainly because of address changes. Still, a list of 4,000,000 would be large enough to meet requirements, and could be quickly updated. It is also worth pointing out that face-to-face registration is not so efficient either. As many as 25 percent of 18-year-olds in some years may have failed to register, and it is highly unlikely that more than a few registrants inform Selective Service of change of address, despite a responsibility to do so.

3. The figures of 15 percent and 40 percent are based on the following conclusions. The Internal Revenue Service reported to Selective Service that only 85 percent of the draft age population files income taxes; thus, up to 15 percent of those eligible might be lost if IRS records were used. The registrant's current address would be available to the government through the master Social Security Administration file. However, the Census Bureau reported that up to 25 percent of the draft age population could be missed by combining the IRS and SSA master lists. This, according to Selective Service, could produce gross inequities (see Presidential Recommendations for Selective Service Reform 1980:17-18). As things turned out, the IRS refused to provide assistance to Selective Service, and state motor vehicle department lists were used to compile the master list of eligible 18-year-old men (see Jacobs and Travis 1985).

4. The twelve specific findings of the Committee are as follows:

   a. Article I, Section 8 of the Constitution commits exclusively to the Congress the powers to raise and support armies, provide and maintain a Navy, and make rules for the government and regulation of the land and Naval forces, and pursuant to these powers it lies within the discretion of the Congress to determine the occasions for expansion of our armed forces, and the means best suited to such expansion should it prove necessary.

   b. An ability to mobilize rapidly is essential to the preservation of our national security.

   c. A functioning registration system is a vital part of any mobilization plan.

   d. Women make an important contribution to our national defense, and are volunteering in increased numbers for our armed forces.

   e. Women should not be intentionally or routinely placed in combat positions in our military services.

   f. There is no established military need to include women in a selective service system.

   g. Present manpower deficiencies under the All-Volunteer Force are concentrated in the combat arms infantry, armor combat engineers, field artillery and air defense.

   h. If mobilization were to be ordered in a wartime scenario, the primary manpower need would be for combat replacements.

   i. The need to rotate personnel and the possibility that close support units could come under enemy fire also limits the use of women in noncombat jobs.

   j. If the law required women to be drafted in equal numbers with men, mobilization would be severely impaired because of strain on training facilities and administrative systems.

k. Under the administration's proposal there is no exemption of mothers with young children. The administration has given insufficient attention to necessary changes in Selective Service rules, such as those governing the induction of young mothers, and to the strains on family life that would result from the registration and possible induction of women.

l. A registration and induction system which excludes women is constitutional.

5. However, it did find that Selective Service had failed to include 96,000 potential residents among U.S. citizens living abroad in U.S. territories or possessions.

6. The original registration bill did not give the Selective Service System the authority to use Social Security records to search for nonregistrants. In *Wolman v. U.S.* (1982), District Judge Gerhard Gessel ruled that the Selective Service System's requirement that draft registrants supply Social Security numbers, violated section 7 of the Privacy Act which bars the federal government from denying any "right benefit or privilege" because of a refusal to disclose Social Security numbers. The Selective Service System obtained that authority when Congress included a provision in the DOD authorization bill for 1982 that allowed the Director of HEW to provide the Selective Service with Social Security numbers for draft-eligible men.

7. Representative Solomon has attached his amendment depriving nonregistrants of federal assistance to other social welfare bills as well. For example, the Job Training Partnership Act of 1983 requires an applicant for local job training to certify that he is registered with Selective Service (Solomon II).

8. Ultimately, the Department of Education relieved the colleges and universities of the responsibility of monitoring compliance, having determined that spot site checks by the Department were adequate to assure a very high rate of compliance.

6

Compulsory and Voluntary National Service: Analysis of the McCloskey Bill and Other Proposals

> If now—and this is my idea—there were instead of military conscription a conscription of the whole youthful population to form for a certain number of years a part of the army enlisted against *Nature*, the injustice [inequality of opportunity] would tend to be evened out, and numerous other goods to the commonwealth would follow.
>
> To coal and iron mines, to freight trains, to fishing fleets in December, to dishwashing, clotheswashing, and window-washing, to road-building and tunnel-making, to foundries and sky-holes, and to the frames of skyscrapers, would our gilded youth be drafted off, according to their choice, to get the childishness knocked out of them, and to come back into society with healthier sympathies and soberer ideas. They would have paid their blood-tax, done their own part in the immemorial human warfare against nature; they would tread the earth more proudly, the women would value them more highly, they would be better fathers and teachers of the following generation. [William James, *The Moral Equivalent of War* (1910)]

Enrolling all the nation's youth in a war against social problems, while at the same time exposing them to discipline, authority and higher moral values, has frequently been endorsed by diverse political and academic figures since the philosopher William James proposed the idea seventy years ago. The Depression-era Civilian Conservation Corps (CCC) embodied some of the spirit and characteristics of a National Service program. During its 9-year lifespan, two and a half million men lived in wilderness camps, expending their energies on environmental achievements which are still evident throughout the country (Salmond 1967). Of course, CCC was not a universal draft; participation was voluntary for males regardless of age or marital status. Even so, CCC was unsuccessful in gaining public recognition as citizen service to the nation because it never overcame its reputation as a welfare program.[1] After U.S. entry into World War II, CCC was discontinued although 151 of its facilities served as Civilian Public

111

Service Camps providing "work of national importance" for approximately 12,000 conscientious objectors performing alternative service in lieu of their military obligation (Selective Service System 1948: 315). Most of these camps were administered by the pacifist churches under an umbrella organization called the National Service Board for Religious Objectors.

The idea of National Service surfaced again during the Kennedy administration, especially with the funding of the Peace Corps and Volunteers in Service to America (VISTA). Donald Eberly, the most vigorous of the modern day National Service proponents was, by the early 1960s, already actively pushing the idea of a full-scale National Service program.

He founded the National Service Secretariat in 1966 and organized the first National Service Conferences in 1966 and 1967 (Eberly 1966; 1968). The definition of National Service formulated at the 1966 conference remains as useful as any other, although, as this article makes clear, National Service is an inclusive, somewhat vague concept, that varies to some extent from formulation to formulation.

> National Service as a concept embraces the belief that an opportunity should be given to every young person to serve his country in a manner consistent with the needs of the nation—recognizing national defense as the first priority—and consistent with the education and interests of those participating, without infringement on the personal or economic welfare of others but contributing to the liberty and well being of all.

This formulation is ambiguous indeed. It does not indicate whether National Service is to be compulsory or voluntary, full-time or part-time, lengthy or brief in duration; nor, of course, does it begin to delimit what counts as "the needs of the nation." There is enough room in this formulation to accommodate the views and interests of very diverse groups, no doubt an advantage politically, but also an impediment to policy analysis.

Eberly and other National Service advocates stressed the fractured, if not disintegrated, moral and sociopolitical consensus in U.S. society.[2] Perceiving a trend toward defining citizenship in terms of rights and entitlements, they emphasized the duties of citizenship (see Janowitz 1983). Concerned with the continuing vitality of the social and political systems, their view, recalling Edmund Burke and other "conservative" political philosophers, was that democracy could not be sustained on a diet of raw self-interest. For these proponents, National Service should be a foray into citizenship building. They hoped and believed that young people would be drawn to a national call to serve (Eberly 1977).[3]

The effort to find an alternative to military conscription during the Vietnam War era brought National Service its greatest support. At a major conference held at the University of Chicago on December 4-7, 1966, National Service was discussed as an alternative to both the draft and an all-volunteer force. Papers were delivered by such luminaries as Albert Biderman, Kenneth Boulding, Erick Erikson, Milton Friedman, Morris Janowitz, and Margaret Mead. (Tax 1967). Mead and Janowitz argued that universalizing the obligation to serve would make the much maligned military draft more equitable and more legitimate. Janowitz believed that those who serve in the armed forces should be encouraged to think of themselves (and be recognized by society) as engaging in National Service, and that to do so would bolster their morale. Similar sentiments were echoed by Secretary of Defense Robert McNamara during this period:

> It seems to me that we could move toward remedying [the draft] inequity by asking every young person in the United States to give two years of service to his country—whether in one of the military services, in the Peace Corps, or in some other volunteer developmental work at home or abroad. . . . It would make meaningful the general concept of security; a world of decency and development—where every man can feel that his personal horizon is rimmed with hope.[4]

When President Johnson appointed his National Advisory Commission on Selective Service (Executive Order 11289), he instructed it "to evaluate other proposals related to Selective Service, including proposals for national service." Ultimately the (Burke) Marshall Commission, as it came to be called, rejected National Service on the ground that it was, at that stage in its formulation, too vague to be considered a viable alternative to military conscription. (Report of the National Commission on Selective Service 1967).

Support for National Service was not limited to those who sought an alternative to conscription. Many National Service activists were interested in dealing with youth problems and revitalizing the concept of citizenship. This group saw in National Service a solution to myriad personal, social, and economic problems afflicting young people. Its adherents argued (and continue to do so) that the country should, indeed must, adopt a comprehensive youth policy that would nourish the nation's most precious resource—its young people. They called for a massive youth rehabilitation and assistance program equivalent to the War on Poverty (see President's Science Advisory Committee 1973; Committee for the Study of National Service 1979).

Yet another reason for advocating National Service was its potential to cure, or at least ameliorate, persistent social and environmental problems: crime, drug abuse, illiteracy, insufficient care for the mentally ill, retarded and elderly, and an ineffective system of criminal justice. Proponents envisioned hundreds of thousands, even millions of young people turning away from self-indulgence and throwing their energies into solving these problems. Indeed, the statements of National Service proponents have a distinctly religious ring—the individual will be redeemed through service to fellowmen.

Over the years, intellectuals, educators, citizens' groups, professional associations and ad hoc conferences have endorsed National Service. So have diverse political figures, including Elliot Richardson, Hubert Humphrey, John Connally, Alan Cranston, Paul Tsongas and Ed Koch. National Service has also been considered in numerous studies of both military manpower and the problems of youth.

In light of this diverse support, it is surprising that National Service has not flourished politically. Perhaps it emerged too soon after President Nixon committed the draft-weary nation to the All-Volunteer Forces (AVF). At the time conscription was widely denounced as "compulsory," "involuntary" and "totalitarian." A civilian draft would have been attacked as a gross infringement of individual freedom.

The President's Commission on an All-Volunteer Force (Gates Commission) rejected National Service on philosophical grounds.

> Above all, mandatory National Service is coercive. Such a system of universal conscription would require all those eligible to serve within a specified period of time. If insufficient numbers proved willing to enlist in the military or volunteer for other onerous types of government service, some would be compelled to serve in these less desirable capacities. In essence, mandatory National Service requires forced labor. Although motivated by genuine interest in the nation's welfare, advocates of mandatory National Service are suggesting a compulsory system which is more consistent with a totalitarian than a democratic heritage. If the service that youth would render is important and valuable enough to merit public support, it can and should be financed through general taxation like other government programs. [1970:175]

Ten years later President Jimmy Carter, in a message to Congress on Selective Service Reform, rejected universal National Service as too expensive, and he dismissed voluntary National Service as dysfunctionally competitive for recruits with the AVF (Presidential Recommendations for Selective Service Reform 1982). President Reagan has dismissed National Service as yet another pernicious proposal of social engineers.[5] Yet, despite all the political setbacks, the idea continues to spark interest, debate and study.[6]

Trouble in the All-Volunteer Force

National Service continues to stimulate a great deal of public attention because of doubts about the AVF. Neither the manpower projections nor cost estimates of the President's Commission on an All-Volunteer Force have held up (Janowitz and Moskos 1979; Bachman, Blair, and Segal 1977; Leviton and Alderman 1977; King 1977). In the mid-1970s, despite substantial pay increases, the armed forces, particularly the Army, found it difficult to attract enough male volunteers. In fact, had the Pentagon not steadily scaled down its manpower requirements, the AVF might not have lasted this long. The problem is more serious in the reserves and National Guard which formerly relied on draft-induced volunteers (Congressional Budget Office, 1978). The reserve forces are undermanned and yet, at the same time, the Pentagon has enhanced their national defense responsibilities (Coffey 1979). In the late 1970s and early 1980s deep economic recession made recruiting easier, but the manpower problem is almost sure to become more acute as the number of males reaching age 18 declines from 2.14 million in 1978 to 1.6 million in 1992, and consequently there is increased competition among the military, industry, and the universities for young people, especially male high school graduates.

The quality of AVF personnel is constantly questioned. Critics point out that college graduates have all but disappeared from the enlisted ranks; the percentage of Army personnel with high school diplomas has declined, although the percentage of American males who finish high school has risen. Each year 40 percent of Army enlistees leave the Army without having completed their three-year enlistments; many are administratively discharged with "bad papers." Drug abuse, crime, and racial tension characterize garrison life in the United States and abroad, particularly in Germany (Bryant 1979).

In 1981, Blacks comprised 29.7 percent of all Army personnel, 32.9 percent of enlisted personnel; they constitute an even larger percentage of current recruits and have a higher reenlistment rate. "Non-whites" together constitute over 40 percent of the men and women in the Army (Moskos 1981). There is much controversy over whether this overrepresentation of minorities is a social or moral problem (Janowitz 1975). Critics contend that it is morally wrong for the economically depressed segment of society to carry a disproportionate burden of the national defense.

Doubts about the quantity and quality of AVF personnel have stimulated controversy over the combat capacity of the AVF. These concerns might have led to reinstatement of draft registration even without the Soviet invasion of Afghanistan. They may well require reinstatement of military conscription before the end of the century.

The Revival of National Service

National Service proponents, particularly those concerned about teenage unemployment, alienation, and other problems, have not given up after conscription was replaced by a volunteer force; they continue to refine and press their ideas. However, most proponents began to think in terms of a voluntary program. Another major conference, organized by Donald Eberly, was held at the Roosevelt Library in Hyde Park, New York in April, 1967. Following the conference, Foundation trustees Franklin D. Roosevelt, Jr. and John A. Roosevelt, issued the following statement:

> We propose the establishment of a national youth service, not as a special or emergency program, but as a regular and ongoing part of America's national commitment to its young people. While the basic commitment must be public, the private sector—including the corporations of America, organized labor, philanthropy, and the churches—has a significant role to play.
>
> We propose that such a program shall be financed and administered on a joint federal-local basis; that it invite the largest measure of local initiative and youth participation; that it consolidate all federal youth service projects; that it be voluntary but subject to a national youth registration that will ensure that every young person is offered counselling and information on the opportunities for education, service, and training available to them. [Eberly 1968]

In January 1979, another citizens' group, the Committee for the Study of National Service, composed of, among others, long-time National Service supporters like Bernard Anderson, Donald Eberly, Harold Fleming, Rev. Theodore Hesburgh, Willard Wirtz, Jacqueline Grennan Wexler, Harris Wofford and Roger Landrum, published its report, *Youth and the Needs of the Nation*. It called for the country to "move toward universal service by stages and by incentives but without compulsion." That same year, the Committee sponsored a major conference in Washington, D.C. The 250 participants, exploring a wide variety of National Service-related issues, came out strongly in favor of a voluntary National Service (Committee for the Study of National Security 1980). About the same time, the Carnegie Council on Policy Studies (1979) in Higher Education endorsed a broad-based volunteer National Service plan, similar to that suggested by the Committee for National Service. Still another Commission, the National Commission on Youth, endorsed the idea of a voluntary national service in 1980.

The two wings of the National Service movement (those concerned with manning the military and those concerned with solving youth problems) have jointly kept the idea alive in Congress.[7] In 1977, Senator Sam Nunn, an acknowledged expert on national defense concerned with the AVF's combat readiness, released a study commissioned by a Senate Subcommittee on Manpower and Personnel entitled "Achieving America's Goals: National Service or the All-Volunteer Force." The report reviewed the AVF'S deficiencies and concluded that some form of National Service is desirable and feasible:

> Any of the wide array of national service programs on which the nation might embark would serve to address some of the basic informational and diagnostic needs of American youth as well as to alleviate some of the present and potential problems of the AVF. A broad-scale program of national service could address and alleviate a wide range of such needs and problems, thus enabling the nation to more effectively pursue its national goals. [King 1977]

Three National Service bills were introduced into the 96th Congress. Paul Tsongas and ten other senators offered a bill to establish a Presidential Commission "to examine the need for and desirability and feasibility of establishing a comprehensive National Service program to meet a broad range of national and local needs." A parallel bill was offered to the House by Representative Leon Panetta. Both Paul McCloskey and John Cavanaugh introduced comprehensive bills to establish National Service systems. Hearings were held in 1979 and 1980.[8] The McCloskey and Cavanaugh bills present actual programmatic designs for National Service. Both bills are incomplete in many respects but close examination by Congress and others will have considerable value in sharpening the National Service debate, moving it from the philosophical and abstract to the concrete. More importantly, an examination of these bills demonstrates the enormous conceptual and practical difficulties which make National Service infeasible.

Formulating a National Service Program

The National Service debate is frustrating because the debaters rarely have the same program in mind, and because almost every writer on the topic favors National Service in principle. Proponents typically praise the principle of National Service, but rarely discuss details beyond a few "possibilities" or "suggestions." If National Service is to be taken seriously, principle must be translated into policies and programs. For that reason, this chapter examines the two National Service plans that have been put before Congress.

Before examining that legislation, however, it is useful to identify some of the issues that must be faced by all National Service planners. I hope to show that it is not possible to subsume all National Service concerns and interest groups under a single umbrella. The National Service concept(s) will not bear that kind of pressure. Each National Service interest group's concerns points toward distinctive, and probably contradictory types of programs. Obviously National Service cannot embody everything, solve everything, and be everything.

Furthermore, National Service as a potpourri of concerns and ideas may well turn out to be more attractive than the sum of its parts. I hope to show how each of the assumptions upon which National Service proponents rely can be questioned, and to demonstrate that each National Service prototype would face very difficult administrative problems.

Why National Service?

National Service as Draft Reform

Those National Service proponents favoring National Service as a draft reform believe that conscripton would be more widely accepted as fair if all young people were required to serve their country in one manner or another (e.g., Janowitz 1967). Logically, this group might be equally satisfied with universal military service.[9] Only if all or substantially all youth serve in one capacity or another will the legitimacy of military conscription be enhanced. It follows that exemptions would have to be closely scrutinized, and that enforcement would have to be effective. But it is hard to imagine a scenario in which everybody would serve. At a minimum, some physical, mental and hardship exemptions would prove compelling.

Even if universality could be assured, however, those draft reformers who advocate National Service cannot be sure that National Service would make military conscription more palatable. Much would depend upon how military conscripts perceived civilian service. If they thought of it as a "racket" or a means for middle class kids to beat the draft, the morale of military conscripts might not be raised. A good deal of attention would need to be paid to balancing the comparative burdens and benefits of civilian and military service. It would surely not do for civilian service to be shorter, better paid, more comfortable, less dangerous, and more advantageous in terms of job training. Indeed, if that occurred, the quality of military recruits might decline still further.

It is worth noting that the National Advisory Commission on Selective Service concluded that "no fair way exists, at least at present, to equate nonmilitary with military service." The policy of the old Selective Service System, was, in so far as possible, to equalize conditions of "alternative service" performed by conscientious objectors with those of military inductees. For example, all conscientious objectors were to work outside their home communities. It was express government policy to compel service away from home and under conditions commonly regarded as "difficult" (see *Columbia Journal of Human Rights Law* 1971). This led to severe administrative difficulties in finding suitable placements, a problem that would arise for a large National Service program.

Some military reformers advocate voluntary National Service because they are concerned about the AVF's combat readiness and its racial and socioeconomic unrepresentativeness. They believe that voluntary National Service would create a moral climate favorable to increasing the number of middle class volunteers for military service. But this may well prove wishful thinking. It seems just as likely that a large scale voluntary National Service would drain off potential military recruits, thereby forcing a return to military conscription; at least this was the Carter Administration's conclusion (see Presidential Recommendations for Selective Service Reform 1980).

Charles Moskos, a frequent academic supporter of National Service, has worked harder than any other writer I know of to deal with the relationship between voluntary National Service and the all-volunteer force. In a *Foreign Affairs* article, he advocates a National Service system in which young men and women would be required to serve without pay for three to six months in a wide variety of local activities if they wished to qualify for future student loans (Moskos 1981). Presumably the advantages of this type of mini-National Service are that young people will come to understand that citizenship entails responsibilities as well as entitlements, and that an army of free laborers will be available to work on various national needs. More importantly, from Moskos' perspective, his proposal relates civilian and military service. Youth will be encouraged to participate actively, and those serving in the armed forces will be more generously rewarded.

But there are several potential drawbacks. Will this kind of exchange— free labor for educational loans—reinforce citizenship values or create resentments? Will lack of compensation exclude a large number of less advantaged youth? Is a three month's tour of duty long enough to accomplish anything useful?

Any volunteer National Service program creates potential problems of the All-Volunteer Force by establishing competitive youth opportunities. A 1978 Congressional Budget Office analysis of the effect of various National Service options on military recruitment concluded that a large scale voluntary National Service might create substantial problems for military recruitment, possibly making military conscription imperative. The same point was made by President Carter in his 1980 report to Congress on Selective Service Reform.

Professor Moskos attempts to counter this negative effect by providing more attractive benefits for military personnel through a generous G.I. Bill.

> A person who enlists in the armed forces for an obligatory period of active duty would receive three academic years of educational support for two years

of service, or four academic years of support for three years of service. The entitlements of an AVF G.I. Bill would include the costs of tuition and fees up to $2,500 per academic year, and a subsistence stipend of $250 per month. Such entitlements would also require an appropriate reserve obligation, say three or four years, following active duty. [1981:28]

Moskos apparently believes that his mini-voluntary National Service would not take recruits away from the armed forces because its benefit package would not be nearly as attractive as military service, at least for middle class youth wishing to finance their college education. Assuming he is correct in calibrating civilian and military benefits, it is arguable that he has so watered down the National Service ideal as to rob it of its basic inspiration. Wouldn't most middle class youth view a three month service obligation merely as a hurdle to obtaining loans? As National Service proponents keep improving the military compensation package, they simultaneously keep trying to make National Service more attractive to middle class youth. The curious result might be an intergovernmental price war over a shrinking number of male high school graduates, the preferred recruits of both the Pentagon and National Service planners.

National Service as Youth Rehabilitation

A second group of National Service proponents advocates National Service as a comprehensive strategy for dealing with youth problems like alienation, unemployment, drug abuse, and unplanned parenthood. The following excerpts from the Report of the Committee for the Study of National Service (1979:7) exemplify this view:

> For most young people today the lack of any challenging experience away from home and outside the classroom that stretches and tests them in the service of their community or their country makes that passage [from adolescence into adulthood] very difficult.

> Some period for action in the larger community, before commitment to a career, appears to be desirable for a substantial portion of students leaving high school or college. They feel the need to explore careers and discover more about themselves.

> For those who can find no work, it [the period of life from adolescence to adulthood] is a transition to walking the streets and waiting for welfare payments.

> Too many sons and daughters of the suburbs are drifting without purpose and their apathy or self-centeredness is seldom cured by schooling.

The authors believe National Service is the answer.

A system of full-time National Service would bring together black and white, rich and poor, young people from the North and South, East and West, city and suburb, small town and farm, those who do not go to college, and those who do. [1979:8]

We have no doubt that there is plenty of work that needs to be done on many fronts requiring human service, where with adequate training and supervision young people could make effective contributions. [1979:8]

The introduction of National Service should strengthen the whole voluntary service sector. [1979:10]

By infusing with purpose all the tasks undertaken, no matter how dirty or difficult, National Service should help break down the present hierarchy of values in which so much necessary work is considered degrading. [1979:10]

The quality of citizenship could also be improved if all or a large part of the younger generation experienced National Service. [1979:10]

Most of the empirical claims of the VNS proponents are open to question, particularly that a vast segment of youth is "alienated."[10] Hundreds of thousands of young people are working full time; hundreds of thousands have begun families. The armed forces recruit approximately 400,000 young men and women each year. Approximately half of all high school graduates go on to higher education. While many National Service proponents denigrate the educational system as a "lock-step" deadening experience, our colleges and universities undoubtedly provide large numbers of students with a positive setting for self-maturation and intellectual growth. Even if large numbers of young people are "drifting without purpose," this should not be considered a disease that needs to be cured. Youths have historically drifted, experimented, and rebelled. Many young people, particularly those in college, will eventually discover purpose through study, careers, volunteer and religious activities, and marriage. And society surely benefits, to some extent, by youthful criticism of the status quo.

Because youth problems are multiple and varied, most National Service proposals motivated by such concerns envision a wide range of placements for participants. Here, however, there is a tension. The more one emphasizes the problems—unemployment, drug abuse, alienation, illiteracy— the more VNS begins to sound like a welfare-type program that aims to do something for young people. The more emphasis is given to unmet national needs, the less valuable National Service might be for individuals with severe deficiencies and problems. This dilemma is frequently finessed by asserting that good service programs will, in addition to solving real national problems, also instill job skills, strengthen the work ethic, and promote the sense of self-worth. The history of the Civilian Conservation Corps should be a warning that the finesse may fail; a welfare program cannot be sold as a National Service program. The AVF's recruitment problems should alert us to the reverse difficulty—a National Service program cannot be successfully sold or administered as a job training program.

Since the justification for this form of National Service is the benefit it can offer to young people, it should follow that no one should be coerced to participate by the threat of sanctions or the promise of future benefits. But, if National Service were voluntary and targeted toward young people with the most severe problems, it would be little different from the current melange of youth programs.

Although the United States has never had a single comprehensive so-called youth policy, it has sponsored a large number of training and vocational programs that in their heyday provided job training and employment for millions of young people. This is hardly the place to review the entire range of federal youth manpower programs, but some perspective is necessary.

The 1962 Manpower Development and Training Act poured government funds into vocational training and led to the creation of a vast network of training facilities. The Emergency Employment Act of 1971 constituted the first purposeful job creation law since the Depression-era Works Progress Administration (see Nathan, Cook and Rowlins 1981; Mirengoff, et al. 1978). The Comprehensive Employment and Training Act of 1973 (CETA), and its subsequent amendments in 1974 (Emergency Jobs and Unemployment Assistance Act) and 1976 (the Emergency Jobs Program Extension Act), and the doubling of enrollees as a result of the Economic Stimulus Appropriations Act of 1977, launched the country far along the road toward universal job training for lower socioeconomic youth. About a half million young people per year were enrolled in CETA before its public service employment programs were terminated in the fall of 1981. The Reagan Administration has cut back on federal youth manpower programs like the Youth Conservation Corps and the Young Adult Conservation Corps. And it let CETA expire in late 1983; but not without replacing it with the Job Training Partnership Act (JTPA). Although the new Act stresses private sector rather than public-sector employment, it bears witness that even in a conservative administration, the government is not prepared to withdraw sponsorship of youth jobs programs. In November 1984, President Reagan vetoed a House bill that would have set up an American Conservation Corps to give unemployed youths jobs in conservation projects. The president rejected the program as providing "make-work" federal jobs and "artificial public sector employment," yet he reiterated his support for JTPA.

The federal government has also sponsored a smaller number of service programs that provide selective opportunities for self-disciplined, highly motivated, and usually well-educated youths in their early 20s: these include the Peace Corps, VISTA, University Year for Action, Youth Challenge Program, and National Student Volunteer Program. These programs have been coordinated and administered through the Action agency, established during the Nixon administration. Finally, the gargantuan student aid program (nearly $7 billion in 1979-80) has made it possible for a large segment of the youth population to attend two- and four-year colleges.

There are at least two great challenges facing a voluntary National Service program aimed at addressing the needs of youth. The first is to design programs that can truly assist disadvantaged youth. Without being excessively pessimistic about the government's capacity "to help people," the failures of many educational and social programs to cure the problems for which National Service is now a proposed solution should permit some skepticism.

A National Service program that promised a year-long placement to everyone would have to establish one or more placements of last resort—perhaps an environmental work corps. The danger is that this kind of program would quickly be defined as a lower class holding action. If that were to occur, its participants could hardly be expected to derive great advantage from it.

The second challenge is to design a program that will be attractive to young people from advantaged backgrounds. As Diane Hedin (1982) has put it, "As a way to channel youths' altruism and idealism, National Service may be an idea whose time has come and gone." She points out that high school youth have lost concern for social issues and responsibilities, as evidenced by a 1979 Gallup poll showing only 15 percent of 18 to 24 year olds to be interested in joining National Service.

Many or most middle class young men and women who wish to serve their country or community may feel that their part-time religious, charitable, and other volunteer activities are sufficient. Or they may feel that after college they will be adequately serving society as doctors, lawyers, teachers or civil servants. This is a point worth emphasizing. Must work be low-skilled and poorly paid to count as "service"? If not, does the work of police officers, firefighters, prison guards, teachers, and social workers count as community or national service?

Those who foresee long years of graduate and professional schooling may be quite reluctant to interrupt their career training. Others who would desire a year-long service experience might gravitate to programs geared toward the middle class, producing a high degree of class segregation in the civilian service programs. Professor Charles Moskos (1971: 7-12) recognized this potential pitfall several years ago.

> A voluntary national service program would probably evolve into a two-track system: a lower one trying to "salvage" poverty-scarred youth, and a higher one offering upper-middle-class youth a channel to resolve identity crises through altruistic endeavors.

> Those national service programs that would appeal to upper-middle-class college youth on a voluntary basis could easily turn into new forms of institutional elitism (in the manner of the Peace Corps and VISTA). At the same time, national service programs directed toward lower class youth would be quickly defined for what they are—welfare schemes in new guises. If America's privileged youth would really like to demonstrate their moral concern for our country's underclasses, they must be willing to put up with an extended period of indignity on a par with those very same underclasses.

> America's upper and upper-middle-class youth must be willing to forsake their class privilege. Since it is virtually certain that such a step would not be self imposed (to any large extent), any effective national service program will necessarily require coercion to insure that all segments of the American class structure will serve. The social equivalent of military service cannot be recapitulated in a voluntary system precisely because it requires a levelling of the classes. Implementation of a regimented but egalitarian national service would put to a harsh but real test the humanistic sentiments so often voiced by today's privileged youth.

National Service and National Needs

A third group of National Service proponents, or at least a third clear position taken by proponents, concentrates on the nation's unmet environmental and human needs (e.g. Sherraden and Eberly 1982). It argues that the United States does not have the resources to deal with soil erosion, reforestation, scenic beautification, day care, and care for the elderly, retarded and other needy groups. Young people are defined as an underutilized or free good that could be mobilized on behalf of the nation. A National Service system inspired by this concern would sponsor programs that provide maximum social payoff rather than maximum payoff to participants.

Granting the accuracy of the diagnosis, one might well ask why it is peculiarly the responsibility of young people to work on the nation's immense environmental and human services problems. If young people were impressed into such service for little or no pay, National Service would truly impose a "hidden" tax on youth, to use the terminology of Milton Friedman and the market economists. If National Service placements paid the minimum wage or higher one might ask why the non-young should be excluded.

Clearly, national needs are not distributed uniformly throughout the United States. Significant environmental projects would be located in wilderness areas, and the bulk of human services projects in the great metropolitan centers. A National Service designed to meet these needs would have to transport a great number of young people to project sites and arrange their housing and living arrangements. In addition to being expensive, this would involve the government in such sensitive matters as managing dormitories and taking responsibility for the participants' health and safety.

Compulsory or Voluntary Service

National Service debaters have paid a great deal of attention to whether service should be compulsory or voluntary, and well they should; the matter is vital. Practically every other question concerning National Service— e.g., size, cost, administrative structure, constitutionality—depends upon its resolution.

Compulsory Service

A compulsory program would be far more complicated to organize and administer than one that is voluntary. As a preliminary matter, there would be serious Thirteenth Amendment problems. While the Selective Service Draft Law Cases (1918) established the legality of a military draft more than sixty years ago, drafting an entire age cohort into civilian as well as military service would pose immense, possibly insurmountable, constitutional barriers (see American Bar Association 1984). Second, a compulsory program would face serious enforcement problems. What would be done about conscientious objectors, resisters, shirkers and the physically, mentally and morally incompetent? Are they to be jailed, denied future government benefits, or punished in some other way? Third, a compulsory program would be enormously expensive, even if participants were only paid a subsistence stipend and even if they all lived at home. Fourth, it would be a gargantuan administrative undertaking. There are approximately four million males and females turning 18 each year. To provide a meaningful civilian job to all those not in the armed forces (approximately three and a half million) for two years, one year or even six months would be, to say the least, an enormous challenge, even more so if all participants had to be placed in their home communities.

A quasi-compulsory program tied to the military draft, like the two legislative proposals discussed later in this chapter, would not have to be as large as one that is universal, but it would still generate complicated exemption and enforcement problems. Since it would be seen as a component of the military draft system, it would have to balance military and civilian placements according to length of service, working conditions, training opportunities, and educational benefits.

Voluntary Service

From the very beginning of the National Service movement, many staunch supporters objected to marrying National Service to the military draft. They defined National Service as the cornerstone of a national youth policy that would facilitate the transition from youth to adulthood. This explains why the decision in the early 1970s to embark on an all-volunteer armed forces was not viewed by National Service advocates as a death blow. Even today many supporters of National Service are sensitive to charges that it is a smokescreen for a military draft. For them, National Service is fully compatible with the AVF or with any other form of military manpower recruitment. In the event of a military draft, some would not even exempt National Service participants.

Voluntary National Service would not require anyone to participate in a civilian service program; however, it might encourage participation through G.I. Bill-type benefits, such as tuition grants for higher education. Most versions of voluntary National Service would guarantee to any young man or woman a service position of one or two year's duration.[11] While local communities would be encouraged to develop all varieties of programs and placements, the emphasis would be on human and environmental service, not on job training. To date, no voluntary program has been as fully described as the McCloskey or Cavanaugh plans.

Voluntary National Service would be far easier to administer than a compulsory national service. There would be no constitutional problems. It could begin on a pilot basis and expand incrementally; administrative problems, although not insignificant, would be easier to solve. Costs would be lower, but a program involving one million young people (a figure frequently suggested) would probably still carry a price tag in excess of $10 billion annually.

In addition to cost, another crucial question that Voluntary Service would have to face is universality. Just as a compulsory plan would have to struggle with the question of whom to exempt, a voluntary program would have to determine whom to exclude. Donald Eberly and others propose a program that would provide a service experience for everyone who wants one. This promise could prove very difficult to fulfill. Some young people are so deficient educationally and vocationally, or are otherwise so handicapped, that they will be undesirable to most sponsors. If the promise is to be kept, some placement of last resort would be an absolute necessity. Large numbers of young people will not be qualified for positions they covet. A few popular programs will be besieged by applicants with acceptable qualifications. National Service could not assure volunteers their first choice nor a placement near home.

What Constitutes National Service?

When it comes to identifying appropriate activities for young people in National Service, there is no dearth of suggestions. We can all think of jobs that need doing; the country needs more human and environmental services of all sorts. Why not have young people serve in day care centers, homes for the elderly, hospitals, schools, and in soil conservation, reforestation, and scenic restoration? Why not assign National Service volunteers to our overburdened and inefficient criminal justice agencies—police, probation, parole, jails, prisons and diversion programs?

Placements like these are most appropriate for a National Service program that seeks justification on grounds of unmet national needs. There seems little doubt that if young people could perform such services adequately, the nation would reap enormous benefits. So we must ask: whether young people could perform adequately? What would they get out of it? What would it cost? Would those young people who are unemployed become more employable after working for a year in a nursing home?

It will be objected that National Service could have enough diverse placements to meet national needs *and* provide valuable job training and other services that would facilitate personal maturation. Maybe it could, but in the final analysis National Service cannot be all things to all people. If it becomes more diverse, it will lose its *raison d'être* and probably its capacity to do anything well. Furthermore, the more that programs differ from one another, the more vulnerable National Service will be to charges of inequity.

Administration of National Service

Very little has been written about the administrative structure of National Service. Donald Eberly and others advocate a decentralized program with as small a centralized federal bureaucracy as possible. Unfortunately, life may not be so easy.

It is almost certain that any large-scale National Service, compulsory or voluntary, will require federal funding. This means some federal control. At a minimum, there will need to be a federal National Service agency of some kind to promulgate rules and regulations—who is eligible, how long participants must/may serve, what agencies can serve as sponsors (public or private), what positions within agencies are appropriate (typing, filing, direct services). There will need to be regulations regarding agency shop agreements, worker's compensation, taxes, and termination for unsatisfactory performance.

If National Service is compulsory or quasi-compulsory, there will be a need for elaborate administrative mechanisms for registering young people, determining exemptions, adjudicating dismissals and determining penalties. Even if National Service is voluntary, some such mechanisms may be necessary, especially if certain benefits attach to successful performance—e.g., college tuition credits, eligibility for student loans, FHA mortgages or employment in the federal government.

If National Service carries with it the promise of student loans or some other G.I. Bill-type benefits, there would have to be some way of determining whether a young man or woman had properly completed the obligation. What should be done about those young people whom employers wish to fire? With federal benefits turning on the completion of service, the "accused" would undoubtedly have to be provided due process protections and several levels of administrative and perhaps judicial appeals. The complicated relationship between the Department of Labor, sponsors, and service deliverers under the CETA program has been blamed for undermining that program (see National Council on Employment Policy 1978: 6). Similarly, the less complicated federal/state and state/local relationships mandated by the Justice Department's Law Enforcement Assistance Administration block grants has been judged ineffective (Twentieth Century Fund Task Force 1976: 123). Any large scale National Service program would entail more complicated intergovernmental and interorganizational relationships than either CETA or LEAA, and might well present administrative challenges beyond the capacity of our legal, governmental, and civil service structures.

What Role Will Women Play in National Service?

If we take as given that women will be excluded from military conscription (see *Rostker v. Goldberg* 1981) and the current limits on the number of female volunteers whom the armed forces can absorb, we reach the following conclusions. A purely compulsory National Service program would be drafting women only for civilian jobs; that would raise severe (probably insurmountable) constitutional problems. A quasi-compulsory program that treated civilian service as a draft exemption would probably be disproportionately filled with men because women would feel no compulsion to join. Indeed, they might feel pressure not to join since, if civilian placements were limited, each woman who signed up would be denying a man a possible draft exemption.

If environmental, conservation services and other National Service programs are organized on an away-from-home basis, and if participants are housed in dormitories, women will have to be placed in their own work camps and living units or be integrated with the men in some way or another. To integrate men and women in camps and dormitories would make National Service vulnerable to two types of criticism: 1) that women are not being sufficiently protected from male predators and 2) that dormitory life is marked by sexual promiscuity, drug abuse and other debauchery. The government could not ignore such criticisms and would certainly have to be able to justify its security procedures and dormitory regulations in Congress and in other forums.

What Is an Appropriate Wage?

Should National Service participants be paid a "subsistence" wage, minimum wage or market wage? Obviously, the answer determines the overall cost and perhaps the feasibility of the program. A subsistence wage opens the program to criticisms that it is exploitive, especially if it is compulsory. It would probably have a negative effect on recruiting; although certain idealists might be attracted to working for subsistence wages, many young people would resent and reject low wages unless they had no better opportunities. Finally, a subsistence wage would almost certainly mean that participants would live at home or perhaps in government provided dormitories. A so-called market wage would probably be prohibitively expensive, despite the support it would have from labor unions. National Service participants would almost certainly be paid the federal minimum wage. But that hardly exhausts the compensation question. Would the federal government or local sponsor have to provide worker's compensation, pension contributions and medical insurance?

How Long a Tour of Duty?

National Service proposals have defined the duration of service anywhere from a few months to two years. The longer the program the greater the number who will not complete it successfully. It is well to recall that during the Depression, a large percentage of Civilian Conservation Corps participants had to be discharged (Salmond 1967). During the early 1970s years the failure rate in the Job Corps was over 30 percent (Leviton and Johnston 1975). Currently, more than one-third of AVF volunteers are dismissed before completing their three-year tour of duty.[12] Even the California Conservation Corps retains only 40 percent of its volunteers for a full year. Seattle's Program for Local Service, which Donald Eberly and others consider a National Service prototype, loses about one-third of its volunteers during their first year of service (Eberly 1977).

The longer the program, the greater the number of placements. A program with a two year tour of duty would, all other things being equal, have to provide twice as many placements as a one-year program. It would therefore be almost twice as expensive. A one year or shorter tour of duty would cost less, but it would be out of sync with the longer military obligation. And if too short, the service experience might provide too few benefits to be attractive to some proponents.

Service in the Community or Service Away from Home

From the perspective of the participant there is a big difference between service performed in the community while living at home and service performed outside the community while living on one's own or in a National Service dormitory. The choice between these two options will effect the overall character of National Service.

Some advocates have pointed to the mixing of young people from all socioeconomic, racial, and ethnic groups as a major advantage—even a goal—of National Service. It is not clear whether they believe that benefits accrue only from off-duty group living or from on-duty working as well. The former would be the more intense interpersonal experience. Sociologist Amitai Etzioni (1978:13) has written:

> A year of National Service, especially if designated to enable people from different backgrounds to live and work together, could be an effective way for people—from parochial and public schools, from North and South, boys and girls, big city and country persons, whites and non-whites—to get to know each other on an equal footing while working together at a joint task. The "total" nature of the situation—being away from home, peers, and "background" communities—and spending time together around the clock, is what promises the sociological impact.

The prototypical National Service organizations, Civilian Conservation Corps, Peace Corps, and VISTA all require service away from home. Aside from the benefits that derive from the programs themselves, there are the broadening effects of travel and contact with different cultures. Those advantages would not accrue to those who fulfill their service obligation while commuting from home.

If National Service is to be performed away from home, attention will have to be paid to housing arrangements. Over the next two decades there will be approximately 3 to 4 million persons turning age 18 each year. If National Service requires one year of service, and if one-half of the participants serve away from home, housing would be required for 1.5 to 2.0 million men and women. VISTA volunteers are normally left to find their own housing; of course, their motivation is high since they are volunteers in a highly competitive program. Even so, they have not always found it easy to locate suitable housing in cities like New York and Washington, particularly when earning a subsistence wage. We should not expect 18-year-olds, involuntarily impressed into a universal National Service, to find their own housing; many will lack the motivation even to try. Therefore, housing would have to be provided by the government or other National Service sponsors. If an away-from-home approach is chosen, dormitories will have to be constructed. This will not only be enormously expensive, but it will also make National Service and/or the sponsoring agency responsible for the quality of life in the dorms. It is well to remember that CCC camps were run by the Army. This hardly seems like a viable present-day option.

The McCloskey and Cavanaugh Proposals

Purpose

McCloskey and Cavanaugh propose to establish a National Service which would cure military manpower problems, expand civilian service opportunities, and create an obligation for young people to serve their country.[13] Both proposals reinstitute a military draft, and, to encourage participation, provide exemptions for those who choose civilian service. In order to establish and administer a nationwide civilian service system, both congressmen proposed the creation of new federal agencies, and new cooperative ventures between federal and state governments and between the National Service agency and local public and private service organizations.

Given that both these plans aim to strengthen military recruitment, it is surprising that neither provides substantial incentives for those who choose to serve in the armed forces. Without such incentives, the number of military volunteers might actually decrease.[14] While a draft assures that overall manpower quotas would be met, many potential recruits from the middle and upper middle classes might be drawn toward what they perceive as more desirable civilian service options.

Under McCloskey's proposal the civilian service obligation is much shorter than the military obligation. A registrant can choose between two years of active duty service, six years in the reserves or one year civilian service. Thus, a young person concerned about disruption of career plans would have an incentive to volunteer for civilian service. Civilian service volunteers would be paid a subsistence stipend, and it is proposed that entry-level military enlistees also be reduced to the subsistence level. A Pfc with less than two years of service would earn far less than what a Pfc in the AVF now earns. The impact of so severe a salary reduction on morale should not be ignored.

McCloskey and other National Service proponents justify the pay cut on the ground that the AVF is too expensive and that savings derived from the pay reduction will be used to subsidize civilian service programs. Furthermore, they believe that monetary incentives are not appropriate for either military or civilian service recruiting. In fact, in their view, monetary incentives may be counterproductive if they promote self-interest at the expense of a spirit of service. Perhaps to sweeten the pill, McCloskey does provide post-service educational benefits for those who successfully complete their military service.

Some aspects of the Cavanaugh plan provide a more favorable deal for military volunteers. A civilian service tour of duty requires twenty-four months, while a volunteer for active duty need serve only eighteen months, and a reservist six months of active duty and thirty-six months in the Selective Reserve. While Cavanaugh may have increased the comparative attractiveness of military service by shortening its duration, a two-year civilian service will double the number of civilian placements that must be provided and double the cost. Furthermore, an eighteen-month active military tour is probably inefficient. The Army has strongly resisted even a two-year initial enlistment, on the ground that the necessity of lengthy training requires a minimum three-year term to be cost effective.

Under the Cavanaugh bill, those serving in civilian positions, which are to be exclusively in the federal bureaucracies, are to receive "subsistence wages"; no mention is made of compensation for military service, presumably leaving in tact current military pay scales. Cavanaugh does not propose to resuscitate the G.I. Bill or provide any other special post-service benefits to make military service comparatively more attractive.

Neither National Service bill guarantees a cure for the ailing AVF. Reinstating the military draft would, of course, assure that manpower quotas would be met, but the quality of enlistees would not be guaranteed. Neither bill provides sufficient incentives for middle class high school graduates to volunteer for military service. The same social segments that now disproportionately volunteer for military service will probably continue to do so under the McCloskey and Cavanaugh proposals. Draftees would only be a small percentage of all recruits (probably no more than 15 percent), and a significant fraction will be members of the lower socioeconomic classes. Thus, the impact of these National Service proposals on the demographic composition of the AVF would be modest.

Universality

Neither the McCloskey nor Cavanaugh plan is universal. McCloskey provides a draft lottery to meet recruitment shortfalls. However, even under the worst case assumptions it is hardly likely that the armed forces would require more than 50,000 draftees per year to supplement the much larger number who volunteer. The AVF did fail to meet force levels by 8,000 to 10,000 in the mid-1970s and by 30,000 in 1979. Yet by the mid-1980s, the AVF was operating at nearly full complement.

Cavanaugh proposes a draft lottery to meet both military and civilian manpower shortfalls. Under his plan, every federal agency must set aside a number of placements for National Service participants equal to 5 percent of its total personnel. Civilian National Service would be performed only in these federal agencies. Volunteers would be accepted, but any vacancies would be filled through the draft lottery. Despite this innovation, the majority of youth would not be needed in the civilian or military services. Neither the requirement nor the opportunity to serve are universal.

Some National Service proponents maintain that the mere creation of a National Service system would stimulate widespread feelings of moral obligation to serve, and predict that civilian and military organizations would be deluged with applications. If that occurred, the McCloskey civilian service would have to be flexible enough to provide opportunities for all who desired a civilian service placement. To meet this contingency, McCloskey proposes to use the Young Adult Conservation Corps, a federal program established in the late 1970s, as a placement of last resort. The Cavanaugh National Service System, on the other hand, could not survive an avalanche of applications because there are limits to the number of unskilled volunteers that the federal agencies could utilize. Other types of service would have to be permitted or many applicants would have to be turned away.

Eligibility. During the Vietnam War era those who opposed the draft decried the inequities, particularly student deferments that permitted many young men to avoid serving altogether. Student deferments were abolished toward the end of the Vietnam War period. However, McCloskey and Cavanaugh both seem to readmit them by the back door. McCloskey would permit a participant to choose to serve at any point between his 18th and 23rd birthdays. Cavanaugh would permit a similar designation, up to age 26. Such deferments increase the chances that some individuals will eventually escape service altogether. It also suggests that some young people would enter civilian service after college when they have greater maturity and more skills. This might accentuate work assignment distinctions within the civilian service.

McCloskey's National Service permits two categories of exemptions: those with permanent physical or mental disabilities, and conscientious objectors. The Cavanaugh plan is identical, except that is speaks of "persons found to be physically, mentally, or otherwise unfit on a permanent basis." It is important to remember that approximately one-third of all otherwise eligible young men are at present unacceptable for military service for physical, mental, or moral reasons. Since the McCloskey proposal does not draft for civilian service, a relatively minor infirmity (i.e., poor vision) which is disqualifying for the military draft also removes any pressure to join the civilian service. The Cavanaugh proposal provides that an individual who is drafted need not be assigned to his preferred category (military or civilian) of National Service, depending upon available positions and individual qualifications. Thus, a draftee found unfit to serve in the armed forces could be conscripted for a federal agency.

The United States has always required conscientious objectors to perform civilian alternative service (see Greenawalt 1971). Those refusing to accept alternative service have been subject to criminal prosecution. McCloskey would apparently expand the scope of conscientious objection to encompass a right of conscientious objection to civilian as well as military service, thereby weakening the universality of his proposal. Individuals would be required to "prove by a clear preponderence of the evidence that service in general in a military and civilian capacity would be a violation of [their] most profound convictions." If the National Service System is required to judge the sincerity of each individual's belief system, this exemption could quickly swallow up the rule. The former judicially imposed standard, similar to this, proved difficult to administer in the late 1960s and early 1970s and may have foreordained the demise of military conscription (see Coffey 1979).

As important as the exemptions recognized by McCloskey and Cavanaugh are the many categories ignored by their proposals.[15] Will mothers of young children, drug addicts, criminals, illiterates—and others who have traditionally been exempt—now be required to serve? However desirable their inclusion would be for equity reasons, it seems doubtful that the armed forces would accept such personnel when there exists a military draft to provide a large pool of qualified young people.

Role of Women. Contrary to the vision of William James, neither the McCloskey nor Cavanaugh bill treats the two sexes differently; both men and women would be equally vulnerable to military conscription and thus have the same incentive to join the civilian service. But the implementation of a sex-blind draft is highly unlikely. The recent draft registration debate showed overwhelming political resistence to the conscription of women. If women could not be drafted, they would be under no compulsion to enlist in civilian service under McCloskey's plan. The majority of young women, particularly middle class women optimistic about their educational and employment options, would probably decide to pursue their civilian careers without interruption. Likewise, Cavanaugh's plan puts no pressure on women to enlist in the armed forces. However, they would be vulnerable to the civilian draft, assuming it somehow survived constitutional attack.

Enforcement. Some young people will attempt to evade their National Service obligation: some will not register, others will not show up for work, or if they do, will be obstructive or disruptive. There will have to be a system of incentives and disincentives to promote cooperation.

If discharge is a readily available sanction for disruptive behavior, the equity-enhancing function of National Service will be undermined. The most obvious sanctions, fines and imprisonment, exhaust judicial resources and trigger moral and political opposition. An alternative sanction is the denial of certain government benefits—loans, social security, mortgages—either for a determinate period or for life. One cannot know what deterrent effect this would have. Conceivably, 17- and 18-year olds may be largely oblivious to such threats.

Traditionally, the United States armed forces have refused to permit draftees to quit, and have utilized dishonorable discharges and occasionally criminal penalties to punish resisters. National Service could adopt a similar policy. But this could have grave social costs. A stigmatizing discharge might be more palatable politically, but its effectiveness would require public and private employers to recognize successful completion of National Service as proof of capacity for reliable employment. The military system of graded discharges is questionable in its own right; one may ask whether it makes sense for the military to create so many "losers" whose career opportunities are further diminished by dishonorable discharges. To put the graded discharge system to work to coerce satisfactory performance in National Service would be counterproductive and ironic. A program designed to help young people could end up stigmatizing them and diminishing their chances for personal and occupational success.

Failure to register under both McCloskey's and Cavanaugh's bills is a criminal offense, punishable by imprisonment. Those who fail to serve satisfactorily in McCloskey's civilian service (i.e., willful disobedience, insubordinate conduct, conviction of a felony or of highly unsatisfactory conduct) would be dismissed from their positions and made subject to a military draft. The dismissal, by itself, would not be regarded as punishment by those who do not want to serve. It is highly questionable whether military service should be used to "punish" civilian service failures. A presupposition of National Service is that military service is the quintessential form of National Service, not a punishment. The armed forces would hardly be enthusiastic about drafting civilian service failures.

Since Cavanaugh's civilian service is less voluntary, it is not surprising that it would punish unsatisfactory performance more stringently. A registrant may be dismissed for any one of five causes: (1) willful disobedience; (2) insubordinate conduct; (3) conviction of a felony; (4) grossly unsatisfactory performance; or (5) absenteeism. Extensive procedural protections surround the dismissal determination. The "accused" is entitled to a hearing, an appeal to the Civilian Service Review Board, and a de novo review in federal district court. If the dismissal is ultimately upheld, the registrant faces lifetime ineligibility for any federal employment, federal loan or loan guarantee under the Small Business Act, federal education grant, scholarship or loan guarantee, or any home mortgage loan or loan guarantee. This is truly Draconian punishment, even more severe than a dishonorable military discharge.

What Counts as National Service

The McCloskey Bill. The McCloskey Bill envisions a broad array of civilian service opportunities in both public and private sectors. The bill defines "qualified service categories" as follows:

Sec. 206(a). With the assistance of such advisory committees as the Director may establish, the Board shall from time to time promulgate regulations designating specific service categories as qualified service categories in which civilian service registrants may serve for the purposes of this Act.

206 (b). An activity shall be considered to be a qualified service category under subsection (a) of this subsection if—

(1) the activity is of substantial social benefit in meeting human, social, or environmental needs of or in the community where registrants are to perform service or is of substantial social benefit to the Nation;

(2) Federal participation in the area is constitutionally permissible under the First Amendment to the Constitution of the United States;

(3) participation of registrants in the activity concerned will not interfere unreasonably with the availability and the terms of employment of sponsors with positions available in that activity;

(4) registrants are able to meet the physical, mental, and educational qualifications that the activity requires; and

(5) the activity is in other respects suitable for the purposes of this Act.

206 (c). Suitable service categories shall include positions in—

(1) the Foundation and State, local, and regional government agencies;

(2) public, private, and parochial schools;

(3) nonprofit hospitals;

(4) law enforcement agencies;

(5) penal and probation systems;

(6) private, nonprofit organizations whose principal purpose is social service; and

(7) seasonable farm labor on commercial farms at which adequate labor by persons who are United States citizens is not available, if and only if the Foundation designates such positions as being suitable for the purposes of this Act.

206 (g). Suitable service categories may not include positions in—

(1) profitmaking business organizations;

(2) labor unions;

(3) partisan political organizations;

(4) organizations engaged in religious functions, unless the position itself does not involve any religious functions;

(5) domestic or personal service companies or organizations; and

(6) except as provided under subsection (c) (7), commercial farms.

The proposed legislation empowers the Foundation to define suitable National Service positions. The "substantial social benefits" standard leaves wide discretion. An enormous range of organizations, including most all governmental agencies, could claim to provide a benefit to the community or the nation. It is hard to imagine any agency that would be excluded, other than those specifically proscribed in Section 206(d). The bill seems to envision civilian service being performed in governmental and private nonprofit agencies rather than in any specially designed organizations such as the Peace Corps or Civilian Conservation Corps.

While the definition speaks of "categories of qualified activities," the specific, but not exhaustive, list of suitable placements specifies particular organizations and agencies. Perhaps these agencies, with uncharacteristic innovation, can generate many stimulating opportunities. But skeptics, until shown differently, will refuse to believe that any and all positions in such agencies could provide a valuable, meaningful, or important National Service experience. Surely, it could not be said that CETA (Titles II & VI, public service employment) provided this kind of experience, despite the program requirement that "participants are . . . [to perform] meaningful and necessary public service work at all times." (see Nathan, Cook and Rawlins 1981)

It will be extremely difficult politically to pick and choose among private organizations applying as National Service sponsors. The statement that "suitable service categories shall include positions in "private, nonprofit organizations whose principal purpose is social service" is vague. Does the

NAACP perform a social service? What about the Boy Scouts, the American Cancer Society, the Sierra Club. and the Humane Society? Could a young man fulfill his National Service obligation by tutoring students in elementary calculus at an exclusive private school? Can social service be for the benefit of an exclusive group or membership, or must it be a public good which everyone can consume?

The inclusion of "seasonable farm labor on commercial farms" is unexpected. This would provide a windfall to commercial farmers, who would obtain free workers. Perhaps the intent is to discourage hiring illegal aliens. If so, this hardly seems a sensible approach to that problem.

Any large scale National Service will also generate concern about job displacement. Will National Service cause public employers to substitute federally paid National Service workers for locally paid government employees? This very issue triggered amendment of the CETA public service employment system to require that CETA workers be assigned to special projects rather than regular public services. Still, the skeptics were never fully convinced. It is far easier to state, as McCloskey does, that "participation of registrants in the activity concerned will not interfere unreasonably with the availability and the terms of employment of employees of sponsors with positions available in that activity," than it is to demonstrate the absence of a job displacement effect.

The Cavanaugh Bill. Cavanaugh's designation of qualified service categories is far less ambiguous than McCloskey's. Federal agencies are required to reserve 5 percent of their positions for National Service personnel; this constitutes the only civilian service option. An individual must choose between two years of service in the federal bureaucracy or take his chances in the draft lottery. If he is drafted, he may still be assigned to his preferred civilian service placement, though there is no guarantee.

The Cavanaugh Bill does not rely upon nonmilitary manpower needs as a rationale for National Service. There is no effort to harness the idealism of youth through special service opportunities, no effort to provide special skills training, and no linking of National Service to critical national needs. Instead, the plan extends the burden of service by impressing volunteers or draftees into the federal bureaucracies.

The Cavanaugh Bill gives no hint of which agency positions are appropriate for National Service participants. Since most participants will be young and unskilled, it will be no easy matter for the federal agencies to absorb them. It would not be surprising if they were assigned to dull makework tasks. Instead of satisfying the "urge to serve" or strengthening citizenship norms, such assignments would probably be viewed negatively and perhaps aggravate the estrangement and alienation of young people.

Administration of National Service

The McCloskey and Cavanaugh National Service proposals both establish new federal agencies to carry out registration and placement. Both bills do away with Selective Service and then recreate it as the "National Service System" (McCloskey) or the "Public Service System" (Cavanaugh). The National Service System's headquarters would be located in Washington, D.C.; its director would be a presidential appointee. The president, with the advice of each governor, is empowered to appoint a National Service director for each state and adminstrators of local placement centers which, under both plans, would be established in each county or comparable political subdivision. Both bills also establish state appeals boards to process disputes over classifications. Both provide for exclusive federal funding. Neither bill mentions living arrangements.

The Cavanaugh Public Service System. The Cavanaugh plan establishes a Civilian Placement Bureau within the Public Service System. The Bureau administrator (who is to be appointed by the Director of the Public Service System) is charged with responsibility for determining the number of federal positions to be filled through conscription and for placing civilian service volunteers and draftees. In making placement decisions, the administrator must consider the qualifications of the registrant, the geographical location of his residence, and his employment preference. Given the typical registrant's age, minimal skills, and the numbers to be processed, it hardly seems likely that the matching process will involve much fine tuning.

A large percentage of federal agency positions are located in Washington, D.C. Thus, hundreds of thousands of registrants must work in Washington. The bill gives no hint of how these civilian service draftees, with their subsistence stipends, will find housing in the tight Washington market.

The McCloskey Youth Service Foundation. McCloskey proposes to establish another independent federal agency, the National Youth Service Foundation, to administer the civilian component of the National Service plan. The Foundation is to consist of a nineteen-member Board of Trustees, and a Director and his staff. It would be charged with administering the National Youth Service Corps and making grants to units of state and local government (grantees) to provide employment opportunities for civilian service registrants in the Corps.

The Foundation's Board of Trustees is directed to make grants to state and local governmental units wishing to develop and encourage civilian service opportunities. There is to be only one local grantee for any "geographic area" (a term left undefined). The grantee is to use these funds (1) to pay stipends to those in the National Youth Service Corps, (2) to encourage governmental and private organizations to become sponsors, or to make more civilian service opportunities available, and (3) for other purposes authorized by the Board. Although the grantees apparently have the authority to pay registrants and to coordinate civilian service opportunities, it is the National Board which determines which agencies and organizations can become sponsors. This is very similar to the CETA program. The charges of local corruption and ineptitude that plagued CETA, and the numerous efforts to tighten federal controls should warn us of the potential pitfalls in this kind of federal/state/local venture (see Van Horn 1979).

McCloskey places the burden of finding a civilian service placement on the individual, although information, presumably on nationwide service opportunites, is to be available through the local placement centers. Because the registrant must find his own position, it is likely that a large proportion of registrants will serve close to their home. If so, the National Service System may not have to supply living quarters. Those registrants who choose to serve in another region of the country will be required to find a residentially based program or locate their own housing. Some sponsors may build dormitories so that they can recruit a substantial number of young people from outside the immediate locale. Neither the National Service System nor the National Youth Service Foundation would be involved directly in managing such living facilities, though the Foundation might regulate and inspect.

As noted earlier, the Young Adult Conservation Corps serves the McCloskey plan as a placement of last resort. Today, it is a small residentially based program, run by the Departments of Interior and Agriculture. Depending upon the number of enrollees, it might have to be vastly expanded to fulfill its new National Service role.

Constitutionality

Compulsory National Service is vulnerable to Thirteenth Amendment attack because, arguably, forced participation in a civilian labor program is precisely the kind of involuntary servitude which the Constitution proscribes (see Black 1967). This argument is most forcefully directed against a National Service that drafts universally and then assigns individuals to military and civilian agencies.[16]

While the Thirteenth Amendment outlaws "involuntary servitude," it is by now well established that military conscription is an exception. National sovereignty itself implies the power to provide for the nation's defense; in any case, the Constitution explicitly empowers Congress to raise and support armies. Chief Justice Earl Warren once referred to this power as "broad and sweeping," declaring that "the power to classify and conscript manpower for military service is 'beyond question'." (*U.S. v. O'Brien* 1968: 377)

The lower federal courts have consistently upheld the federal government's authority to demand civilian alternative service from conscientious objectors.[17] In the leading case of *Howze v. United States* (1959), the Ninth Circuit Court of Appeals rejected a conscientious objector's Thirteenth Amendment challenge to alternative service.

> Compulsory civilian labor does not stand alone, but is the alternative to compulsory military service. It is not a punishment, but is instead a means of preserving discipline and morale in the armed forces. The power of Congress to raise armies and to take effective measures to preserve their efficiency, is not limited by either the thirteenth amendment, or the absence of a military emergency.

Both the McCloskey and Cavanaugh National Service proposals envision more civilian labor than the traditional alternative service that conscientious objectors have been obligated to perform.[18] The crucial Constitutional question is whether these plans are linked closely enough to the recruitment of military manpower to come within Congress's broad power to "raise armies."[19]

There seems little doubt about the legality of McCloskey's proposal. It does not force anyone to perform civilian labor. All young people are made vulnerable to a military draft, which as previously noted, is beyond constitutional question. If the individual is physically or mentally unfit or can establish his conscientious opposition to any form of National Service, his obligation is extinguished. If not, he can avoid the military draft only by enlisting in an approved civilian service program. In effect, this plan does no more than extend to everyone an option that has long been available to conscientious objectors.

It could be argued that McCloskey's military draft is a mere subterfuge for impressing youth into a civilian labor program. This argument would have some weight if draft calls were bloated beyond military need in order to compel participation in the civilian service, or if there was some other kind of manipulation. However, McCloskey's plan aims to recruit military manpower in a way that is efficient, rational and legitimate from society's standpoint, and at the same time, to maximize the individual's options.

Cavanaugh's proposal is constitutionally dubious because it establishes a draft for the federal civilian bureaucracies. Even if the military met all of its recruitment needs, young men and women would still be drafted to serve in various federal agencies if there were not enough civilian volunteers. Proponents could argue that the program is vital to the recruitment of military manpower and therefore within Congress' power to take necessary and proper steps to raise armies. They could defend the civilian agency draft on the ground that it promotes volunteerism for the armed forces, presuming that many young people will desire to avoid civilian service. The agency draft might also be justified on the ground that it will improve the morale of military personnel by expanding the obligation to serve the nation to a greater number of young people, thereby emphasizing the value and importance of service.

While these arguments may require various leaps of faith, it is by no means clear that the Supreme Court would reject them.[20] It should be remembered that in *Rostker v. Goldber* (1981), the Court accepted very dubious reasoning for male-only draft registration. Justice Rehnquist's majority opinion repeatedly stressed that on national defense matters the Court will show almost complete deference to congressional judgments.

> This is not, however, merely a case involving the customary deference accorded congressional decisions. The case arises in the context of Congress' authority over national defense, and perhaps in no other area has the Court accorded Congress greater deference.

Conclusion

Are There Military Advantages to National Service?

The McCloskey and Cavanaugh National Service bills must ultimately be judged on what they contribute to the armed forces of a democratic society. Both bills would eliminate military recruitment problems, since any shortfalls would be made up through a draft. But the same result could be reached without National Service, by implementing a military draft to make up for shortfalls in the number and quality of volunteers.

National Service proponents claim that a draft coupled with civilian service would reduce inequity in a system in which a small number of draftees are called upon to make great personal sacrifices while the vast majority of young people make none whatever. There are several responses to this claim. Under National Service plans like those of McCloskey and Cavanaugh, large numbers of young people, and most women, could avoid any type of service. Those who do perform civilian service will be living and working in a multitude of settings, but very few will find themselves in circumstances even roughly equivalent to military draftees.

The impact of a civilian service system on the morale of military personnel is hardly clear. No doubt it would depend upon whether the nation is at war and the availability of various military benefits. If military morale is the key concern, more might be achieved by higher pay, a more generous

G.I. Bill, and post-service employment preferences than by increasing the number of young people participating in human service and environmental programs.

Are There Nonmilitary Advantages to National Service?

Many nonmilitary claims are made for National Service, especially that it will assist young people to mature. Such claims should be regarded skeptically. Our foster homes, juvenile institutions, and even public schools hardly breed confidence in the government's ability to identify and solve the problems of youth. Beside that, many young people are not "in trouble." They would likely resent being impressed into civilian service programs and if they were, many would have negative experiences. Furthermore, expanding federal youth programs to include a greater percentage of middle and upper class youth might divert resources from programs geared to the least advantaged young people. If the goal is to help young people "in trouble" or "in need," money might better be spent on improved foster care, family planning, job training, remedial education, juvenile corrections, and public sector employment.

Notes

1. Another New Deal program, the National Youth Administration (NYA) was larger than CCC, but received less aclaim. It provided mostly part-time work and work-study for males and females between sixteen and twenty four years old (see Sherraden and Eberly 1982).
2. Since the mid-1960s, Eberly has written continuously and lobbied prodigously in behalf of the idea; his intense commitment and remarkable energy has kept National Service alive in the federal bureaucracies, before Congress, in the academic community, and before the public. (See Eberly 1967: 110-16; 1970; 1971: 65-69; 1977: 43-66; Sherraden and Eberly 1977: 445-66; 1982)
3. Senator Cranston stated before the Senate Subcommittee on Child and Human Development (March 13, 1980):

   A national service program might well provide both the stimulus and the opportunity that Americans need to demonstrate, once again, the compassion and the generosity that have contributed to our Nation's greatness. It could create anew that sense of unity and purpose which has bound our diverse population together in years past and which seems to be missing today except in times of immediate crisis.

   Another example is from the sociologist and social policy analyst, Amitai Etzioni (1978:13):

   In a period of growing alienation and cynicism, Americans badly need opportunities for meaningful positive involvement with their society. Thus the criterion for including a particular form of service in the program should be its societal usefulness; that is, promotion of values that transcend the mere advancement of one's own self interest.

See also Howard Didsbury, Jr. (1976:306):

Idealism, enthusiasm and a desire to contribute to society are not lost causes with today's youth. The fundamental problem is the death of meaningful, challenging opportunities to allow young people to express their social concerns. H.G. Wells would describe it as "the present waste of youthful seriousness."

4. This statement was printed in the *New York Times* (May 19, 1966: 11) from a speech delivered before the American Society of Newspaper Editors, Montreal, Canada (May 18, 1966).

5. "The basic question to be resolved is, what kind of society will we have? Will it be one that is made up of millions of individuals who are presumed responsible till proven otherwise and who make rational decisions which recognize the common good and lead to a desire to help others? Or will we have a society in which the individual is reduced to the level of a statistic to be manipulated by society engineers with a compulsive need to see total order around them?" (*Shrevesport (La.) Times*, April 10, 1979)

6. New York City has established a demonstration youth volunteer service to recruit 18-year-old residents to perform important, needed services for one year. The City Volunteer Corps is designed to test the feasibility of a large-scale urban youth service in New York City and in the nation. Among the program's objectives are the personal development of the volunteers and the integration of young people from all income levels and walks of life. The volunteers will receive a small weekly stipend and scholarship aid, as well as acquire training and skills to enhance their employability. Projects will include physical improvement of the city, human services and counselling, and emergency assistance (National Service Corporation for New York City, Outline of Program, October 1984).

7. There have been various legislative proposals for the study or establishment of National Service since the 1960s. Senator Daniel Brewster introduced a bill on March 7, 1967 to establish an Advisory Commission on National Service (S. 1213) "to determine the feasibility and desirability of an expanded national service system for citizens able and willing to serve in non-military activities designed to help the United States to combat disease, ignorance, and poverty at home and abroad." On February 28th, 1968 Senators Kennedy, Brewster, Case, Hart, Mondale, Yarborough, Nelson, and Tydings intoduced S. 3052 to establish a study commission to carry out a detailed one year study of the feasibility and desirability of a national service corps. The Youth Power Act, introduced on April 22, 1969 by Senators Hatfield and McGovern would have established a National Youth Service Foundation and National Youth Service Council. The former would have been empowered to "make grants to or to contract with public or private nonprofit agencies for recruitment and training of 17- to 27-year-olds, for periods up to 2 years.

8. They include the Hearing on National Service Legislation Before the Military Personnel Subcommittee of the Committee on Armed Services, House of Representatives, 96th Cong., 2nd Sess., 1980; Hearing Before the Subcommittee on Child and Human Development of the Committee on Labor and Human Resources, United States, 96th Cong., 2nd Sess., 1980 (establishment of a Presi-

dential Commission on National Service and a National Commission on Volunteerism). National Service has also been mentioned at many congressional hearings concerned with the status of the All-Volunteer Force.
9. The idea of conscripting all able-bodied American boys for six months or a year of military training has, if anything, a longer and even more distinguished pedigree than National Service. General Hugh Scott, Chief of Staff, vigorously urged the idea in 1916. In the post-World War II period, Presidents Truman and Eisenhower both favored it over selective service (see O'Sullivan and Meckler 1974). Eisenhower explained his support as follows:

> First, there are the long term military advantages. After a few years of UMT, we would have always a huge reserve of young men with sound basic military training. The R.O.T.C. would turn out better officers; the National Guard would be far more efficient. In case of a great emergency, all these men would be ready for combat after a brief refresher course, and in the event of nuclear attack—the Lord forbid!—a disciplined body of young men in every community would be a priceless asset.
>
> Second, although I certainly do not contend that UMT would be a cure for juvenile delinquency, I do think it could do very much to stem the growing tide of irresponsible behavior and outright crime in the United States. To expose all our young men for a year to discipline and the correct attitudes of living inevitably would straighten out a lot of potential trouble makers. In this connection—although I am sure that in saying this I label myself as old fashioned—I deplore the beatnick dress, the long unkept hair, the dirty necks and fingernails now affected by a minority of our boys. If UMT accomplished nothing more, it might be worth the price tag—and I am not altogether jesting when I say this. To me a sloppy appearance has always indicated sloppy habits of mind.
>
> The armed forces have not favored UMT, at least since World War II, emphasizing the need for fully active forces rather than for forces capable of being made combat ready with the aid of reserves.

The Gates Commission pointed out:

> Universal Military Training resembles mandatory National Service, for it contemplates conscription of all those eligible. It is undesirable for generally the same reasons as mandatory National Service. For one thing, it would impose on the military more untrained personnel than can be productively employed. A one-year tour of duty—the usual term proposed—is prohibitively expensive in view of the very short period an individual would serve after receiving costly training (Report of the President's Commission on an All-Volunteer Force 1970: 175).

10. The Congressional Budget Office's (1978:34) effort to ascertain the degrees of youth alienation led to the conclusion that:

> Evidence of levels of alienation among youth is sketchy but suggestive of the need for social commitment and service. Almost 48 percent of male college freshmen and 41 percent of females believe that there is little they can do to change society. About one in seven noncollege youth (15 percent), 11 percent of college enrollees, consider themselves to be second-class citizens. Aliena-

tion among disadvantaged youth—for example, black teenagers in urban ghettos—is particularly high.
There is much to quarrel with in this brief paragraph. If youth are "alienated" (a highly ambiguous term) why conclude that social commitment and service will help? Maybe what is needed is better economic opportunity or more political power. Is it surprising that 15 percent of young people consider themselves "second-class citizens?" More than 15 percent are poor and disadvantaged, uneducated, and clearly "not making it." This reflects a problem that goes beyond race and class. To state the statistic the other way around could be heartening, i.e., 85 percent reject the notion that they are second-class citizens.

11. The most specific planning has come from Donald Eberly. See in particular his "A Model For Universal Youth Service" prepared for the Universal Youth Service conference sponsored by the Eleanor Roosevelt Institute, April 9-10, 1976. Mr. Eberly would guarantee a service opportunity for everyone who wants one.

12. See testimony presented by B.T. Collins, Hearing Before the Subcommittee on Child and Human Development of the Senate Committee on Labor and Human Resources, 96th Cong., 2nd Session, on Establishment of a Presidential Commission on National Service and A National Commission on Volunteerism, March 12, 1980.

13. The McCloskey Bill (H.R. 1730 2[b]) states: "It is the purpose of this Act to establish a program under which all citizens of the United States are asked to perform 1 or 2 years of either military or civilian service between the ages of 18 and 30, but in which no one is required to serve except to the extent that the needs of the military require that some persons be inducted for military training and service." The Cavanaugh plan (H.R. 3603) contains no statement of purpose, but is clearly addressed to the problem of recruiting military manpower. "A Bill to establish a Public Service System under which the young people of the United States shall be subject by random selection to induction for civilian, military, or military reserve service."

14. The problem of balancing military and civilian obligations can lead to curious results. McCloskey provides that a registrant who is dismissed from civilian service after completing only half his obligation need only serve one year of military service (§213). This would be highly undesirable from the military's standpoint.

15. McCloskey allows deferment for (1) temporary unfitness and (2) family hardship (H. R. 1730 § 105[a]). Cavanaugh does allow deferment for (1) the mother of any child who provides regular care to such child, (2) pregnant women, and (3) those for whom service would be a family hardship. (H.R. 3603 §6[d] [1]).

16. Many commentators over the years have suggested that the United States armed forces expand its role far beyond national defense to take on critical environmental and social needs (see e.g., Albert Biderman 1971:47-58). If Biderman's proposal were adopted, one wonders whether a universal national service system could be justified under the Congressional power to "raise armies." After all, the Constitution does not specify what the role of the Army is to be. It is interesting to note that conscientious objectors, serving alternative service during World War I, were technically drafted into the armed forces and then assigned to compulsory civilian service. In World War II the system was changed; conscientious objectors were never drafted.

17. The Military Selective Service Act of 1967 provided for those conscientious objectors opposed to participation in both combatant and noncombatant roles to serve in a civilian capacity that contributed to the "maintenance of the national health, safety, or interest," (50 U.S.C. App. §456 [j] [1976]). The term of alternative service was twenty-four months (32 C.F.R. 1660.10 (1981); see *Harv. Civ. Rts.—Civ. Lib. L. Rev.* 1971).

18. Apparently, a legal analysis of National Service carried out by the Justice Department in the Carter administration reached the conclusion that "the Congress could, consistent with the Constitution, implement a national youth service program having general characteristics similar to any of the programs outlined in four basic models." These models include both the McCloskey and Cavanaugh proposals (Selective Service Reform Message from the President of the United States transmitting his Proposal for Selective Service Reform, Together with a Draft of Proposed Legislation to Amend the Military Selective Service Act To Allow the Registration of Both Men and Women, pursuant to Section 811 of Public Law 96-107, 1980: 46).

19. Congress would not seem to have any other authority to require National Service, although it has been suggested that such a program could be justified under the same power that gives state governments the right to require compulsory education (see Cullinan 1967). This argument is not convincing for a number of reasons. First, the states, not Congress, have the power to require compulsory education. Second, education is not work, and hardly "involuntary servitude." Third, compulsory education traditonally expires at age 16; National Service would impose governmental authority at least till the late teens.

20. The Supreme Court has upheld state statutes that require uncompensated labor on the ground that the services were exceptional, e.g., *Butler v. Perry* 1916 (road-building); *Robertson v. United States* 1897, (seamen's contracts). Furthermore, a number of courts have held nonmilitary labor obligations constitutional when the commitments of time and energy were significantly less than that proposed in the national service programs, e.g., *Kasey v. Commissioner* 1972 (preparation and filing of income tax returns); *Williamson v. Vardeman* 1982 (requirement that attorneys represent indigent defendants); *Hurtado v. United States* 1973 (requirement that citizens testify in criminal cases); *Boblin v. Board of Education* 1975 (requirement that students perform "cafeteria duty" in public schools); see American Bar Association 1984: 17-21.

7

Veterans and Civil-Military Relations

The status of armed forces veterans constitutes an important facet of a society's civil-military relations. Veterans are neither military personnel nor pure civilians. They are ex-soldiers, who for most purposes play civilian roles, but who maintain some reservoir of experiences and emotions which at times become relevant for various civil-military issues. The shared experience of having borne arms for the nation, especially in wartime, sets the precondition for group consciousness and group action. The veteran is also a chameleon. He blends into civilian life, but may on occasion revert to his former military status especially when it is to his advantage.

Veterans may pose a political problem in that they have the potential to become a powerful vociferous interest group on behalf of narrow veterans' issues or larger political and ideological issues. They also pose an economic challenge if their demands for bonuses, compensations, and benefits conflict with the larger society's taxing and fiscal priorities. Veterans can also affect military recruitment and national commitments.

The first part of this chapter surveys the range of civil-military relations that veterans affect. In addition it calls attention to the problem of defining "veteran" in the current environment marked by large military forces-in-being which are frequently called upon for shows of force or limited combat. The second part of the chapter shines a spotlight on Vietnam veterans arguing that they are not nearly so unique or so troubled-ridden as some commentators claim.

Who Is a Veteran?

Who is a veteran is significant because *veteran* is a social construct that imports strong symbolic meanings and paves the way for numerous economic benefits. In most modern societies anxious about military organization and defense, veterans must be accorded honor, gratitude, and entitlements. Entitlements can be justified on a number of grounds: helping veterans readjust to civilian society; bringing veterans up to the position they would have achieved had their civilian careers not been interrupted by military service; fulfilling a societal debt of gratitude to a uniquely deserving group that can never be adequately compensated for its sacrifice; making military service more attractive to current and future recruits.

Until quite recently, the term *veteran* referred to military personnel who returned from war. Of course, those who returned in the custody of the military police could not be equated with "veterans in good standing"; such persons were excluded from popular and legislative definitions. The military's authority to award bad conduct and dishonorable discharges which disqualify an individual from veterans benefits is a significant social control power.

Most all of those who served during the Revolutionary, Civil, Mexican, and two world wars were clearly war veterans. That many who served during wartime did not actually engage in combat seemed to be overlooked, leading to the frequent complaint that in peacetime toy soldiers tend to drive out real soldiers. There are countless stories and literary depictions of men who never saw combat of any kind exaggerating and fabricating war records for personal aggrandizement during their careers as veterans. To make matters more complicated, since the emergence of mass warfare in the nineteenth century, some segments of wartime civilian populations have sacrificed and suffered as much as soldiers. Thus, the claims of some veterans to special benefits and entitlements could be seriously questioned. In fact, a government's policy toward its veterans might be subsumed under the more general issue of its responsibilities to all its citizens for damages and injuries sustained during wartime.

Historically, those who served in peacetime were not thought of as veterans, although they may have fought against Indians, pirates or other adversaries. What distinguished such personnel was not only peacetime service, but their status as professional soldiers (professional soldiers had their own system of pensions and compensation for disability). The term veterans seems to have attached to citizen soldiers who served during wartime and reverted to civilian status after the war. No distinction seems to be made between draftees and volunteers, but it seems a worthy hypothesis that veterans' benefits are strongly supported as a quid pro quo for involuntary military service.

Inevitably, the problem of defining veterans has become more complicated since World War II with the decline of mass mobilization, the rise of large forces-in-being, the outbreak of frequent so-called limited wars, and the ever declining ratio of combat to support troops. There could be no doubt that those men returning home after combat in Korea were veterans under anybody's definition. But what of their comrades who were stationed in Europe or in the United States? Should they also be regarded as veterans? Likewise, what of military personnel, who served at home or abroad during the Vietnam War era? Despite its being suggested from time to time, U.S. society has not attempted to reserve veteran status for combat veterans. All those who served for a few months during the Korean War period counted as veterans for purposes of the G.I. Bill and other benefits. In 1966, a momentous step was taken: veteran status was accorded to all personnel who served in the United States armed forces during the period of peace extending from the Korean War to the beginning of the Vietnam War. When members of today's All-Volunteer Force complete their enlistment contracts, they too become official veterans eligible for entitlements.

The distinction between peacetime and wartime has lost its meaning. The post-World War II period has produced massive peacetime armed forces for the first time in history. At the same time, the meaning of the term *peacetime* has become hopelessly ambiguous. Peacetime includes periodic combat missions, at least for small numbers of men. For all peacetime forces there is strong emphasis on combat readiness; contemporary military forces must be continuously combat ready in order to deter war. If conflict should break out, they must be deployable anywhere in the world. In a sense, such troops are continually engaged in fighting for peace.

Veterans Benefits

Special benefits have been accorded to veterans as long as there have been wars.[1] Roman soldiers were given extensive land grants and other perquisites. Certain European countries gave their destitute veterans the right to beg on the public highways. Benefits of one kind or another have been a feature of U.S. society since the Revolutionary War. The justification for such benefits has never been entirely clear, perhaps varying with different veterans' program. The bonuses promised to soldiers in the Continental army were clearly motivated by the desire to aid recruitment and retention. Compensation for the combat disabled unquestionably reflects acceptance of a moral responsibility to those who lost their ability to work in the course of serving their country. The pensions that were extended a half century later to all surviving Revolutionary War soldiers and their widows perhaps reflected appreciation and nostalgia for the founding generation, and a desire to lift some elderly patriots out of poverty.

The Civil War veterans (with the assistance and prodding of the Grand Army of the Republic) obtained old soldiers' homes that evolved over time into the sprawling 172 V.A. system. Disabled World War I veterans received better vocational rehabilitation than veterans of earlier wars, but their problems readjusting to civilian life convinced many political leaders that a more comprehensive benefits program had to be planned. The 1944 G.I. Bills provided extensive benefits to aid readjustment including academic and vocational educational benefits, housing assistance, unemployment compensation, and job training (see Mosch 1975; Ross 1969). Readjustment benefits, which typically extend well beyond the cessation of hostilities have been a significant feature of U.S. veterans policy ever since.

Veterans' Political Attitudes and Status

The attitudes, values, and morale of armed service veterans are bound to have political consequences for the larger society. Veterans can demoralize and destabilize a society through criticism, bitterness, relentless demands, and even rebellion. They can envitalize a society through idealism, community spirit and hard work. Patriotic veterans' organizations can buoy up military and governmental institutions and make it easier to formulate and further national commitments. On the other hand, hyperpatriotic veterans' organizations can provide a base for political extremism.

Whether or not veterans are integrated into or alienated from their society depends on their military experiences and their reception by civilian society. A large portion of veterans of most wars probably feel, at least initially, somewhat disillusioned, cynical and dissatisfied. This may be a consequence of combat, the misery of the battlefield (see Waller 1944), and the awkward process of readapting to a society that has itself changed while the veteran served in the armed forces.[2]

Even the World War II soldier, who enjoyed the satisfaction of achieving unconditional surrender over the enemy harbored serious grievances against the military (Stouffer, et al. 1949). No doubt the experience of a losing army is far more demoralizing and traumatic. Troops experiencing military defeat are likely to blame "politicians," civilian shirkers, fifth columnists, and their officers. Even victorious soldiers, however, may feel that they were exposed to unnecessary deprivations and risks for the vainglory of politicians and generals, and that while they made immeasurable sacrifices, civilian workers and businessmen flourished. Even those soldiers whose wartime experiences were satisfactory may leave the armed forces deeply disillusioned and embittered because of perceived inequities and insensitivities in the demobilization process. These negative feelings about the military as an institution are not incompatible with a certain nostalgia for army days and the comraderie of army buddies.

The enormous sacrifice exacted from soldiers during combat no doubt triggers great expectations about postwar honors and rewards, particularly if victory is achieved. These expectations are often cultivated by political and military leaders anxious to keep up the morale of the men in the field.

It is not surprising that after demobilization many veterans feel unappreci-ated and cheated. It would be naive to think that such feelings are ex-tinguished by political rhetoric and ticker tape parades. Veterans are initially concerned about jobs, not parades. Postwar civilian society may also be concerned about jobs, particularly about the negative effect that large numbers of job-seeking veterans will have on the economy.

Throughout U.S. history civilian voices have warned that returning vet-erans will corrupt the morals of the society they fought to protect. Civilians are likely to be anxious to forget war in order to get on with the process of reestablishing civilian lifestyles and patterns of consumption.[3] One need only recall the frustration and bitterness of Revolutionary War veterans who justly felt cheated out of the bonuses and pensions the Continental Congress had promised them, or the World War I doughboys who failed in large measure to obtain their bonuses, despite their pathetic march on Washington, D.C. in 1932. It is quite likely that in wartime soldiers cling to an idealized picture of their family, friends, community and nation. All too often the picture is shattered when they encounter disloyalty, petty squab-bling, hypocrisy, greed, and cynicism.

The claims that veterans make on the body politic are fueled by right-eous indignation.[4] Some veterans may well be convinced that the society is supremely indebted to them for its survival, and that no benefits or positive discriminations are undeserved. Others of a more cynical bent may simply believe that, like other interest groups, they are entitled to whatever gov-ernmental largesse they can obtain.

Given the trauma and disillusion of combat and the dashed expectations of return to civilian life, the assimilative tasks of military and civilian institutions are truly daunting. The 1956 President's Commission on Vet-erans' Pensions (1956: 54) sounded a familiar theme when it cited the following observation by the journalist Stanley Frank:

> When World War II ended . . . we were confronted with a domestic crisis that was a graver threat to our national unity than any attack mounted by the enemy. No one knew the solution to a problem as old as war—the returning soldier embittered against the society he fought to protect. The answer never had been found by any country. World War II, involving nearly twice as many men as all our previous wars combined, was a monstrous time bomb that could have split the country into two divisive factions.

The political impact of veterans on their society depends, of course, on numbers as well as temperament. A small group of intensely alienated veterans may be no more than a thorn in the side of a large nation, while a massive number of embittered, disgruntled, or even dissatisfied veterans, constituting a significant percentage of the entire male population, would be an extraordinarily significant political force. The political challenge is to reintegrate veterans into civilian society, and to "cool out" their demands. The quicker veterans come to see themselves as civilians rather than ex-soldiers, the better. Of course, the institutionalization of special veterans' programs and preferences has the opposite effect. They make it symbolically rewarding and economically profitable to maintain one's identity as an ex-soldier.

Whatever veterans "crisis" exists immediately after a war dissipates over time as the veteran and soldier identity weakens for increasing numbers of men, and ultimately as the veterans generation first assimilates and over time begins to die off. War veterans necessarily constitute an ever decreasing percentage of the citizenry unless they are replenished by veterans from a new war. In that case, there are likely to be conflicts of interest between the veterans cohorts. The shrinking number of veterans will have declining political strength; but their demands will be less expensive to meet. It seems ironic that it has taken several decades for veterans of most of the nation's wars to obtain their maximum benefits.

The Economic Impact of Veterans

Closely related to veterans' political impact on civilian society is their economic impact. The costs of pensions and social services to veterans ultimately surpass the actual cost of fighting a war. These costs are not spread out evenly over postwar years. They tend to be highest right after the war when readjustment benefits fall due and many decades later when declining health and finances create demands for free medical care and pensions.

By the late 1920s and early 1930s veterans expenditures consumed approximately 30 percent of the federal budget. While that figure has declined to less than five percent of federal outlays during the 1980s (due to vast increases in other types of federal expenditures), 25 billion dollars is not an insubstantial sum. The V.A. has the third largest budget of any federal agency and the second largest number of employees. Compensation for service-connected disabilities and hospital care constitutes approximately 75 percent of the current V.A. budget.

It is difficult for a society to oppose its veterans' demands because the veterans' political and moral position, especially that of veterans disabled in combat, is so compelling. A small minority of all veterans, the combat disabled, tend to symbolize the veterans' cause. United States veterans' benefits have always assigned top priority to the combat disabled, but efforts to deny substantial benefits to able bodied veterans have failed.[5] Furthermore, the tendency has been to define *service-connected disability* very liberally. Any injury that befalls a soldier while in the service, even while off duty, is defined as service connected. Congress has, since the 1920s, established presumptions that certain post-service illnesses are service connected.

Supporting veterans is like supporting motherhood and apple pie. To oppose veterans' bills is considered politically ill-advised, even suicidal. Additionally, to oppose veterans' claims is, in a sense, to oppose the interests of the military establishment which no doubt desires that veterans be well respected and well treated. Of course, at some level veterans' expenditures will compete with current defense expenditures, and may create incentives for some personnel to leave the active duty armed forces.

Inevitably, veterans interests must collide with the interests of other groups— taxpayers, the poor, active duty personnel. Sometimes such conflicts remain submerged, hardly noticed by competing interest groups. At other times, they bubble to the surface. One example is the realization by women's groups in the 1970s that veterans' employment preferences significantly limit women's job prospects.[6]

Veterans have been so successful in pressing their economic demands because of their numbers and effective organizational structure. There are approximately 30 million veterans in the United States. That means that as many as half of all families are attached to a veteran. By 1990, 60 percent of the male population over sixty-five will be veterans. Numbers alone suggest that veterans can be an interest group of significantly powerful potential. They have already realized a great deal of their potential under the auspices of the American Legion, Veterans of Foreign Wars, and several other organizations. Approximately 25 percent of all veterans belong to one of the organizations. The American Legion has thousands of posts in cities, towns, and villages all over the country. They are a focus of social and community activity and a base for grassroots political lobbying. (See Duffield 1931; Jones 1946; Minott 1962; Mosley 1966).

The veterans' organizations have a close working relationship with the Veterans Administration. The American Legion is given free space in the V.A.'s Washington headquarters and its personnel regularly represent veterans seeking to pursue claims with the V.A.. The veterans' organizations are also extremely active congressional lobbyists. Veterans' bills are among the most popular in the U.S. Congress. Like the V.A., the Congressional committees charged with examining veterans legislation define themselves as veterans advocates. Rather than reducing the V.A.'s budget requests, which is the usual way of handling federal agencies, congressional committees frequently recommend all that is asked for, and, on occasion more (see, e.g., Levitan and Alderman 1973: Ch. 1).

Given the moral and political strength of veterans' groups, it is appropriate to ask how a modern society can limit or "cool out" the demands of its war veterans. Here one might consider the cooptation of the veterans organizations and their inherent fiscal conservatism. (Indeed the American Legion was begun by high civilian and military leaders in order to prevent the World War I veterans' movement from going in other, especially Bolshevik, directions). It is possible that the veterans' organizations could get more for their constituents than they have done, but their close relationship with the Veterans Administration and Congress no doubt reinforces their inclination to be "reasonable" (Levitan and Alderman, 1973: 23). Veterans' groups do not see themselves as adversaries of the United States government or the V.A. They have also been wary of appearing too greedy lest they trigger the kind of backlash that led to the Economy Act of 1933.[7] Problems have also arisen when, on occasion, the organizations have been divided among themselves on key proposals.

The Military Impact of Veterans

So far we have been speaking of veterans as if their formal ties to the military had been completely severed. But veterans could also be kept within the military family for several years or even longer, as has occurred under various reserve forces formulae (after World War II, for example, U.S. soldiers retained a reserves obligation; some were recalled for the Korean War). Under such circumstances, the veteran is not fully a civilian; he remains within the military family, subject in part to military control, discipline and justice, and perhaps eligible for various military perquisites like access to special shops and stores.

Veterans impact on the miltary as well as on civilian society. They inevitably return home with a set of attitudes and beliefs about military service that are passed along to family and friends. They no doubt play an important role in shaping public opinion on such matters as the desirability of serving in the armed forces and of committing armed forces in international conflicts.

Alienated, antimilitary veterans could lobby against making national commitments or committing troops. An army of disaffected war veterans might serve to lower the attractiveness of miltary service, to hinder recruitment, and to raise the level of distrust about the military. Contrariwise, large and powerful promilitary veterans' groups could encourage young men to enlist, help to maintain and improve the status of military careers, provide public support for large military expenditures and for using the armed forces in conflict situations.

Vietnam Veterans

Between 1965 and 1973 approximately 3 million Americans served in Vietnam. The typical tour of duty for a draftee or short term enlistee was one year. Thus, men trickled into Vietnam as individuals, accumulated time, and at the end of a year were transferred to a base in the United States or elsewhere to complete their obligation. From the outset of U.S. involvement, those who opposed the war painted a bleak picture of a so-called veterans problem. Predictions about the maladjustment of Vietnam veterans were offered in terms of a classic tragedy. Just as U.S. forces had brutalized South Vietnam and its people, American G.I.'s would be brutalized by the experience, and return home to wreak havoc and violence on American society; a brutal society would be destroyed by its own forces of external aggression. This tragic scenario was supported, to some extent, by some veterans' groups which strongly opposed the war and wished to atone for their contribution to it. Their members dressed in ragged military uniforms and performed guerilla theatre in the street (see Hellmer 1974). They testified to the prevalence of American atrocities in Vietnam, and expressed the view that the Vietnam veteran could not and should not adjust to American society. The mass media also supported the tragic scenario by giving headline treatment to crimes committed by Vietnam veterans, and by presenting alarming accounts of drug use and addiction among veterans.[8]

Other critics of the war stressed the damage that had been done to the veterans and their need for extensive rehabilitation. (see, e.g., Figley, ed. 1978) Perhaps the point here, conscious or unconscious, was to heighten societal guilt, if not for the destruction of the Vietnamese people then for the victimization of America's sons and brothers. Critics, many academically based researchers, claimed that Vietnam war veterans suffered from postcombat trauma, drug problems, confusion, aimlessness, and all sorts of physical problems. Not surprisingly, this picture did not go unchallenged in Congress, the Veterans Administration, and the academy.

A decade has passed since the end of the war; much of the emotion over the veterans problem has receded. The vast majority of veterans have long since relegated their veteran status to memory. In 1982, a monument to military personnel who died in the war was erected in Washington, D.C.[9]

On May 7, 1985, the Vietnam veterans at long last received the ticker-tape parade they had always wanted. According to the *New York Times* (May 8, p. 1), a million spectators lined 5th Avenue to throw confetti and cheer. The time is now ripe for a new look at whether the Vietnam veterans constitute a unique social problem.[10]

Spirited debaters have argued about the morale and combat effectiveness of the U.S. soldier in Vietnam. Gabriel and Savage (1973), among others, have charged that in the early 1970s American military forces in Vietnam were dissolving, discipline had disintegrated, platoons regularly refused to carry out combat assignments, fraggings were a constant worry, drug abuse was epidemic, awol's and desertions reached record levels, and the average soldier tried to avoid dangerous assignments. Naturally, there are those who strongly disagree.

There can be no clearcut resolution of this debate. No doubt morale and combat effectiveness varied across branches, divisions, brigades, companies, and even platoons. Still, in my view, while the Gabriel and Savage account is exaggerated, the experience of U.S. forces was very negative, especially after 1969. Perhaps for the first time in American history there was a visible antiwar movement within and around the armed forces, and antiwar sentiments were commonplace. Compared with other wars, a larger number and far larger proportion of young men who served in Vietnam left the service antimilitary, antisociety, and personally troubled.

This hardly means, however, that the Vietnam veterans who began to appear in the late 1960s and 1970s were killers, human time bombs, or potential revolutionaries, as they were sometimes portrayed. Nor, despite extensive drug use in Vietnam, did large numbers become part of the addict subculture after they left the service. To keep matters in perspective, we should not forget that alienation, intense antigovernment feeling, drug use and personal anxiety were prevalent among the entire generation of young people during this period.

Most of those who have written about Vietnam veterans assert that they are different from veterans of any other war because they returned home in a trickle rather than in a triumphant wave, and because they were ignored or, even worse, despised rathered than revered. It is sometimes said that the larger society blamed the soldiers for losing the war, or for committing atrocities, or simply projected its own war guilt onto the soldiers. All of these charges are exaggerated.

It is true that Vietnam veterans were not treated to ticker tape parades as were the veterans of the two world wars, but neither were the Korean War veterans who are unaccountably ignored by many writers. Like the Vietnam veterans, the Korean War veterans trickled back into American society after completing their rotation in the war zone, and they too failed to achieve a decisive unconditional victory. In any case, too much can be made of the absence of ticker tape parades. Surely, many veterans of the world wars, especially World War I, must have viewed such symbolic recognition cynically when they found themselves without work and lagging occupationally and socially behind those in their cohort who avoided military service altogether.[11] In the decade following World War I, the plight of many veterans became quite desperate.[12]

Nor is it accurate to say that Vietnam veterans were generally dishonored and despised; this view may be biased by observations at a few liberal colleges and universities. Families and communities organized tributes and homecoming celebrations for their sons and neighbors. The vast majority of Americans did not blame the Vietnam veterans for losing the war or for committing atrocities. Poll data show that, to the extent that blame was laid, it was put at the doorstep of civilian political leaders. Not even the Mai Lai massacre produced profound antimilitary or antiveteran feeling. Most Americans tended to dismiss the massacre as a justified response to provocation or as a misguided action by a single unstable officer. It is true, of course, that the Vietnam War was unpopular, but previous wars, especially World War I and Korea may seem far more popular in retrospect than they were at the time.

As seems to be the case after every war, the Vietnam veterans did indeed experience difficulties (greater difficulties than Vietnam-era veterans who did not serve in Vietnam) in finding civilian employment, despite new job training and placement programs initiated by the Department of Defense and the Veterans Administration, and liberalized unemployment benefits. To a large extent, this situation was the result of the national economy's stagflation. Ten years later, Vietnam veterans do not have significantly higher unemployment rates than non-Vietnam veterans in their age cohort (Center for Policy Research, 1981:197). Surprisingly, Vietnam veterans are earning more than their peers who did not go to Vietnam, and black Vietnam veterans are much more successful economically than their non-veteran peers. It cannot be demonstrated that Vietnam service produced a lasting economic disadvantage for those who served. While the evidence is too flimsy at this point to accept the opposite conclusion—that Vietnam veterans were made better off by their military service—such a conclusion has frequently been reached by students of earlier groups of veterans.

Much writing, commentary, and study during and immediately after the war concerned the mental and emotional problems of Vietnam veterans. Despite lower rates of psychiatric breakdown in the war zone than in previous U.S. wars, certain mental health personnel claimed that Vietnam veterans were experiencing or would experience massive problems (see Figley, ed. 1978). Some of these specialists posited the existence of a post-Vietnam stress disorder that explained certain violent crimes committed by Vietnam veterans. Lawyers soon urged the courts to recognize this syndrome as a partial defense to a criminal charge, but the courts were generally unpersuaded. I do not believe that there is any solid reason to believe that Vietnam veterans are more violent and more criminogenic than others in their age cohort (Center for Policy Studies 1981: 373-377).

The inservice antiwar movement carried over after separation from service. Vietnam Veterans Against the War sought to make American society accept its war guilt. It urged veterans to maintain their veteran identity for political reasons and so that they could work through the trauma of having fought in an illegitimate war. Certain antiwar psychiatrists, most visibly Yale's Robert J. Lifton, initiated veterans' "rap groups," a type of group therapy and political consciousness raising. Without working through one's war experiences and feelings, according to Lifton, there could be no release from the guilt that most Vietnam survivors experience (see Lifton 1973). Lifton's work has been enormously influential among psychiatrists and psychologists working with and studying Vietnam veterans. It is hardly surprising that many Vietnam veterans accepted the view of themselves as troubled, guilt ridden, and ill-adjusted; no doubt, in the manner of a self-fulfilling prophesy, this made it harder to reassimilate into civilian society.[13]

Dire predictions of psychiatric and emotional breakdown never materialized. The definitive 1981 five-volume study of the Vietnam veterans by the Center For Policy Research did find that Vietnam veterans experience greater stress and mental and emotional difficulties than service personnel who served elsewhere than in Vietnam during the same time period. But the differences are neither large nor dramatic.

The Vietnam Veterans and the Veterans Administration

Another claim frequently made by antiwar and veterans' activists is that the V.A. and veterans' organizations were insensitive and unresponsive to the Vietnam veterans, and that, for their part, the Vietnam veterans were disaffected from the V.A.. Thus, critics claimed that Vietnam veterans would not come to the veterans' hospitals for help with psychiatric problems, that the veterans' hospitals were poorly set up to respond to both drug problems and acute combat injuries, and that the V. A. was unresponsive, even hostile, to disability claims, particularly those attributed to agent orange.

It is far beyond the scope of this chapter to present a comprehensive assessment of the responses of Congress and the V.A. to the Vietnam veterans (see Levitan and Alderman 1973: Ch. 4). If, however, our government had truly turned its back on Vietnam veterans, that would have constituted an extraordinary break with the last half-century trend of providing increasingly generous benefits to war veterans. Not surprisingly, it is not true. In part the criticism and discontent can be attributed to the lack of realism of some critics who compare the V.A. with an imaginary picture of how a bureaucracy "should" function. The massive V.A., despite its unquestioned commitment to helping veterans, suffers from all of the ills that afflict large governmental bureaucracies: inflexibility, petty-mindedness, resistance to change, paperwork snarls, and internecine warfare. I say this not to excuse any failures, but to place the criticisms in perspective.[14] Unlike other social welfare bureaucracies, the V.A. (whether by legislation, rulemaking or politics) administers its programs very liberally, resolving most policy and factual disputes for the benefit of the veterans. It also enjoys the practically unique position of having as much money as it needs to carry out its programs.

One's overall assessment of the Veterans Administration will be determined, to a large extent, by one's assumption about the capacity of bureaucracies to solve problems. For example, it may be unfair, as Paul Starr (1974) has done, to charge the Veterans Administration with failure to meet the needs of drug abusers. One is hard-pressed to find many examples of successful drug abuse programs; it would be an understatement to say that addicts are a notoriously intractable and difficult group to treat. It is not surprising that the Veterans Administration was slow to come up with reasonable programs to assist addicts and other drug abusers. Likewise, to take another of Starr's criticisms, it may well be true that the Department of Defense's employment readjustment programs "failed to meet its goals or live up to its promises," but few, if any, of the Department of Labor's job training programs since the early days of the Great Society can be pointed to as clear successes.

Critics originally pointed out that the Vietnam veterans used the G.I. Bill educational and retraining benefits at a much lower rate than veterans of earlier wars. This was cited as evidence of alienation and the irrelevance of traditional government policy. Over time, however, benefits were increased substantially, and within several years the use of the G.I. Bill by Vietnam veterans surpassed use by previous generations of veterans; in the final analysis, approximately 75 percent of Vietnam veterans utilized their academic and vocational education benefits.

Starr does make a valid point when he notes that Vietnam veterans found the V.A., particularly its hospital system, primarily geared toward treating older World War II veterans, many of whom were chronically ill or disabled.[15] The V.A. should hardly be indicted for this. The World War II veterans were (and remain) the largest group of veterans in the United States. As they age, more and more turn to the V.A. for medical care. In the mid-1960s, the V.A. hospital system was understandably concerned with caring for the elderly and chronically incapacitated, and somewhat unprepared to deal with acute combat injuries, particularly in the early years of the war. But, as Starr also notes, major strides were made to retool the system to respond to the younger patients. Because of medical advances, the war-injured Vietnam veteran was far better cared for than his predecessors. President Carter's appointment of Vietnam veteran and triple amputee Max Cleland, as head of the Veterans Administration certainly attests to his Administration's desire that Vietnam veterans receive top priority in the V.A. system. Indeed, many World War I and World War II

V.A. hospital patients began to complain that Vietnam veterans were receiving disproportionate attention and resources.

It may well be true that the V.A. could not respond effectively to the emotional and mental problems of many returning veterans. But we must bear in mind the depressing record of civilian public mental health bureaucracies. It is sad that there are insufficient mental health resources, and that most resources are spent on those with most money. Despite superior resources, it is hard even for the V.A. to recruit talented psychiatrists and psychologists. It is also unfortunate that the promise of mental health treatment remains unfulfilled. There are no guaranteed cures; despite treatments many seriously ill patients fail to improve.

Congress responded to the charge that Vietnam veterans were disaffected from the V.A. hospitals by establishing outreach centers across the country. The V.A. consistently fought these centers, probably seeing them as a challenge to its traditional institutional and management structures (National Academy of Sciences 1977; V.A. Response 1977), but the centers have survived. Whether the outreach centers will or should become permanent V.A. fixtures is another question.

Agent Orange Controversy

During the years following the Vietnam War some Vietnam veterans began complaining of a wide variety of rashes, illnesses, neurological and psychiatric problems, sexual dysfunctions, cancers, miscarriages by their wives, and chromosomal abnormalties in their children.[16] Over time, more men connected their medical problems with their war experiences and, more specifically, to contamination by dioxin, a toxic substance present in agent orange, a chemical defoliant extensively used by U.S. forces to clear the jungles of South Vietnam.[17]

The V.A. claimed that there was insufficient scientific or statistical evidence to support the claim that agent orange had caused these health problems. Other than the skin disease chloracne, the V.A. refused to recognize alleged agent orange illnesses for purposes of medical care or service connected disability compensation.[18] The V.A.'s attitude has frequently been cited as evidencing a certain insensitivity if not hostility toward veterans. This is a distorted interpretation. The V.A. and the Veterans of Foreign Wars have opposed recognition of agent orange claims that American Legion and Vietnam Veterans of America have favored, on the ground that to do otherwise would undermine the principle that compensation should only be paid to those with proved combat-related injuries. They argued that the legislation would politicize the compensation program. They are concerned about opening the floodgates too wide and possibly jeopardizing the whole compensation system. In the past Congress has legislated that certain diseases (e.g. malaria, tuberculosis) are service connected if they appear within a year or two of separation from service. What makes the agent orange claims different is the amorphousness of the supposed disease(s). Practically any veteran's disability or illness, physical, genetic or psychological, can and has been blamed on agent orange. Taken to the limits of its logic, the acceptance of the claimants' position on agent orange would entitle all Vietnam veterans to free V.A. medical care and disability compensation.

The veterans relentlessly pressed their position with the V. A., Congress, and in the courts. Agent orange became a kind of rallying point for the waning Vietnam veterans' movement of the late 1970s and early 1980s. The cause probably benefitted enormously from the environmental (anti-dioxin) consciousness of the period and especially from a powerful television documentary which strongly supported the veterans' position.

The veterans achieved a major victory in 1981 when, despite the opposition of the veterans' organizations and the V.A., Congress gave the V.A. discretionary authority to provide hospital and nursing home care for agent-orange type illnesses despite the lack of sufficient scientific evidence to show that such illnesses were caused by agent orange exposure (The Veterans Health Care Training, and Small Business Loan Act of 1981, P.L. 97-72, 95 Stat. 1047). A veteran needed only to show that he could have been exposed to agent orange in order to receive treatment; in other words, service in Vietnam during the period in which agent orange was in use creates a sufficient presumption to justify a right to free treatment. By October, 1983, 125,649 veterans had received an initial physical examination based upon complaints of agent orange contamination. (See GAO, 1983) The legislation also provides for a massive scientific study of agent orange to be carried out by the Center for Disease Control. The study is not expected to be completed until the late 1980s.

Although this federal legislation represented a substantial victory, the veterans remained ineligible for disability compensation for alleged agent orange illnesses and injuries. However, they continued to file disability claims, more than 18,500 by October 1983; only the small number of claims based upon chloracne were granted. They also persisted in their lobbying. In 1984, a divided House Committee on Veterans Affairs favorably reported a bill to authorize temporary disability payments to Vietnam veterans suffering from soft tissue sarcomas, porphria cutanea, and chloracne, unless it could be shown that these diseases had been contracted by causes other than agent orange exposure during military service (The Agent Orange and Atomic Veterans Relief Act of 1984 [H.R. 1961]).

The veterans claiming agent orange injuries also sought compensation from the agent orange manufacturers of whom Dow Chemical was the largest. The manufacturers vigorously contested the suits. Legal skirmishing dragged on for years. The companies argued that there was no reliable scientific evidence to support a finding that agent orange causes the types of injuries of which the veterans complain. Furthermore, they disputed the ability of individual plaintiffs to prove that their particular illness or injury had been caused by agent orange in Vietnam, rather than by other factors traceable to the claimant's civilian environment or genetic endowment. Indeed, the companies pointed out that the Vietnam veterans had undoubtedly been exposed to many types of chemicals and diseases in Vietnam. Finally, the companies claimed that if the courts were to find them responsible for the veterans' health problems, ultimate liability should rest with the federal government which had contracted with the chemical companies for the production of agent orange; the companies argued that to cripple financially the manufacturers of agent orange (the suits alleged damages amounting to tens of billions of dollars) would chill all sorts of future defense contracting during wartime.

The companies sought to make the federal government a party to the suit by a familiar technique of impleading. The government, in turn, successfully sought dismissal as a party on the basis of a 1950s Supreme Court decision, *Feres v. United States* (1950), which had held that the federal government was not liable in private lawsuits (under the Federal Tort Claims Act) to injured armed services personnel. The Court concluded that veterans were meant to be compensated by the Veterans Administration programs, not by the courts in private lawsuits.[19] To hold otherwise, it was suggested, would jeopardize U.S. military effectiveness by permitting subordinates to challenge their superiors' decisions in civil courts.[20]. In subsequent litigation, however, a few lower courts held that the families of injured servicemen were not barred by *Feres* from suing the federal government, if they themselves had sustained some injury. The agent orange litigation amounted either to a head-on assault on the *Feres* doctrine or an effort to find further exceptions and qualifications.

As even this brief account suggests, the agent orange lawsuits emerged as one of the most complicated pieces of litigation in U.S. history. There were novel legal issues concerning federal jurisdiction, class actions, and governmental immunity for injuries caused to active duty military personnel and their families. There were thousands of plaintiffs and potentially hundreds of thousands more (including Australian veterans). On the other side, there were more than a dozen chemical companies with complicated and confusing claims about whether, when, what kind, and how much defoliant they had produced, and how much of what they had produced had actually been dropped on South Vietnam. There were also the unresolved and massively complex scientific issues concerning the basic questions, how toxic is agent orange and what kinds of health problems, if any, can be caused by various levels of exposure? Even if all these problems could be overcome, there remained the awesome problem of proving that any particular individual's illness was caused by agent orange contamination in Vietnam.

The lawsuit dragged on. How to manage the extraordinarily complex litigation challenged some of the nation's best legal and judicial minds.[21] Finally in 1984, under the leadership of federal district judge Jack Weinstein of the Eastern District on New York, the case was settled for $180 million, to be contributed by the the various manufacturers according to a formula of the defendants' design.[22] The settlement involves no finding that agent orange is responsible for any of the injuries experienced by the plaintiffs. A mechanism will be set up whereby veterans can apply for compensation from this fund, but the fund's custodians will have to keep in mind that many more veterans and their families will make claims now that money is available, and that many who are not now suffering any ill health will undoubtedly develop problems linkable to agent orange over the next decade or decades.

Many veterans have criticized the settlement for being too small. While there is undoubtedly a case to be made for this view, one cannot help sensing that more is at stake here than the amount of money available to compensate alleged agent orange victims. There is the symbolism of a settlement which, once again, resulted in something less than an unconditional victory for the Vietnam veterans. And there may also be a sense that with the settlement of the case there are no more issues to keep the Vietnam veterans movement alive.

Notes

1. No exhaustive survey of American veteran benefits could be presented in such a short chapter. The Veterans Administration lists and describes these programs in more than 70 pages in one of its many brochures urging veterans to take advantage of their entitlements. (See Fact Sheet on Federal Benefits for Veterans and Dependants.) There are disability pensions for those who have been disabled while serving in the armed forces, whether or not their injury occurred in combat. A very liberal approach is taken on the question of whether a particular illness or injury is service connected. For example, tuberculosis which is diagnosed within two years of terminating military service is automatically treated as service connected for purposes of veterans benefits. The surviving relatives of servicemen who are killed also receive pensions. Those veterans who are disabled in civilian life are entitled to pensions when they reach age 65, or at any age if they are destitute. All veterans and their families since 1975 are entitled to free treatment from the massive veterans' hospital system for any illnesses or injuries, service connected or not. Veterans are also provided with

life insurance, and with special loan programs. There are lifetime hiring preferences in the federal civil service and in most of the states.
2. As for the World War I veteran, see Waller, 1944: 95.

   The soldier is glad to come home, but he comes home angry. In the early months of 1919, the writer talked with a great many other demobilized soldiers on Chicago streets. Although he had felt something of the serviceman's rebellion, he was as astonished as any civilian at the intensity of their fury. They were angry about something; it was not clear just what. The writer questioned many of them, but found not one who could put his grievances into understandable form. But there was never any mistaking their temper. They hated somebody for something. There were angry men on West Madison Street in 1919, and as one learned later, there was rancor on Market Street in St. Louis and at Eighth and Race in Philadelphia, and in all the little angry knots where soldiers gathered were bitterness and disillusion and discontent.
3. Waller (1944: 178) reports that "A hero of the 1918 A.E.F. tells the following story of his return to New York City: "We had a parade but it was nothing like we had seen in the movies. The guys who didn't see any action got the great applause. By the time we got back, the country was fed up with these war heroes . . . I remember I met a girl I knew and thought she would treat me like a hero. She acted as though she had seen me the day before."
4. "From 1919 to the outbreak of war in 1941, veterans demanded that society repay them for their wartime sacrifices. Each successful demand seemed to increase, not decrease, their sense of unredeemed sacrifice." (Ross 1969:6)
5. Presidents Wilson, Coolidge, Hoover and Roosevelt all tried to limit benefits for able-bodied veterans. Congress frequently overrode presidential vetoes of veterans spending measures. In vetoing a 1935 veterans bill, President Roosevelt observed that "able-bodied Veterans should be accorded no treatment different from that accorded to other citizens who did not wear a uniform during the World War. (Ross 1969: 18)
6. Women's groups tried unsuccessfully to have these preferences declared unconstitutional. (see Personnel Administrator of Massachusetts v. Feeney, 1980)
7. The 1933 Economy Act (P.L.2, 73 Cong. March 26, 1933), passed during President Franklin Roosevelt's first hundred days, gave the president sweeping power to revise veterans' benefits. F.D.R. used this authority to make substantial cuts. (See Ross 1969: 25-28)
8. Similar fearful and negative stereotypes about violent veterans have arisen during each of America's wars. Speaking of World War II, Willard Waller (1944: 286) wrote: "Even now the newspapers contain frequent stories of crimes committed by shell-shocked or psychoneurotic veterans, and these cases are certain to multiply when demobilization turns loose some millions whose personalities have been warped by their experiences."
9. The Vietnam War Memorial was itself the focus of extraordinary controversy. The winning design, a simple black V-shaped marble sculpture, was criticized by some Vietnam veterans as being "a tribute to Jane Fonda" in that it reflected shame and guilt rather than pride. Antiwar veterans more or less liked the memorial, perhaps seeing in it the symbolic closure necessary to put the war behind them. On Veterans Day 1984, a second more "realistic" and more "affirmative" memorial was placed near the first memorial.

10. Although the debate over the mindset and adjustment problems of the Vietnam veterans tends to treat Vietnam veterans as a homogeneous category, those who actually served in the Vietnam war zone did not share a unitary experience. For example, some served on ships or in administrative positions in relatively secure military bases. Perhaps only about fifteen percent of those who served in Vietnam experienced combat, although a far larger percentage lived under the threat of enemy attack. Furthermore, because the Vietnam War lasted such a long time (as compared with other American wars), it is likely that the experiences of military personnel differed according to date of service. It is probably accurate to say that service in Vietnam was a far more positive experience in the early years (1965-1968) than later on (1969-1973) when antiwar feeling became increasingly widespread and intense, and the possibility of obtaining the enemy's unconditional surrender seemed more and more unrealizable.

11. See Havighurst, et al. 1951:70. "Welcoming ceremonies of a more formal nature appeared to disturb the veteran less [than family celebrations]—perhaps because he felt such functions were largely irrelevant to his actual return to civilian life."

12. Even veterans of World War II, America's most popular war, were seriously disgruntled about the demobilization process and often discouraged about the difficulties of readjusting to civilian life.

> During years of travel and repression in the military environment, he had dreamed of coming home—and when he did return, it was to a home with a housing shortage, a clothing shortage, a beer shortage, a shortage even of automobiles with which he might have gratified his post service restlessness. (Havighurst, 1951: 85)

13. Paul Starr (1973: 35) comments: "Certainly many veterans are ill at ease about their experiences in the war, but it would be wrong to suggest that guilt is a prevalent emotion among them. It is, however, very prevalent among these who write about Vietnam veterans.

14. Levitan and Alderman (1973: 164) put the matter far more positively:
> Given the caveat that some skeletons may remain hidden in the closets, the public record of the V.A. is surprisingly free of blemishes. The difficulties which have been noted in the delivery of some services are bound to be part of a large bureaucratic organization. In most cases V.A. services are effectively delivered, with a maximum of respect for the recipient and a minimum of delay from government intricacies. Contrary to the conventional wisdom about the rigidity that engulfs long-established bureaucratic organizations, the V.A. officialdom remains unusually sensitive to the needs of its clientele.

15. The V.A. hospital system provides free health care to veterans with service-connected illnesses and disabilities. It treats all of their medical problems, not just those that are service connected. The V.A. hospital system is also open to any veteran who is 65 or over, or receiving a veteran's pension, or is deemed medically needy. For the most part, a veteran's signed statement claiming to be medically needy is taken as conclusive on the issue.

16. These include changes in skin color; chloracne rashes; photosensitivity; migrain headaches; recurring nausea; vomitting, dizziness, and diarrhea; numbness and tingling in the extremities; intolerance to alcohol; loss of sex drive; neurological and psychological problems, including violent rages, mood

swings and memory lapses; sudden debilitating weight loss; premature aging; miscarriages of wives; birth defects in children; cancers.

17. U.S. air forces began spraying herbicides on the dense jungles of South Vietnam in the early 1960s in order to destroy the foliage which provided camouflage and food for the enemy. Between 1965 and 1970 approximately 10 million gallons of agent orange was sprayed over 10 percent of the land mass of the country. Any U.S. soldier could have been exposed to agent orange through skin contact or by eating or drinking contaminated food or water. There have been numerous hearings on agent orange in both houses of Congress. See Agent Orange Update, Hearings before the Senate Comm. on Veterans Affairs, 96th Congress, 2d. Sess. 799 (1980); House Committee on Veterans Affairs 1984.

18. The results of one preliminary epidemiological study (known as Ranch Hand) show no statistically significant health effects for Air Force personnel actually involved in spraying agent orange over Vietnam between 1962 and 1971. See report (98-S92) accompanying Agent Orange and Atomic Veterans Relief Act of 1984.

19. *Stencel Aero Engineering Corp. v. United States*, 431 U.S. 666 (1977) extends *Feres* to third party cases in which the plaintiffs could not recover directly from the government.

20. This decision hints at some very interesting questions. What should be the government's responsibility to its military and civilian citizens for injuries sustained during wartime? Should the government be responsible for injuries sustained due to negligent military orders and tactics, negligent security, or poorly performing equipment? Should war contractors even bear responsibility for defective or injurious weapons and other machinery?

21. The massive agent orange litigation generated numerous judicial opinions as it progressed. See in Re Agent Orange, 475 F. Supp. 928 (E.D.N.Y. 1979); In Re Agent Orange, 506 F. Supp. 753 (E.D.N.Y. 1980); In Re Agent Orange, 635 F. 2d 987 (2d Cir. 1980); In Re Agent Orange, 534 F. Supp. 1046 (E.D.N.Y. 1982); In Re Agent Orange, 571 F. Supp. 481 (E.D.N.Y. 1983). The settlement was announced on May 7, 1984. See the account in the *New York Times*, May 8, 1984, B4.

22. In re "Agent Orange" Product Liability Litigation, MDL, No. 381 (JBW), 597 F. Supp. 740 (1984); In re "Agent Orange" Product Liability Litigation, MDL No. 381 (JBW), 603 F. Supp. 239 (1985).

List of Legal Cases

Alexander v. Trustees of Boston University, 584 F. Supp. 282 (D. Mass. 1984), revs'd 766 F.2d 630 (1st cir. 1985).
Bemis v. Whalen, 341 F. Supp. 1289 (S.D. Cal. 1972).
Boblin v. Board of Education, 403 F. Supp. 1095 (D. Hawaii 1975).
Brown v. Glines, 444 U.S. 348 (1980).
Burns v. Wilson, 346 U.S. 137 (1953).
Butler v. Perry, 240 U.S. 328 (1916).
Cafeteria Workers v. McElroy, 367 U.S. 886 (1961).
Carlson v. Schlesinger, 511 F.2d 1327 (D.C. Cir. 1975).
Chappell v. Wallace, 103 S. Ct. 2362 (1983).
Committee for G.I. Rights v. Callaway, 518 F.2d 466 (D.C. Cir. 1975).
Crawford v. Cushman, 531 F.2d 1114 (2nd Cir. 1976).
Culver v. Secretary of the Army, 559 F.2d 622 (D.C Cir. 1977).
Daigle v. Warner, 490 F.2d 358 (9th Cir. 1973).
Doe v. Selective Service System, 557 F. Supp. 937 (D. Minn. 1983).
Feres v. United States, 340 U.S. 135 (1950).
Fillette v. United States, 401 U.S. 437 (1971).
Flower v. United States, 407 U.S. 197 (1972).
Giles v. Secretary of the Army, 627 F.2d 554 (D.C. Cir. 1980).
Gilligan v. Morgan, 413 U.S. 1 (1973).
Greer v. Spock, 424 U.S. 828 (1976).
Harmon v. Brucker, 355 U.S. 579 (1958).
Hildebrand v. State, 507 P.2d 1323 (Okla. Crim. App. 1973).
Howze v. United States, 272 F.2d 146 (9th Cir. 1959).
Hubert v. State, 504 P.2d 1245 (Okla. Crim. App. 1972).
Hurtado v. United States, 410 U.S. 578 (1973).
In re Grimley, 137 U.S. 144 (1890).
Jabara v. Webster, 691 F.2d 272 (6th Cir. 1982), cert. denied, 104 S. Ct. 193 (1983).
Kasey v. Commissioner, 457 F.2d 369 (9th Cir.), cert. denied, 409 U.S. 869 (1972).
Kinsella v. Singleton, 361 U.S. 234 (1960).
Laird v. Tatum, 408 U.S. 1 (1972).
Luther v. Bordon, 48 U.S. (7 How.) 115 (1845).

Martin v. Mott, 12 Wheat. 19 (1872).
McElroy v. Guagliardo, 361 U.S. 281 (1959).
Middendorf v. Henry, 425 U.S. 25 (1976).
Mulloy v. United States, 398 U.S. 410 (1970).
Novak v. Rumsfeld, 423 F. Supp. 971 (N.D. Cal. 1976).
O'Callahan v. Parker, 395 U.S. 258 (1969).
Orloff v. Willoughby, 345 U.S. 83 (1953).
Ostereich v. Selective Service Board, 393 U.S. 233 (1968).
Parisi v. Davidson, 405 U.S. 34 (1972).
Parker v. Levy, 478 F.2d 722 (3rd Cir. 1973).
Parker v. Levy, 417 U.S. 733 (1974).
Personnel Administrator of Massachusetts v. Feeney, 442 U.S. 256 (1979).
Reid v. Covert, 354 U.S. 1 (1956).
Relford v. United States Disciplinary Commandant, 41 U.S. 355 (1971).
Robertson v. United States, 165 U.S. 275 (1897).
Rostker v. Goldberg, 453 U.S. 57 (1981).
Schlesinger v. Councilman, 420 U.S. 738 (1975).
Secretary of the Navy v. Huff, 444 U.S. 453 (1980).
Selective Service Draft Law Cases, 245 U.S. 366 (1918).
Selective Service System v. Minnesota Public Interest Research Group, 104 S. Ct. 3348 (1984).
Spock v. David, 469 F.2d 1047 (3rd Cir. 1972).
Stencel Aero Engineering Corp. v. United States, 431 U.S. 666 (1977).
Sugarman v. Dougall, 413 U.S. 634 (1973).
Toth v. Quarles, 350 U.S. 11 (1955).
United States v. Alderman, 22 U.S.C.M.A. 298 (1973).
United States v. Alsup, 17 M.J. 166 (C.M.A. 1984).
United States v. Banks, 380 F. Supp. 363 (D.S.D. 1974).
United States v. Berry, 1 U.S.C.M.A. 235 (1952).
United States v. Booker, 5 M.J. 238 (C.M.A. 1977).
United States v. Brown, 23 U.S.C.M.A. 162 (1974).
United States v. Casper, 541 F.2d 1275 (8th Cir. 1976).
United States v. Catlow, 23 U.S.C.M.A. 142 (1974).
United States v. Clay, 1 U.S.C.M.A. (1951).
United States v. Courtney, 24 U.S.C.M.A. 280 (1976).
United States v. Daniels, 19 U.S.C.M.A. 529 (1970).
United States v. Donohew, 18 U.S.C.M.A. 149 (1969).
United States v. Douglas, 23 U.S.C.M.A. 178 (1976).
United States v. Dumas, 23 U.S.C.M.A. 278 (1975).
United States v. Harvey, 19 U.S.C.M.A. 539 (1970).
United States v. Jacoby, 11 U.S.C.M.A. 428 (1960).

United States v. Jaramillo, 380 F. Supp. 1375 (D. Neb. 1974), appeal dismissed, 510 F.2d 808 (8th Cir. 1975).

United States v. Jordan, 24 U.S.C.M.A. 156 (1976).

United States v. Larionoff, 431 U.S. 864 (1977).

United States v. Lockwood, 15 M.J. 1 (C.M.A. 1983).

United States v. O'Brien, 391 U.S. 367 (1968).

United States v. Red Feather, 392 F. Supp. 916 (D.S.D. 1975). aff'd sub. nom. *United States v. Casper*, 541 F.2d 1275 (8th Cir. 1976), cert. denied, 430 U.S. 970 (1977).

United States v. Rinehart, 8 U.S.C.M.A. 402 (1957).

United States v. Rivera, 6 M.J. 535 (N.C.M.R. 1978).

United States v. Roberts, 25 U.S.C.M.A. 39 (1976).

United States v. Rowel, 24 U.S.C.M.A. 137 (1976).

United States v. Russo, 23 U.S.C.M.A. 511 (1975).

United States v. Schmucker, F.2d (6th Cir. 1983).

United States v. Seeger, 380 U.S. 163 (1965).

United States v. Trottier, 9 M.J. 337 (C.M.A. 1980).

United States v. Walden, 490 F.2d 372 (4th Cir. 1983), cert. denied, 416 U.S. 983 (1984).

United States v. Wappler, 2 U.S.C.M.A. 398 (1953).

United States v. Ware, 24 U.S.C.M.A. 102 (1976).

United States v. Wayte, 549 F. Supp. 1376 (C.D.# Cal. 1982).

United States v. Wayte, 710 F.2d 1385 (9th Cir. 1983).

United States v. Wayte, 105 S.Ct. 1524 (1985).

United States v. Welsh, 398 U.S. 333 (1970).

Williamson v. Vardeman, 674 F.2d 1211 (8th Cir. 1982).

Wolman v. United States, 542 F. Supp. 84 (D.D.C. 1982).

Youngstown Sheet and Tube Co. v. Sawyer, 343 U.S. 579 (1952).

References

Agent Orange Update. Hearings Before the Senate Committee on Veterans Affairs. 96th Congress, 2d. Sess. 799, 1980.

Albright, Penrose L. Speech before the Federal Bar Association's Annual Convention, San Juan, P.R. Reported in *United States Law Week* 46 (1977): 2262.

American Bar Association. *The Constitutionality of a Mandatory Non-Military National Service Obligation.* 1984.

American Criminal Law Review 13 "The Posse Comitatus Act: Reconstruction Politics Reconsidered." (1976): 703-35.

American Federation of State, County, and Municipal Employees. "Public Sector Dispute Resolution." Adopted at the 23rd AFSCME International Convention, June 1978.

Army Lawyer. "The 1984 Manual for Courts-Martial: Significant Changes and Potential Issues." (July 1984): 1-58.

Bachman, Jerald G.; Blair, John D.; and Segal, David R. *The All-Volunteer Force: A Study of Ideology in the Military Force.* Ann Arbor: University of Michigan Press, 1977.

Bennet, Douglas J. Jr. "Congress in Foreign Policy: Who Needs It?" *Foreign Affairs* 57 (1978): 40-50.

Bernard, William Spencer, ed. *American Immigration Policy: A Reappraisal.* 1st ed. New York: Harper, 1950.

Bickel, Alexander M. *The Morality of Consent.* New Haven: Yale University Press, 1975.

Biderman, Albert, D. "Toward Redefining the Military." *Teachers College Record* 73 (1971) 47-58.

Black, Charles. "Constitutional Problems in Compulsory National Services." *Yale Law Report* (1967): 19-21.

Blackman, John L. *Presidential Seizure in Labor Disputes.* Cambridge: Harvard University Press, 1967.

Bryant, Clifton D. *Khaki-Collar Crime: Deviant Behavior in the Military Context.* New York: Free Press, 1979.

Bundy, McGeorge. "Vietnam, Watergate and Presidential Powers." *Foreign Affairs* 58 (1979-80): 397-407.

Bureau of the Census. *United States Department of Commerce Statistical Abstract of the United States.* 1976.

Carliner, David. *The Rights of Aliens: The Basic ACLU Guide to an Alien's Rights.* New York: Avon, 1977.

Carnegie Council on Policy Studies in Higher Education. *Giving Youth a Better Chance: Options for Education, Work and Service.* San Francisco: Josey-Bass, 1979.

Carter, James Earl. Selective Service Reform Message from the President of the United States transmitting his Proposal for Selective Service Reform, Together with a Draft of Proposed Legislation to Amend the Military Selective Service Act to Allow the Registration of Both Men and Women pursuant to Section 81, of Public Law 96-107. Washington, D.C.: Government Printing Office, 1980.

———. "Undocumented Aliens: Message to the Congress." *Weekly Compilation of Presidential Documents* 13 (1977): 1170-75.

Cartright, David, and Thurmond, Strom. "Unions in the Military: Pro and Con." Washington, D.C., American Enterprise Institute, 1977.

Center for Policy Research, Legacies of Vietnam: Comparative Adjustment of Veterans and their Peers: A Study Proposed for the Veterans Administration, Washington, Government Printing Office, 1981.

Chase, James. "Foreign Policy and the Democratic Process: Is a Foreign Policy Consensus Possible?" *Foreign Affairs* 57 (1978): 1-16.

Choper, Jesse. *Judicial Review and the National Political Process: A Functional Reconsideration of the Role of the Supreme Court.* Chicago: University of Chicago Press, 1980.

Coffey, Kenneth J. *Strategic Implications of the All-Volunteer Force: The Strategic Defense of Central Europe.* Chapel Hill: University of North Carolina Press, 1979.

Columbia Survey of Human Rights Law. "Invalid Disruption Rules for CO Alternative Service." 1971, 3:136-168.

Committee for the Study of National Service. *Youth and the Needs of the Nation.* Washington, D.C.: The Potomac Institute, 1979.

———. *National Youth Service: What's at Stake?* Washington, D.C.: The Potomac Institute, 1980.

Committee on Military Justice and Military Affairs of the Association of the Bar of the City of New York. A Bill to Improve the Military Justice System. 1976.

Committee on the Uniform Code of Military Justice, Good Order and Discipline in the Army, *Report to the Honorable William M. Brucker, Secretary of the Army.* 1960.

Connally, John. Statement on "Meet the Press," June 1, 1975. Reported in *National Service Newsletter* (January 30, 1976): 4.

Comptroller General of the United States. *Report to the Congress, Military Jury System Needs Safeguards Found in Civilian Federal Court.* 1977.

Cook, A. *The Armies of the Street: The New York City Draft Riots of 1863.* Lexington: University Press of Kentucky, 1974.

Cooke, John S. "Highlights of the Military Justice Act of 1983." *The Army Lawyer* (February 1984): 40-47.

———. "The United States Court of Military Appeals, 1975-77: Judicializing the Military Justice System." *Military Law Review* 76 (1977): 43-163.

Cooper, R.D.L. *Military Manpower and the All-Volunteer Force,* a report prepared for Defense Advanced Research Projects Agency. Santa Monica, CA: Rand Corporation, 1977.

Corwin, Edward S. *The Constitution* (revised by H.W. Chase and C.R. Ducat), 14th ed. Princeton: Princeton University Press, 1978.

———. *The President, Office and Powers, 1787-1948.* 3rd ed. New York: New York University Press, 1948.

Criminal Law Reporter. "New Task Forces." 33 (1983): 2291.

Cullinan, Terrence. "National Service and the American Educational System." *The Draft: A Handbook of Facts and Alternatives,* ed. Sol Tax. Chicago: University of Chicago Press, 1967.

Department of Defense. Letter from Secretary Caspar Weinberger to Vice President George Bush. July 13, 1982.

Department of State. *Instruction to Counsels*, XXXVIII, No. 9, July 25, 1964.

Didsbury, Howard F., Jr. "Youth, Community Service and the Future." *The Futurist* 10 (1966): 305-6.

Domestic Council Committee on Illegal Aliens. *Preliminary Report of the Domestic Council Committee on Illegal Aliens*. 1976.

Drug Law Reporter 1 (1983): 36.

——. 1 (1983): 48.

Duffield, Marcus. *King Legion*. New York: J. Cape and H. Smith 1931.

Dulles, Foster Rhea. *Labor in America*. 3rd ed. New York: Thomas Y. Crowell, 1966.

Eberly, Donald J. "A Universal Youth Service." *Social Policy* 7 (1977): 43-66.

——. "National Youth Service." *New York Affairs* 4 (1977): 64-73.

——. "A National Service Pilot Project." *Teachers College Record* 73 (1971): 65-79.

——. "The Estimated Effect of a National Service Program on Public Service Manpower Needs, Youth Unemployment, College Attendance and Marriage Rates." New York: Russell Sage Foundation, 1970.

——. "Guidelines for National Service." *The Draft: A Handbook of Facts and Alternatives*, ed. Sol Tax. Chicago: University of Chicago Press, 1967.

Eberly, Donald J., ed. *National Service: A Report of a Conference*. Report of the Second National Service Conference. New York: Russell Sage Foundation, 1968.

——. *A Profile of National Service*. Report of the First Conference. New York: Overseas Educational Service, 1966.

Edelman, Peter B. "The Impact of National Service on Youth Employment" in *National Service: Social Economic and Military Impacts*, eds. Michael W. Sherraden and Donald J. Eberly, New York: Pergamon Press, 1982.

Emerson, Thomas I. "Toward a General Theory of the First Amendment." *Yale Law Journal* 72 (1963): 877-956.

Engdahl, David E. "The New Civil Disturbance Regulations: The Threat of Military Intervention." *Indiana Law Journal* 49 (1974): 581-617.

Ervin, Sam J. "Military Administrative Discharges: Due Process in the Doldrums." *San Diego Law Review* 10 (1972): 9-35.

Etzioni, Amitai. "National Service for Youth." *Human Behavior* 5 (1978): 13.

Evans, Daniel. Washington State of State Address, January 10, 1973, Reported in *National Service Newsletter* (February 1973): p. 2.

Federal Bar Association. Annual Convention. San Juan, Puerto Rico. 45 U.S.L.W. 2263, November 29, 1977.

Feld, M.D. "Military Professionalism and the Mass Army." *Armed Forces and Society* 1 (1975): 191-214.

Figley, C.R. *Stress Disorders Among Vietnam Veterans*. New York: Bruner-Muzel, 1978.

Ford, John N. "Officer Selection Boards and Due Process of Law." *Military Law Review* 70 (1975): 137-88.

Franck, Thomas M. and Edward Weisband. *Foreign Policy by Congress*. New York: Oxford University Press, 1979.

Franklin, Frank George. *The Legislative History of Naturalization in the United States*. New York: Arno Press, 1969.

Frex, Alton. *A Responsible Congress.* New York: McGraw-Hill, 1975.

Furman, H.W.C. "Restrictions Upon the Use of the Army Imposed by the Posse Comitatus Act." *Military Law Review* 7 (1960): 85-129.

Gabriel, Richard A., and Paul L. Savage. *Crisis in Command: Mismanagement in the Army.* New York: Hill and Wang, 1978.

_____. "Cohesion and Disintegration in the American Army: An Alternative Perspective." *Armed Forces and Society* 2 (1976); 340-76.

Gallup Opinion Index. *Report No. 175.* Princeton, N.J.: The Gallup Poll, 1980.

_____. *Report No. 169: National Service Programs.* Princeton, N.J.: The Gallup Poll, 1979.

Gelb, Leslie H., and Anthony Lake. "Congress: Politics and Bad Policy." *Foreign Policy* 20 (1975): 232-38.

Generous, William T., Jr. *Swords and Scales: The Development of the Uniform Code of Military Justice.* Port Washington, N.Y.: Kennikat Press, 1973.

Gentel, William D. *Police Strikes: Causes and Prevention.* Washington, D.C.: International Association of Chiefs of Police, 1979.

Godson, Roy. *Intelligence Requirements for the 80's: Elements of Intelligence.* Washington, D.C.: National Strategy Information Center, 1979.

Goodfellow, Charlotte E. *Roman Citizenship.* Lancaster, PA: Lancaster Press, 1935.

Government Accounting Office. "V.A.'s Agent Orange Examination Program: Action Needed to More Efficiently Address Veteran's Health Concerns." Washington, D.C.: Government Printing Office, 1983.

_____. "Alternatives to Current Draft Registration Program Needed Unless Level of Compliance Improves." FPCD 82-20, Washington, D.C.: Government Printing Office, April 14, 1982.

_____. "Actions to Improve Parts of the Military Manpower Mobilization System are Underway." FPCD 80-58, Washington, D.C.: Government Printing Office, July 22, 1980.

_____. "Evaluation of the Recent Draft Registration." FPCD 81-30, Washington, D.C.: Government Printing Office, December 19, 1980.

_____. "Weaknesses in the Selective Service System's Emergency Registration Plan." FPCD 79-89, Washington, D.C.: Government Printing Office, August 29, 1979.

Government Operations Committee. Hearings before the House Subcommittee on Government Information and Individual Rights. 97th Cong., 2nd Sess., 1982.

Government Operations Committee Report. *Military Assistance to Civilian Narcotics Law Enforcement.* H.R. No. 921, 97th Cong., 2nd Sess. 1982.

Grayson, Brett L. "Recent Developments in Courtmartial Jurisdiction: The Demise of the Constructive Enlistment." *Military Law Review* 72 (1976): 117-135.

Greenawalt, R. Kent. "All or Nothing at All: The Defeat of the Selective Conscientious Objection." *Supreme Court Review* (1971): 31-68.

Haas, Richard. *Congressional Powers: Implications for American Security Policy* (Adelphi: Papers no. 153). London: International Institute for Strategic Studies, 1979.

Haessig, Arthur G. "The Soldier's Right to Due Process The Right to be Heard." *Military Law Review* 63 (1974): 1-44.

Halbrook, Stephen P., "Military Enforcement of Drug Laws Under the Posse Comitatus Act." 1-11 Drug Law Rep. 121-129.

Hamilton, Lee H., and Michael H. Van Dusen. "Making the Separation of Powers Work." *Foreign Affairs* 57 (1978): 17-39.

Hansen, Donald W. "Discharge for the Good of the Service: An Administrative and Judicial Potpourri." *Military Law Review* 74 (1976): 99-185.

Harvard Civil Rights–Civil Liberties Law Review 9 (1974): 227-324. "Punishment of Enlisted Personnel Outside the UCMJ: A Statutory and Equal Protection Analysis of Military Discharge Certificates."

_____. 6 (1971): 505-24. "Swords Into Plowshares: Alternative Service Requirement for Conscientious Objectors."

Harvard Law Review. 81 (1968): 1771-1817. "Congress, the President and the Power to Commit Forces to Combat."

_____. 83 (1970): 1038-1280. "Developments in the Law—Federal Habeas Corpus."

Havighurst, Robert. The American Veteran Back Home: A Study of Veteran Readjustment, N.Y.: Longnams Green, 1951.

Hauser, William L. *America's Army in Crisis: A Study in Civil-Military Relations.* Baltimore: Johns Hopkins University Press, 1973.

Hazard, Henry B. "Administrative Naturalization Abroad of Members of the United States." *American Journal of International Law* 46 (1952): 259-71.

Hearings on the Constitutional Rights of Military Personnel before the Senate Subcommittee on Constitutional Rights. 87th Cong., 2d Sess., 1962.

Hearings before the House Committee on the Budget's Task Force on Defense and International Affairs. Washington, D.C.: Government Printing Office, 1980.

Hearings on Military Justice before the Senate Subcommittee of the Armed Services Committee. 89th Cong., 2d Sess., 1966.

Hedin, Diane. "The Views of Adolescents and Young Adults on Civic Obligation and National Service" in *National Service*, eds. Michael W. Sherraden and Donald J. Eberly, 1982

Helmer, John. *Bringing the War Home: the American Soldier in Vietnam And After.* N.Y.: Free Press, 1974.

Henderson, Gordon D. "Courts-Martial and the Constitution: The Original Understanding." *Harvard Law Review* 71 (1957): 293-324.

Henkin, Louis. *Foreign Affairs and the Constitution.* Mineola, N.Y.: Foundation Press, 1972.

Hoffman, Stanley. "A View From at Home: The Perils of Incoherence." *Foreign Affairs* 57 (1978): 463-91.

Hofstadter, Richard. and Wallace, Michael. *American Violence: A Documentary History.* New York: Knopf, 1970.

House Committee on Veterans' Affairs, "Agent Orange and Atomic Veterans Relief Act.: 98th Cong., 2d Sess., H.R. 98-592, January 25, 1984.

House Judiciary Committee. Hearings before the Subcommittee on Courts, Civil Liberties, and the Administration of Justice. No. 45, April 14 and May 22, 1980.

Jacobs, James B., and Retsky, Harold G. "Prison Guard." *Urban Life* 4 (1975): 5-29.

Jacobs, James B., and Travis, Jeremy. "Compliance Strategies For Draft Registration," *University of Arizona Law Review*, 1986.

Jacobs, James B., and Zimmer, Lynn. "The 1979 Montana Prison Strike: A Case Study." Unpublished paper, Cornell University, 1980.

James, William. "The Moral Equivalent of War." *International Conciliation*, No. 27, February 1910.

Janowitz, Morris. *The Reconstruction of American Patriotism.* Chicago: University of Chicago Press, 1983.

_____. "The Citizen Soldier and National Service." *Air University Review* 31 (1979): 2-16.

_____. "Military Institutions and Citizenship in Western Societies." *Armed Forces and Society* 2 (1976): 185-204.

_____. "The All-Volunteer Force as a 'Sociopolitical' Problem." *Social Problems* 22 (1975): 432-49.

_____. *Military Conflict*. Beverly Hills: Sage Publications, Inc., 1975.

_____. "National Service: A Third Alternative?" *Teachers College Record* 73 (1971): 13-26.

_____. "American Democracy and Military Service." *Trans-Action* 4 (1967): 5-11, 57-59.

_____. "The Logic of National Service." *The Draft* ed. Sol Tax, Chicago University of Chicago Press 1967.

_____. *The Professional Soldier*. Glencoe, IL: Free Press, 1960.

Janowitz, Morris, and Moskos, Charles. "Five Years of the All-Volunteer Force 1973-1978." *Armed Forces and Society* 5 (1979): 171-218.

Johnston, Michael. "Patrons and Clients, Jobs and Machines: A Case Study of the Uses of Patronage." *American Political Science Review* 73 (1979): 385-98.

Jones, Bradley K. "The Gravity of Administrative Discharges: A Legal and Empirical Evaluation." *Military Law Review* 59 (1973): 1-25.

Jones, Richard S. *A History of the American Legion*. Indianapolis: Bobbs-Merril, 1946.

Journal of International Law and Politics. 16 (1984): 353-413. "Trends in U.S. Extraterritorial Narcotics Control: Slamming the Stable Door After the Horse Has Bolted."

Judiciary Committee Report. H.R. 71, Part II, 97th Cong., 2nd Sess. 1982.

Kettner, James H. *The Development of American Citizenship, 1608-1807*. Chapel Hill: University of North Carolina Press, 1978.

King, William R. *Achieving America's Goals: National Service or the All-Volunteer Armed Forces?* Report prepared for the Senate Subcommittee on Manpower and Personnel of the Senate Armed Services Committee. Washington, D.C.: Government Printing Office, 1977.

League of Women Voters, *Changing of the Guard: Citizen Soldiers in Wisconsin Correctional Institutions*. Madison, Wisconsin: League of Women Voters, 1978.

Levitan, Sar A., and Alderman, Karen C. *Old Wars Remain Unfinished: The Veterans Benefits System*. Baltimore: Johns Hopkins University Press, 1973.

_____. *Warriors at Work: The Volunteer Armed Force*. Beverly Hills: Sage Publications, 1977.

Levitan, Sar A., and Johnston, Benjamin H. *The Job Corps: A Social Experiment That Works*. Baltimore: Johns Hopkins University Press, 1975.

Lifton, Robert Jay. *Home from the War: Vietnam Veterans, Neither Victims Nor Executioners*. New York: Simon & Schuster, 1973.

Lonn, Ella. *Foreigners in the Union Army and Navy*. Baton Rouge: Louisiana State University Press, 1951.

Lonn, Ella. *Foreigners in the Confederacy*. Chapel Hill: University of North Carolina Press. 1940.

Lowenstein, Edith, ed. "Recent Amendments to Selective Service Regulations Affecting Aliens." *Interpreter Releases* 49 (1972): 274-80.

MacMullen, Ramsay. *Soldier and Civilian in the Later Roman Empire*. Cambridge: Harvard University Press, 1963.

Marquette Law Review 65 (1982): 660-93. "Free Speech in the Military."

Marshall, Geofrey. "The Armed Forces and Industrial Disputes in the United Kingdom." *Armed Forces and Society* 5 (1979): 270-80.

Maynes, Charles W., and Richard H. Ullman. "Ten Years of Foreign Policy." *Foreign Policy* 40 (1980): 3-17.

McCollum, James K., and Robinson, Jerald F. "The Law and Current Status of Unions in the Military Establishment." *Labor Law Journal* 28 (1977): 421-30.

McNamara, Robert S. Speech to the American Society of Newspaper Editors: Montreal, Canada, May 18, 1966, quoted in the *New York Times*, 19 May 1966, p. 11.

Mead, Margaret. "Women in National Service." *Teachers College Record* 73 (1971): 59-64.

_____. "A National Service System as a Solution to a Variety of National Problems" in *The Draft*, ed. Sol Tax (1967): 99-109.

Meeks, Clarence, I. "Illegal Law Enforcement: Aiding Civil Authorities in Violation of the Posse Comitatus Act." *Military Law Review* 70 (1975): 83-136.

Meyers, Bruce. "Soldiers of Orange: The Administrative, Diplomatic, Legislative and Litigatory Impact of Herbicide Orange in South Vietnam." *B.C. Environmental Affairs Law Review* 8 (1982): 157-199.

Michigan Law Review. "From *Feres* to *Stencel*: Should Military Personnel Have Access to FTCA Recovery?" 77 (1979): 1099-1126.

Military Law Review 103 (1984): 79-104. "Significant Decisions of the Court of Military Appeals: 1982-1983."

Minott, Rodney G. *Peerless Patriots: Organized Veterans and the Spirit of Americanism.* Washington, D.C.: Public Affairs Press, 1962.

Mirengoff, William; Rindler, Lester; Greenspan, Harry; and Sereblom, Scott. *CETA: Assessment of Public Service Job Manpower and Civilian Youth Programs.* Washington, D.C.: Government Printing Office, 1978.

Morehouse, Ward, III. "F.B.I. Readying for Anti-Draft Wave on Campus This Fall," *Christian Science Monitor* 72 (June 23, 1980): p. 4, col. 1.

Morgan, Edmund M. "The Background of the Uniform Code of Military Justice." *Vanderbilt Law Review* 6 (1952-53): 169-85.

Morris, Milton D., and Mayio, Albert. *Curbing Illegal Immigration*, a staff paper. Washington, D.C.: Brookings Institution, 1982.

Mosch, Theodore R. *The G.I. Bill: A Breakthrough in Educational and Social Policy in the United States.* Hicksville, New York: Exposition Press, 1975.

Moskos, Charles C., Jr. *The American Enlisted Man: The Rank and File in Today's Military.* New York: Russell Sage Foundation, 1970.

_____. "The Social Equivalent of Military Service," *Teachers College Record* 73 (1971): 7-12.

_____. "Making the All-Volunteer Force Work: A National Service Approach." *Foreign Affairs* 60 (1981): 17-34.

Mosley, Raymond, Jr. *The American Legion Story.* New York: Duell, Sloan & Pearce, 1966.

Muller, Steven. "Our Youth Should Serve." *Newsweek* 92 (1978).

Murdock, Eugene Converse. *One Million Men: The Civil War Draft in the North.* Madison, State Historical Society of Wisconsin, 1971.

_____. *Patriotism Limited 1862-65: The Civil War Draft and the Bounty System.* Kent, Ohio: Kent State University Press, 1967.

Nathan, Richard; Cook, Robert F.; and Rawlins, V. Lane. *Public Service Employment: A Field Evaluation.* Washington, D.C.: The Brookings Institution, 1981.

National Academy of Sciences. *Study of Health Care for American Veterans.* 95th Congress, 1st Sess. Senate Committee on Veteran Affairs, Print No. 4, 1977.

National Advisory Commission on Civil Disorders. *Report.* New York: New York Times, 1968.

National Advisory Commission on Selective Service. *In Pursuit of Equity: Who Serves When Not All Serve?* Washington, D.C.: Government Printing Office, 1967.

National Association of Attorneys General, Committee on the Office of Attorney General. *Legal Issues Concerning the Role of the National Guard in Civil Disorders.* Raleigh, N.C.: The National Association of Attorneys General, 1973.

National Commission on Youth. *The Transition of Youth to Adulthood: A Bridge too Long: a Report to Educators, Sociologists, Legislators, and Youth Policymaking Bodies.* Boulder, CO: Westview, 1980.

National Council on Employment Policy. *The Case for CETA Reauthorization: Continued Decentralization,* 1978.

National Council on Women in the United States. *Women in National Service,* 1967.

National Service Secretariat. *National Service Newsletter.* Washington, D.C.

Newsweek. "Social Security: Old Computers." 1982, 99,11:61.

North, D. and Houstoun, M. *The Characteristics and Role of Illegal Aliens in the U.S. Labor Market: An Explanatory Study.* Washington, D.C.: Linton, 1976.

Northwestern University Law Review. "Agent Orange as a Problem of Law and Policy" 77 (1982): 48-83.

Ocheltree, Keith, ed. *Six Strike Stories.* Chicago: Public Personnel Association, 1969.

Ostan, William S. "Unionization of the Military: Some Legal and Practical Considerations." *Military Law Review* 77 (1977): 109-42.

O'Sullivan, John., and Meckler, Alan M., eds. *The Draft and Its Enemies: A Documentary History.* Urbana: University of Illinois Press, 1974.

Peterson, Andrew A. "Deterring Strikes by Public Employees: New York's Two-For-One Salary Penalty and the 1979 Prison Guard Strike." *Industrial and Labor Relations Review* 34 (1981): 545-62.

Pisano, Vittorfranco S. *Contemporary Italian Terrorism: Analysis and Countermeasures.* Library of Congress Law Library, 1979.

Presidential Recommendations for Selective Service Reform. A Report to Congress Prepared Pursuant to P.L. 96-107, 96th Con., 2nd Session Washington, D.C.: Government Printing Office, 1980.

President's Commission on an All-Volunteer Force. *Report of the Commission.* Washington, D.C.: Government Printing Office, 1970.

President's Commission on Veteran's Pensions. *A Report on Veteran's Benefits in the United States, Veterans in Our Society: Data on the Conditions of Military Service and on the Status of the Veteran.* 84th Cong., 2nd Sess., Staff Report No. IV, House Committee Print No. 261, June 21, 1956.

President's Science Advisory Committee Report of the Panel on Youth, Office of Science and Technology, Executive Office of the President, 1973.

Rabin, Robert L. "Do You Believe in a Supreme Being—The Administration of the Conscientious Objector Exemption." *Wisconsin Law Review* (1967): 642-84.

Randall, James Garfield. *Constitutional Problems Under Lincoln.* rev. ed. Urbana: University of Illinois Press, 1951.

Rehnquist, William. Internal White House Memorandum to Assistant to the President, John Erlichman. Unpublished Memorandum, March 22, 1970.

Richardson, Elliott. Commencement Address at the University of Connecticut, June 5, 1972. Reported in *National Service Newsletter* (June 1972): p. 1.

Riker, William. *Soldiers of the States: The Role of the National Guard in American Democracy.* Washington, D.C.: Public Affairs Press, 1957.

Roh, Charles E., Jr., and Upham, Frank K. "The Status of Aliens Under United States Draft Laws." *Harvard International Law Journal* 13 (1972) 501-17.

Ross, David R., *Preparing For Ulysses: Politics and Veterans,* N.Y.: Columbia University Press, 1969.

Roundtable Discussion on the Use of the Military in the Control of Illegal Drugs. *Report of the Proceedings.* January, 1984.

Russell, Francis. *A City in Terror: The 1919 Boston Police Strike.* New York: Penguin, 1977.

Salmond, John A. *The Civilian Conservation Corps, 1933-1942: A New Deal Case Study.* Durham, N.C.: Duke University Press, 1967.

Schlucter, David A. "The Enlistment Contract: A Uniform Approach." *Military Law Review* 77 (1977): 1-64.

Schuck, Peter H. "The Transformation of Immigration Law." *Columbia Law Review* 84 (1984): 1-90.

Select Commission on Immigration and Refugee Policy. *U.S. Immigration Policy and the National Interest,* 1981.

Selective Service System. *Outline of Historical Background of Selective Service.* Washington, D.C.: Government Printing Office, 1948.

Senate Committee on Labor and Human Resources. 96th Cong., 2d Sess. *Presidential Commission on National Service and A National Commission on Volunteerism,* 1980.

Shaw, William. "The Interrelationship of the United States Army and National Guard." *Military Law Review* 31 (1966): 39-84.

Sherman, Edward F. "Congressional Proposals for Reform of Military Law." *American Criminal Law Review* 10 (1971) 25-49.

———. "The Military Courts and Servicemen's First Amendment Rights." *Hastings Law Journal* 22 (1971): 325-73.

———. "Judicial Review of Military Determinations and the Exhaustion of Remedies Requirement." *Virginia Law Review* 55 (1969): 483-540.

———. "Revised Military Code: A Qualified Assessment." *Trial,* 5 (1968-69): 44-46.

Sherraden, Michael W., and Eberly, Donald J. *National Service: Social, Economic and Military Impacts.* New York: Pergamon Press, 1982.

———. "National Service: Alternative Strategies." *Armed Forces and Society* 3 (1977): 445-66.

Siemer, Deanne; and Effron, Andrew. "Military Participation in United States Law Enforcement Activities Overseas: The Extraterritorial Effect of the Posse Comitatus Act." *St. John's Law Review* 54 (1979): 1-54.

Society Symposium 18 (1981): 28-60. "The Rise and Fall of the Volunteer Army."

Solomon, L.D. "An Interview with Willard Wirtz." *New York Affairs* 4 (1977): 74-85.

Southern California Law Review 5 (1979): 1453-1511. "The National Emergency Dilemma: Balancing the Executive's Crisis Powers with the Need for Accountability."

Starr, Paul. *The Discarded Army: Veterans After Vietnam: The Nader Report on Vietnam Veterans and The Veteran's Administration.* Washington, D.C.: Center for Study of Responsive Law, 1974.

Stouffer, Samuel, et al. *The American Soldier: Combat and Its Aftermath, II.* Princeton: Princeton University Press, 1949.

Subcommittee on Manpower and Personnel of the Armed Services Committee of the United States Senate. *Hearings.* Washington, D.C.: Government Printing Office, June 20, 1978 and November 19, 1979.

Swearer, Howard. "An Idea Whose Time Has Come." *Brown Alumni Monthly* 82 (1981): 27-30.

Task Force on the Administration of Military Justice in the Armed Forces. *Report.* 1977.

Tax, Sol. ed. *The Draft: A Handbook of Facts and Alternatives.* Chicago: University of Chicago Press, 1967.

Terry, Sara. "Diverse Coalition of Draft Foes Maps Fresh Strategy." *Christian Science Monitor* 12 (June, 1980): 4.

Texas Tech Law Review. "Don't Call out the Marines: An Assessment of the Posse Comitatus Act." *Texas Tech Law Review* 13 (1982): 1467-93.

Tribe, Lawrence H. *American Constitutional Law.* Mineola, N.Y.: Foundation Press, 1978.

Twentieth Century Fund. Task Force on the Law Enforcement Assistance Administration. *Law Enforcement: The Federal Role.* N.Y.: McGraw-Hill, 1976.

U.S. Congressional Budget Office. *National Service Programs and Their Effects on Military Manpower and Civilian Youth Problems.* Washington, D.C.: Government Printing Office, 1978.

U.S. National Advisory Commission on Civil Disorders. *Report.* New York: New York Times Co., 1968.

U.S. News and World Report. 92 (1982): 84. "Social Security Takes Aim at Its Creaky Computers."

U.S. Veterans' Administration. *Fact Sheet on Federal Benefits for Veterans and Dependents.*

U.S. Veteran's Administration, Department of Medicine and Surgery. *The Vietnam Veteran in Contemporary Society: Collected Materials Pertaining to the Young Veterans.* Washington, D.C., May 1972.

U.S. Veterans Advisory Commission. *Report.* Washington, D.C.: Government Printing Office, 1968.

Useem, Michael. *Conscription, Protest and Social Conflict.* New York: John Wiley and Sons, 1973.

Van Arsdol, Maurice, et al. "Non-apprehended and Apprehended Undocumented Residents in the Los Angeles Labor Market: An Exploratory Study." Unpublished, University of Southern California Dept. of Sociology and Anthropology, 1979.

Van Horn, Carl E. "Evaluating the New Federalism: National Goals and Local Implementors." *Public Administration Review* 39 (1979): 17-22.

Waller, Willard, W., *The Veteran Comes Back*, N.Y.: The Dryden Press, 1944.

Veterans Administration Response, September 22, 1977. Senate Committee Print No. 7, 1977.

Villenez, Wayne J., and Kasarda, John D. "Veteran Status and Socio-economic Attainment." *Armed Forces and Society* 2 (1976): 407-20.

Wall Street Journal. (July 1982): p. 23, col. 4. "Social Security Walks Electronic High Wire as It Tries to Fight Computer Failure, Fraud."

Weigley, Russel Frank. *History of the United States Army.* New York: Macmillan, 1967.

Weinberger, Caspar. Letter to President of Senate George Bush, 1982.

Westmoreland, William. "Military Justice—A Commander's Viewpoint." *American Criminal Law Review* 10 (1971): 5-8.

Whelan, Christopher. "*The Law and the Use of Troops in Industrial Disputes.*" Working Paper No. 2, Wolfson College, Oxford: Centre for Socio-Legal Studies, March 1979.

———. "Military Intervention in Industrial Disputes." *The Industrial Law Journal* 8 (December 1979): 222-34.

Willis, John T. "The United States Court of Military Appeals: Its Origin, Operation and Future." *Military Law Review* 55 (1972): 39-93.

———. "The Constitution, The United States Court of Military Appeals and the Future." *Military Law Review* 57 (1972): 27-97.

Wilson, James Q. *Varieties of Police Behavior: The Management of Law and Order in Eight Communities.* New York: Atheneum, 1972.

Winthrop, William Woolsey. *Military Law and Precedents.* 2nd rev. ed. 1920 reprint. Washington, D.C.: Government Printing Office.

Wisconsin League of Women Voters. *Changing of the Guard: Citizen Soldiers in Wisconsin Correctional Institutions.* Madison, WI: League of Women Voters, 1978.

Wofford, Harris. "Toward a Draft Without Guns." *Saturday Review* 19 (October 15, 1966): 53.

Wulf, Melvin L. *The National Guard and the Constitution.* New York: American Civil Liberties Union, 1971.

Yale Law Journal. "Honored in the Breach: Presidential Authority to Execute the Laws with Military Force" 83 (1973): 130-52.

Yankelovich, Daniel. "Farewell to President Knows Best." *Foreign Affairs* 57 (1978): 670-93.

Yankelovich, Daniel, and Kaagan, Larry. "Assertive America." *Foreign Affairs* 59 (1980): 696-713.

Yarmolinsky, Adam. *The Military Establishment: Its Impacts on American Society.* New York: Harper & Row, 1971.

Zimmer, Lynn and Jacobs, James B. "Challenging the Taylor Law: Prison Guards on Strike." *Industrial and Labor Relations Review* 34 (1981): 531-44.

Index

Administrative regulations of the armed forces: Article 15 of, 12-13; discharges and, 10-12; due process rights and, 8-10; judicial deference to abuse of, 22; for social control, 11-13

AFSCME. *See* Organized labor

Agent Orange, 162-65, 167n16-22, 168n19-22

Air Force. *See* Military

Air traffic controllers' strike (1981), 75n1

Aliens: in all-volunteer force, 44; in American Revolution, 32, 34, 38; bibliography of congressional acts about, 49-50; in Civil War, 32, 34, 35, 36-37, 38, 45n4; eligibility for armed services of, 31, 32-34, 45n2; illegal, 36, 40, 45, 46n8, 48n24; in Mexican War, 32; as officers in armed forces, 34-36, 46n7; in War of 1812, 32; in World War I, 33, 34, 37, 38; in World War II, 33-34, 35, 37, 39, 47n13. *See also* Citizenship

All-volunteer force. *See* AVF

American Council on Education, 105

American Revolution, 32, 34, 38, 151

Ansell, Samuel T., 6

Armed Forces Reserve Act (1952), 34

Army: intelligence operations, 79; national guard as reserves for, 69-70. *See also* AVF; Military; Military law; Military service

Articles for the Government of the Navy, 5

Articles of War, 5

Aspin, Leslie, 104

Atlantic Council panel on draft registration, 94-95

AVF (all-volunteer force): aliens in, 44; citizenship and, 44-45; discipline and, 26-28; military law and, 26-29; national service and, 114, 116-17, 132; problems with, 93-95, 114-15, 116-17, 132; quality of, 94, 95, 115, 132; recruitment for,

16-17, 94, 95, 114-15, 132. *See also* Draft system

Bayh, Birch, 23

Bemis v. Whalen (1972), 16

Bickel, Alexander, 43, 44

Bill of Rights, 7-8

Boards of review, armed forces, 23

Brademas, John, 105

Brown v. Glines (1980), 21, 28

Burns v. Wilson (1953), 17

Carlson v. Schlesinger (1975), 30n5

Carter (Jimmy) administration: draft registration and, 95, 96-97; national service, 114

Cavanaugh proposal for national service, 117, 131-42, 146n13

CCC (Civilian Conservation Corps), 111-12

CETA (Comprehensive Employment and Training Act, 1973), 122, 137, 138, 140

Chappell v. Wallace (1983), 21

Citizenship: all-volunteer force and, 44-45; as reward for military service, 38-41, 47n15-19; definition of, 42-43; draft system and, 33, 36-38, 46n10-12; military service and, 36-38, 99, 106-7; national service and, 112; qualifications of military officers, 34-36; as reward for military service, 38-41, 47n15-19. *See also* Aliens

Civil War: aliens in, 32, 34, 35, 36-37, 38, 45n4; military service during, 36-37, 38; veterans, 151

Civilian Conservation Corps. *See* CCC

Civilian influence on military: congress as, 22-24; contractual nature of military service as, 13-17; extension of rights as, 5-10; federal courts as, 17-22; legal aspects of, 5-30; shift from criminal to ad-